MODERN BRITISH PLAYWRITING: THE 1980s

VOICES, DOCUMENTS, NEW INTERPRETATIONS

Jane Milling is Senior Lecturer in Dram. She is co-author, with Deirdre Heddon, of *Devising Performance: A Critical History* (Palgrave, 2005) and series editor, with Graham Ley, of Theatre and Performance Practices (Palgrave). Her articles on Restoration and eighteenth-century performers and women writers have been published in *Theatre Survey, Restoration and Eighteenth Century Theatre* and *Theatre Notebook.*

Dr Milling has also worked on a series of Arts and Humanities Research Council-funded projects under the Connected Communities programme, including 'Participatory Arts for Well-Being: Past and Present Practices' and 'Understanding Everyday Participation'.

MODERN BRITISH PLAYWRITING: THE 1980s

VOICES, DOCUMENTS, NEW INTERPRETATIONS

Jane Milling

Series Editors: Richard Boon and Philip Roberts

Methuen Drama

Methuen Drama

1 3 5 7 9 10 8 6 4 2

First published in Great Britain in 2012 by Methuen Drama

Methuen Drama, an imprint of Bloomsbury Publishing Plc

Methuen Drama
Bloomsbury Publishing Plc
50 Bedford Square
London WC1B 3DP
www.methuendrama.com

Copyright © 2012 by Jane Milling

General Preface copyright © 2012 Richard Boon and Philip Roberts
'Howard Barker' copyright © 2012 Sarah Goldingay
'Jim Cartwright' copyright © 2012 David Lane
'Timberlake Wertenbaker' copyright © 2012 Sara Freeman

The rights of the author and contributors to be identified as the authors of this work have
been asserted by them in accordance with the Copyright, Design and Patents Act, 1988

Paperback ISBN 978 1 408 12959 3
Hardback ISBN 978 1 408 18213 0

Available in the USA from Bloomsbury Academic & Professional, 175 Fifth Avenue/
3rd Floor, New York, NY 10010

A CIP catalogue record for this book is available from the British Library

Typeset by Mark Heslington Ltd, Scarborough, North Yorkshire
Printed in the UK by MPG Books Ltd, Bodmin, Cornwall

CONTENTS

GENERAL PREFACE

This book is one of a series of six volumes which seek to characterise the nature of modern British playwriting from the 1950s to the end of the first decade of this new century. The work of these six decades is comparable in its range, experimentation and achievement only to the drama of the Elizabethan and Jacobean dramatists. The series chronicles its flowering and development.

Each volume addresses the work of four representative dramatists (five in the *2000–2009* volume) by focusing on key works and by placing that work in a detailed contextual account of the theatrical, social, political and cultural climate of the era.

The series revisits each decade from the perspective of the twenty-first century. We recognise that there is an inevitable danger of imposing a spurious neatness on its subject. So while each book focuses squarely on the particular decade and its representative authors, we have been careful to ensure that some account is given of relevant material from earlier years and, where relevant, of subsequent developments. And while the intentions and organisation of each volume are essentially the same, we have also allowed for flexibility, the better to allow both for the particular demands of the subject and the particular approach of our author/editors.

It is also the case, of course, that differences of historical perspective across the series influence the nature of the books. For student readers, the difference at its most extreme is between a present they daily inhabit and feel they know intimately and a decade (the 1950s) in which their parents or even grandparents might have been born; between a time of seemingly unlimited consumer choice and one which began with post-war food rationing still in place. Further, a playwright who began work in the late 1960s (David Hare, say) has a far bigger body of work and associated scholarship than one whose emergence has come within the last decade or so (debbie tucker green, for example). A glance at the Bibliographies for the earliest and latest volumes quickly reveals huge differences in the range of secondary material available to our authors and to our readers. This inevitably means that the later volumes allow a greater space to their contributing essayists for original research and scholarship, but we have also actively encouraged revisionist perspectives – new looks – on the 'older guard' in earlier books.

So while each book can and does stand alone, the series as a whole offers as coherent and comprehensive a view of the whole era as possible.

Throughout, we have had in mind two chief objectives. We have made accessible information and ideas that will enable today's students of theatre to acquaint themselves with the nature of the world inhabited by the playwrights of the last sixty years; and we offer new, original and often surprising perspectives on both established and developing dramatists.

Richard Boon and Philip Roberts
Series Editors
September 2011

Richard Boon is Emeritus Professor of Drama at the University of Hull

Philip Roberts is Emeritus Professor of Drama and Theatre Studies at the University of Leeds

ACKNOWLEDGEMENTS

I would like to thank series editors Richard Boon and Philip Roberts for their unflagging wit and wise advice. The guest contributors Sara Freeman, Sarah Goldingay and David Lane have been a source of great insight and scholarship, and Cathy Turner and Graham Ley generously offered ideas, critique and their well-stocked libraries. I would like to thank Mark Dudgeon for his patient care, and the staff at Methuen Drama. And grateful thanks should go to Howard Barker and to Sarah Daniels for their generous gift of time and creative words, and to Jim Cartwright, Timberlake Wertenbaker, Mel Kenyon and A.J. Associates.

INTRODUCTION TO THE 1980S

1. Domestic life

At home

- UK population increased from 56.4 million in 1981 to 57.4 million in 1991; today it stands at around 60 million.[1]
- There were 350,000 marriages in 1981, only 306,800 in 1991. The number of cohabiting couples doubled from 13 per cent in 1986 to 25 per cent in 1998.
- In 1987, in the vast majority of households the cleaning (72 per cent), washing and ironing (88 per cent), and cooking (77 per cent) were done by women. Yet the divorce rate has remained fairly steady since the early 1980s at around 145,000 divorces per year.[2]
- Babies born to parents outside marriage accounted for 8 per cent of total births in 1970, and only 12 per cent in 1980. But by 1990 this had markedly increased to 28.3 per cent. This upward trajectory continued: in 2008 45 per cent of births were outside marriage.
- Number of births to teenage mothers in England and Wales fell from 81,000 in 1980 to 72,000 in 1990. Media hysteria notwithstanding, numbers have continued to decline.[3]
- Between 1981 and 1991 there was a shortage in the housing stock in part because single-person households rose from 22 per cent to 27 per cent, with older women as the largest group. Households of three or more people declined. Lone-parent households increased, with 88 per cent of children living with two parents in 1981, down to 83 per cent in 1991. Numbers have remained at about this level.
- 1980 Housing Act introduces council tenants' 'right to buy' their house at a discount. Proceeds go to local authorities, but

income cannot be used to build new housing stock. In 1971 less than half of all households were owner-occupied; by the end of the 1980s 67 per cent were owner-occupied.[4]

- Mortgages became easier to acquire: pre-1980s most mortgages were supplied by mutual building societies, with strict rules on lending against deposits and close control on the number of mortgages. After the 1979 Banking Act, banks move into mortgage sector.

- 1986 Building Societies Act allowed competition between building societies and commercial banks and created a process for building societies to demutualise. This was very profitable for the managers and initial shareholders, although of less benefit to borrowers and savers with the societies. In the competitive environment, 'salary to loan' multiples for mortgages increased from 2.5 times salary to 5 (or more) times salary.[5]

> Those houses we own we decorate with salmon and peach paint, neon geometric wallpaper and carpets, black metal furniture, wicker sofas, pastel cushioning, built-in 'country-style' kitchens, tiled work surfaces, brass-look taps, vertical blinds, ceiling fans and houseplants, particularly cheeseplants.

- Between 1980 and 1989 there was a 205 per cent growth in house prices.[6]
- House prices slumped in 1989, leaving many householders in 'negative equity'.
- In 1988, mortgage interest tax relief is removed, so the monthly cost of mortgage payments goes up. Bank of England base interest rates rise to 13 per cent in 1988, reaching 15 per cent from October 1989 to October 1990. In 1990 mortgage costs peaked at 30 per cent of household income.
- In 1990 43,900 houses were repossessed, up from just 5,000 in 1980.[7]
- April 1990: Community Charge replaced the local government 'rates', increasing costs by 34 per cent. (This was reversed the

following year by 30 per cent, funded by increase in VAT from 15 per cent to 17.5 per cent.)

Average price of household goods in pence			
	1970	1980 (percentage increase vs 1970)	1990 (percentage increase vs 1970)
rump steak per kilo	125	507 (306)	813 (550)
cod fillet	47	238 (406)	574 (1,121)
white loaf	8.8	37 (320)	65 (639)
milk pint	4.7	17 (262)	31 (560)
imported butter	10.1	44 (336)	65 (544)
eggs dozen	23.2	72 (210)	121 (422)
pint bitter	10	50 (400)	109 (990)
carrots	7.3	29 (297)	59 (708)
bananas	16.8	59 (251)	114 (579)
instant coffee	22.7	101 (345)	131 (477)

- We shopped more at out-of-town supermarkets – there were 280 such supermarkets in 1980 and 775 in 1990. But not on Sundays – thanks to the 'Keep Sunday Special' campaign. The 1986 government Shops Bill was defeated. Sunday shopping arrives in 1994.
- Car ownership increased: 59 per cent of households have access to a car in 1981, 68 per cent in 1991, and by 2010 75 per cent of households have a car.

> The 1980s saw increased ownership of deep freezers, microwave ovens, landline telephones, dishwashers, continental quilts, sandwich toasters, electric power showers and jug kettles. Entertainment-based electronic goods rapidly advance: most households have colour television with a TV remote control. In 1983 18 per cent of households have a VHS recorder, by 1989 60 per cent do. By the end of the decade, new arrivals include the personal computer (19 per cent), CD player (16 per cent), Sony Walkman™ portable cassette player, Nintendo Game Boy™, portable music centre or 'ghetto blaster'.

- 1983 Mental Health Act requires local authorities to discharge mentally ill people from psychiatric hospital settings into smaller sheltered housing units, without any funding for the transition or its increased costs. This policy is dubbed 'Care in the Community'.[8]

- Until 1980 local authority old people's homes provided most residential care for older people. 1980: Supplementary Benefits (Requirement) Regulations meant people entering private care got board and lodging payments, pensioners on income support used taxpayers' public funds to enter private-sector care. 1983–85: private residential places grew by 60 per cent (1980 local authority: 134,500 places; private: 37,400; voluntary: 45,300). 1985–90: private places rose by 82 per cent (1990 local authority: 125,600; private: 155,600; voluntary: 40,000). Provision of private residential care peaked in 1990, as new legislation reduced the financial incentive from the early 1990s.[9]

At work

- 1979: unemployment at 1.4 million; by 1982 it was more than three million and stayed at that level until 1987, due to economic recession, high inflation and industrial restructuring.
- In 1984, 25 per cent of unemployed males aged sixteen and over had been out of work for more than two years, and 55 per cent of unemployed women aged fifty and over had been unemployed for over a year. In the mid-1980s the statistics were massaged when 'long-term unemployment' was redefined at fifty-two weeks instead of twenty-six weeks.
- The percentage of women in the workforce rose from around 65 per cent in 1981 to 73 per cent in 1991. Much of the increase in women's work between the early 1970s and early 1990s is in part-time employment. The pay gap is constant through the 1980s – women's gross hourly pay remained at about 75 per cent of men's.
- 1980: average annual male wage is £6000. In 1986, median weekly earnings for a single man are £127.78, for a single woman £89.53.[10]
- What you earned seemed to buy you less in the early 1980s

– in 1980 the annual inflation rate is over 20 per cent, in 1986 it is down to 2.4 per cent, by 1990 it is back to 10.9 per cent.

- 1984: only 65 per cent per cent of adults have a current bank account.
- Union membership peaks in 1979. TUC membership is twelve million in 1979, 10.3 million by 1984, reflecting job losses in heavily unionised sectors, although this still means 55 per cent of the employed population are in a union. By 2000 TUC membership is eight million, largely because the financial and service industries are poorly unionised.[11]

2. Education

1980: Education Act 1980 creates the 'assisted places' scheme (public money pays independent school fees for children on low incomes who score well in entrance exams, around 6,000 places per year), gives parents greater powers on governing bodies and over admissions, and removes the obligation on local education authorities to provide school milk and meals.

1981: Education Act 1981 requires local education authorities to assess and provide for children with special educational needs, encourages 'mainstream' integration.

- Over 1980s, 25+ per cent rise in children gaining five O-levels or GCSEs at C or above.
- The number of children in post-sixteen education rose slightly between 1979 (36 per cent) and 1988 (44 per cent). Of those sixteen-year-olds who left school, predominantly from low-income families, few had qualifications. Children from the highest parental income percentile increased their participation in post-sixteen education and higher education by 11 per cent over the 1980s, children with the lowest parental incomes increased their participation by 1 per cent.[12]

1982: Technical and Vocational Education Initiative established a decentralised set of projects to encourage fourteen- to eighteen-year olds into work experience or technical courses. This proved a successfully taken-up initiative.

1983: Youth Training Scheme (YTS) started, offering one year of on-the-job training, run by Manpower Services Commission. Replaces the Youth Opportunity Programme. YTS students were paid a small wage, £35 per week (unemployment, housing and other benefits were withdrawn); included thirteen weeks' study away from the job.

- BTEC Business and Technical Education Council vocational qualifications introduced.

1985: Swann Report *Education for All*, centrally concerned with Afro-Caribbean children, recommended multicultural education, following the lead of many local education authorities, particularly the Inner London Education Authority (ILEA), to address racism at the level of curriculum materials and positive imagery. The National Association for Multicultural Education changes its name to the National Anti-Racist Movement in Education, in order to press for structural reform to address underachievement and the limited employment of black and Asian teachers.

1986: Corporal punishment banned in state schools; you can still be beaten at public school.

- Kenneth Baker becomes Minister for Education.
- General Certificate of Secondary Education (GCSE) introduced to replace the split between O-level (aimed at the top 20 per cent of ability range) and CSEs (aimed at the next 40 per cent of ability range). Major change includes the introduction of coursework assessment, not just examinations.
- National Vocational Qualifications (NVQs) for training introduced.
- YTS places expanded and extended to two years.

- University Grant Committee responsible for higher education funding tries to determine how to organise its shrinking budget. The Research Assessment Exercise is introduced, to quantify academic research against performance indicators.

1988: Social Security Act 1988 requires all sixteen- and seventeen-year-olds not in education or employment to register for YTS.

Education Reform Act 1988 introduces:

A *National Curriculum* for state primary and secondary schools (private fee-paying schools were excepted). This was principally intended to standardise subject content and assessment. Additional examinations and tests are introduced at age seven, eleven and fourteen, which do not result in qualifications for pupils but are fed into school league tables. Core subjects are English, maths and science. The science curriculum was altered to replace individual science disciplines with a single qualification or 'double science', which was designed as a preparation in biology, chemistry and physics at GCE level.

An *educational market* is created – theoretically parents could choose which school their child attended, but this rarely happens.

Schools were allowed to become '*grant-maintained*', taking control of previously publicly owned land and buildings, receiving grants directly from central government rather than the local education authority, and running their own admissions policies, i.e. they can be selective and are not obliged to serve all children of their local area, nor excluded children, nor children with special educational needs, nor 'looked-after children' (children in care). The best-performing state schools and grammar schools took advantage of this 'opt-out'.

A ranking of all secondary schools by exam results in the '*league tables*' is introduced – without the 'value-added' measure, so no indication of relationship between children's circumstances at arrival and their relative achievement (i.e. large inner-city schools with 70 per cent children with English as a second language are assessed in the same way as grant-maintained, selective schools).

1988: Local Government Act includes the homophobic Section 28, which rules that a local government shall not 'promote the teaching in any maintained school of the acceptability of homosexuality as a pretended family relationship'. This ran counter to many local education authority policies, which were deliberately anti-discriminatory on the basis of 'sexual orientation'. No prosecutions were ever brought but, as it was not clear whether schools could be prosecuted or only local authorities, many erred on the side of caution in their teaching about homophobic discrimination and gay rights.

- During the 1980s it was still possible to study at a polytechnic – a tertiary education college which balanced academic and vocational teaching, specialising in engineering, applied science and applied arts. Degrees were monitored and awarded by the Council for National Academic Awards and professional bodies in law, architecture, planning, civil engineering, etc. Polytechnics also offered a high number of 'sandwich' courses and part-time 'day-release' schemes.
- In 1980, 13 per cent of young people are in full-time higher education,[13] 15 per cent in 1988–89, with a significant increase to come in the early 1990s. In 2011 around 40 per cent of the student-age population go to university. In 1980 the male-to-female ratio at university was 2:1, in 2010 the student body is 55 per cent male, 45 per cent female. Funding for universities per place fell in the 1980s by 10 per cent, i.e. more students were educated for less.

3. Culture

New words for the decade:

acid house (repetitious music to wave your arms to); AIDS (Acquired Immune Deficiency Syndrome); BOGOF (buy one get one free); bonk-buster (popular novel with lots of bad sex); botox (poison injected to produce temporary paralysis of face); cred (reputation on the street); crowd-surf (or 'stage-dive', densely packed audience catch leaping rock stars); dinkys (double income no kids); dis (to show disrespect, usually met with violence); email; Eurosceptic (politician resistant to idea of EEC); gazunder (to suddenly reduce house price offer); ghetto blaster (portable music centre, initially linked to black music); to handbag (coerce through verbal assault, after Margaret Thatcher); hip-hop (youth culture including rap, graffiti, break-dancing); hole-in-the-wall (ATM cashpoint); nimby (not in my back yard); outsource (obtain goods or services from external suppliers); paintball (corporate bonding through shooting colleagues with paint pellets in woods); plonker (foolish person, from TV series *Only Fools and Horses*); power-dress (female executive attire, suits with big shoulder pads); power walk (not just walking, power walking); ram raid (robbery conducted by driving vehicle through window); rent-a-quote (mediatised politician); Semtex (plastic explosive of choice); shopaholic (but not on Sundays); to veg (do nothing, usually in front of television); wannabe (admirer of celebrity); wigger (white person who emulates black hip-hop culture); yomp (to march with heavy packs over difficult terrain); yuppie (young urban professional person).

Things we ate and drank:

Aqua Libra (weak melon-flavoured fizzy drink); Balti (northern Pakistan cuisine served, via Birmingham, in round-bottomed pans); cambozola; ciabatta (invented 1982 to get more air, less flour into bread); microwaveable ready meals; nouvelle cuisine (teeny portions on huge plates); panna cotta; tiramisu; tricolour pasta salad.

Music
Songs you couldn't avoid in the 1980s:

Michael Jackson 'Thriller' (1983), 'Billie Jean' (1983), 'Bad' (1987); Phil Collins 'In the Air Tonight' (1981), 'Take a Look at Me Now' (1984); Stevie Wonder 'I Just Called to Say I Love You' (1984); Prince 'Purple Rain' (1984), 'Kiss' (1986); Talking Heads 'Once in a Lifetime' (1981); Rick Astley 'Never Gonna Give You Up' (1987); Belinda Carlisle 'Heaven is a Place on Earth' (1987); Bangles 'Walk Like an Egyptian' (1986), 'Eternal Flame' (1989); Eddy Grant 'I Don't Want to Dance' (1982), 'Electric Avenue' (1982); Elton John 'I Guess that's

Why They Call It the Blues' (1983), 'I'm Still Standing' (1983); Sade 'Smooth Operator' (1985).

Big-hair rock:

Van Halen 'Jump' (1984); Yes 'Owner of a Lonely Heart' (1983); Bruce Springsteen 'Dancing in the Dark' (1984), 'Born in the USA' (1984); AC/DC 'You Shook Me All Night Long' (1980); Def Leppard 'Love Bites' (1988); Whitesnake 'Is This Love' (1987); Status Quo 'In the Army Now' (1986); Starship 'We Built This City' (1985); Europe 'The Final Countdown' (1986); Foreigner 'I Want to Know What Love is' (1984); Dire Straits 'Industrial Disease' (1982), 'Money for Nothing' (1985); J. Geils Band 'Centrefold' (1982); Survivor 'Eye of the Tiger' (1982); Tina Turner 'What's Love Got to Do with It' (1984); Toto 'Africa' (1982); bald rock: Queen 'Another One Bites the Dust' (1980).

Black hip-hop:

Run-D.M.C. 'Walk This Way' (1986); Public Enemy 'Fight the Power' (1989), 'Black Steel in the Hour of Chaos' (1988); Salt-N-Pepa 'Push It' (1988); Grandmaster Flash and the Furious Five 'Rock the House' (1985); Afrika Bambaataa 'Planet Rock' (1982).

Songs of protest:

Jackson Browne 'Lives in the Balance' (1986) anti-war, anti-globalisation; Phil Collins 'Another Day in Paradise' (1989) homelessness; Peter Gabriel 'Biko' (1980) Steve Biko's death, 'Games without Frontiers' (1980) anti-war; The Specials 'Free Nelson Mandela' (1984); Nena '99 Luftballons' (1982) anti-arms race; Grandmaster Flash 'The Message' (1982) racism and black poverty; Tracy Chapman 'Behind the Wall' (1988) domestic violence; Dire Straits 'Brothers in Arms' (1982) anti-Falklands War; Cars 'Drive (Who's Gonna Take You Home)' (1985) the track played under images of the famine in Ethiopia, used as the broadcast for Live Aid; Police 'Invisible Sun' (1981) Northern Ireland; U2 'Sunday Bloody Sunday' (1983)

Northern Ireland; House Martins 'Johannesburg' (1987) anti-apartheid; Sting 'Russians' (1985) anti Cold-War rhetoric; Dead Kennedys 'We've Got a Bigger Problem Now' (1981) anti-Reagan, 'Kill the Poor' (1980) anti-poverty; Labi Siffre 'Something Inside So Strong' (1987) anti-apartheid.

New Romantics:

Adam and the Ants 'Stand and Deliver' (1981); Spandau Ballet 'True' (1983); the objectionably sexist Duran Duran 'Rio' (1982), 'Wild Boys' (1984); Talk Talk 'Life's What You Make It' (1985); Culture Club 'Do You Really Want to Hurt Me' (1982).

British post-punk/new wave/electronic/synthpop:

The Cure 'The Lovecats' (1983); Joy Division 'Love Will Tear Us Apart' (1980); New Order 'Blue Monday' (1983); Thompson Twins 'Hold Me Now' (1983); Depeche Mode 'People are People' (1984); Soft Cell 'Tainted Love' (1981), 'Say Hello, Wave Goodbye' (1982); Heaven 17 'We Don't Need This Fascist Groove Thang' (1981), 'Crushed by the Wheels of Industry' (1983); Gary Numan 'Cars' (1979); Eurythmics 'Sweet Dreams are Made of This' (1983); Human League 'Don't You Want Me Baby' (1981); meets alternative indie gothic emo: The Smiths 'Heaven Knows I'm Miserable Now' (1984).

Pop:

The Police 'Every Little Thing She Does is Magic' (1981); U2 'New Year's Day' (1983); Blondie 'Call Me' (1980); Men at Work 'A Land Down Under' (1981); Cyndi Lauper 'Girls Just Want to Have Fun' (1985); Madonna 'Holiday' (1983), 'Like a Virgin' (1984), 'Into the Groove' (1985); Bananarama 'Really Saying Something' (1982); Wham! 'Wham Rap (Enjoy What You Do)' (1983); Frankie Goes to Hollywood 'Relax' (1983); Bowie 'Let's Dance' (1983).

Two-tone ska revival, in response to rising racial tensions:

The Specials 'Ghost Town' (1981); Madness 'Baggy Trousers' (1980), 'House of Fun' (1982); Bad Manners 'Lip up Fatty' (1980); The Beat 'Mirror in the Bathroom' (1980).

Books

Bestselling books of the decade:

Cosmos Carl Sagan; *The Beverly Hills Diet* Judy Mazel; *Jane Fonda Workout*; *No Bad Dogs* Barbara Woodhouse; *It Shouldn't Happen to a Vet* James Herriot; *A Brief History of Time* Stephen Hawking.

Award-winning fiction:

Hawksmoor Peter Ackroyd; *A Child in Time* Ian McEwan; *Midnight's Children*, *The Satanic Verses* Salman Rushdie; *Schindler's Ark* Thomas Keneally; *Life and Times of Michael K.* J. M. Coetzee; *Hotel du Lac* Anita Brookner; *The Bone People* Keri Hulme; *The Old Devils* Kingsley Amis; *Moon Tiger* Penelope Lively; *Oscar and Lucinda* Peter Carey; *The Remains of the Day* Kazuo Ishiguro.

Art

Advertising entrepreneur Charles Saatchi dominates art collecting in 1980s, with London exhibitions particularly of US artists, *New York Art Now* (1987).

1984: Turner Prize for Young Artists begins.

1987: Van Gogh's 'Irises' sells for £27 million, then the highest price paid for a painting, indicating bullish art market. Purchaser was Australian entrepreneur Alan Bond. Sotherbys loan him half the money, he has trouble repaying, revealing auction houses' and art dealers' culpability in inflating prices.

Travel

Passengers travelling through UK airports made forty-three million journeys in 1980, by 2004 this is 167 million.[14]

1983: Front seat belts in cars made compulsory.

The popularity of the air-fare-inclusive short-haul package holiday to Europe peaks in the mid-1980s.[15] To offset the mass tourism approach, independent travel and the *Lonely Planet* guides also rise in popularity.

Leisure

First out-of-town covered shopping centres developed: Brent Cross, London (1976), Merry Hill in Dudley, West Midlands (1985), the Metrocentre, Tyne and Wear (1986), and Parc Trostre, Llanelli (1988).

Must-have toys of the decade:

Rubik's Cube – invented in 1974 by Hungarian professor of architecture, Erno Rubik, a pivotable cube with nine coloured stickers on each face; to solve the puzzle each face must be a solid colour (international rights sold 1980).

Pac-Man – first major arcade game also to appear as handheld electronic game, a circle face eats dots around a maze, chased by four ghosts (1980).

Donkey Kong – first true platform computer game where a monkey or carpenter Mario jump over obstacles and collect objects to win (1981).

Care Bears – lurid pastel-coloured teddy bears with inspirational messages on their tummies (1981).

Trivial Pursuit (1982) – same arguments every Christmas.

My Little Pony – pink and purple plastic ponies with brushable manes and myriad accessories (1983).

Cabbage Patch Kids – ugly flat-faced fabric dolls, concealed in fabric cabbages (peak frenzy 1984).

Transformers – the ultimate comeback aliens masquerading as trucks (1984).

Nintendo Entertainment System – second-generation video-game consoles arrive playing *Super Mario Bros* (1985).

Teenage Mutant Ninja Turtles – action heroes in a half-shell (1987).

Nintendo *Game Boy* handheld LCD screen arrives. Plays *Tetris* game where coloured blocks drop from top of screen (1989), now used to treat post-traumatic stress disorder.

4. Media

TV

1981: MTV launched. First music video channel, created market for music video.

1982: Channel 4 starts broadcasting, partly publicly subsidised by the Independent Broadcasting Authority and partly funded by ITV companies from advertising rights. The channel had a public-service remit. The first programme to air was the anagram game show *Countdown*. The channel introduced Liverpool-based soap opera *Brookside*.

1983: BBC Breakfast Time and TV-am begin first early-morning TV programming.

1984: BBC Drama ceases commissioning single plays for 'Play for Today', and develops filmic approach under Screen One and Screen Two, first hit with Anthony Minghella's *Truly, Madly, Deeply* (1990).

1985: BBC Drama leads the field in drama series *Edge of Darkness* and *The Singing Detective* (1986). BBC soap opera *EastEnders* launched. Christmas Day special 1986 (when Dirty Den issued Ange with divorce papers) draws 30.15 million viewers, highest TV audience for any programme of the 1980s.

1986: Rupert Murdoch of NewsCorp creates right-wing US network Fox Broadcasting Company.

1989: Rupert Murdoch launches Sky Television in 1989, subscription services and produces the sudden appearance of dishes on the sides of houses. It was financially disastrous in the first years of operation.

Film

Films everybody saw in the 1980s:

Airplane (1980), a slapstick comedy about an airplane crash, 'but that's not important right now'.

Star Wars Episode V: The Empire Strikes Back (1980), Luke Skywalker, Princess Leia and Han Solo battle dark forces of the Empire, 'Luke, I am your father'.

Raiders of the Lost Ark (1981), Steven Spielberg directs, Harrison Ford swashbuckles against a Nazi battalion digging up the ark of the covenant in Egypt.

E.T. The Extra Terrestrial (1982), a cute alien with a light-up finger meets boy who helps him 'phone home'. ET is lured indoors by Reese's Pieces peanut butter toffees in the first major product placement. Highest-grossing film of the 1980s.

Blade Runner (1982), Ridley Scott's cult dystopia, where rogue organic robot 'replicants' are hunted by Harrison Ford.

Gandhi (1982), a very serious Richard Attenborough directs biopic of Mahatma Gandhi with Ben Kingsley.

War Games (1983), young hacker Matthew Broderick helps the US military supercomputer understand the futility of the Cold War nuclear policy of Mutually Assured Destruction.

Flashdance (1983), dancing Jennifer Beals as an unlikely welder.

Ghostbusters (1984), comic trio Bill Murray, Harold Ramis and Dan Aykroyd run an agency to control ghosts, 'Who you gonna call?'

Beverley Hills Cop (1984), Eddie Murphy is the first headline black actor, plays a comedy detective.

The Terminator (1984), indestructible Arnold Schwarzenegger is back from a future run by machines to kill a rebel human, 'I'll be back'.

Footloose (1984), Kevin Bacon loosens up a local town through the medium of expressive dance.

The Breakfast Club (1985), drama about five irritating US teenagers bonding in detention.

Back to the Future (1985), Michael J. Fox in comedy sci-fi involving a DeLorean DMC-12 sports car as a time machine.

Top Gun (1986), Tom Cruise flies jet fighters in US Navy recruitment video.

Witness (1985), Harrison Ford as detective forced to hide in an Amish community.

Full Metal Jacket (1987), Stanley Kubrick directs Matthew Modine as a rooky in the Vietnam War.

Who Framed Roger Rabbit (1989), Bob Hoskins investigates a cartoon character's murder; live-animation interaction reignited interest in animation features, 'I'm not bad I'm just drawn that way'.

The Color Purple (1985), Steven Spielberg directs Oprah Winfrey in the adaptation of Alice Walker's Pulitzer Prize-winning novel about African-American women in the early twentieth century.

Fatal Attraction (1987), Michael Douglas chooses to have an affair with an obsessional Glenn Close – the rabbit gets it.

Do the Right Thing (1987), directed by and stars Spike Lee. The dark comedy charts tension between Italian and black communities in Brooklyn, which escalates when a young black man is killed by police.

Newspapers

1981: Rupert Murdoch buys *The Times* and *The Sunday Times*; both papers lurch further to the right politically. Robert Maxwell buys the British Printing Corporation.

1982: 'Gotcha', *Sun* headline on sinking of the Argentine ship *General Belgrano*.

1983: Eddie Shah runs Messenger group of sixty regional newspapers. Has long dispute with print unions in Warrington over unionisation.

1984: During miners' strike the *Sun* prepares a front page with Arthur Scargill under the headline 'Mine Führer'; the print workers refuse to print the edition.

Robert Maxwell buys the left-wing *Daily Mirror* and Mirror Group Newspapers. He comes to own *Sunday Mirror*, and Scottish *Daily Record* and *Sunday Mail*.

1986: Rupert Murdoch introduces electronic printing and moves operations from central London to Wapping in east London with the loss of many printer jobs; 6,000 workers are sacked for striking. A year-long picket of sacked workers is unsuccessful in getting reinstatements.

Sun headline 'Freddie Starr Ate My Hamster'. Max Clifford makes up this story.

In response to Murdoch and Maxwell's control of the press, the *Independent* newspaper is launched, produced by Newspaper Publishing plc. Circulation of 400,000 in 1989.

Eddie Shah launches *Today* newspaper, smaller format than broadsheet, full colour. Paper folds 1996.

Sun falsely accuses Elton John of using rent boys, and Piers Morgan writes a feature entitled 'The Poofs of Pop' (1988).

1988: Robert Maxwell launches ill-fated, transnational paper, the *European*.

1989: *Sun* leads with false headline on the Hillsborough football disaster, 'The Truth: some fans picked pockets of victims; some fans urinated on the brave cops; some fans beat up PC giving kiss of life'. The newspaper still does not sell well in Liverpool.

Fashion

Hair is big: the mullet (short on top, long permed hair at back); the shaggy perm; crimping; backcombing; the side ponytail; the rat's tail (crew cut with one long, measly strand of hair growing down your back); close-cropped beards; late-1980s 'designer stubble'; wet-look perms; very high coifs; the Princess Diana flick.

Rolled-up sleeves on an oversized pastel jacket, worn over a T-shirt; shoulder pads; skin-tight jeans with batwing jumpers; primary-colour evening dresses on *Dallas* and *Dynasty*; lace fingerless gloves; pixie boots; legwarmers; dayglo neon workout tights/body suits/leotards (to suggest imminent jazzercise, aerobics or step class); net skirts; the shell suit (shiny, dayglo, nylon tracksuit designed to give impression of relentless athleticism, modelled by Jimmy Savile); pedal pushers (cropped trousers); Doc Marten boots; torn T-shirts; branded, designer trainers in many colours; pre-faded stonewashed jeans; and for that European aristo-brat look circa 1988, block primary colour polo shirts and capri pants from Benetton.

Deeley boppers (hairbands with objects on springy antennae 1982); bits of lace tied around anything; huge dayglo plastic earrings in geometric shapes; non-matching neon socks; bandanas; electric blue eyeliner and mascara; wide leather bracelets and metal bangles, woven friendship bracelets; digital watches with built-in calculators; plastic, cheerful-coloured, Swiss Swatch™ watches (1985).

Comedy

1979: The Comedy Store, first stand-up comedy club opens in London. Improvisational playing style develops into TV's *Whose Line is It Anyway?* (1988).

Not the Nine O'Clock News, TV comedy sketch show runs till 1982.

1983: Jongleurs comedy clubs open Europe-wide.

1984: *Spitting Image*, TV political satire sketch show, with puppets. *Saturday Live*, based on US *Saturday Night Live*, televised stand-up.

Alternative politically correct comedy emerges (different from club comics and other traditional solo comedy), attacks racism, misogyny, homophobia, right-wing politicians: Alexei Sayle, Ben Elton, Dawn French, Jennifer Saunders, etc.

Celebrity culture

British 'front-page' culture further developed by British tabloid press – leading commercial celebrity, Princess Diana.

5. Science, technology and industry

Science

1980: The hepatitis-B vaccine invented; most babies vaccinated, cuts liver cancer rates.

1981: The scanning tunnelling microscope invented by Gerd Binnig and Heinrich Rohrer (awarded Nobel Prize for Physics 1986), uses beams of electrons, rather than light, to produce 3-D images of features smaller than the wavelength of light. It can also manipulate individual atoms – in 1990 Eigler and Schweizer spell IBM in thirty-five atoms of xenon. Applications for data storage, customised atomic structures and nano electronic circuitry still being explored.

Human growth hormone genetically engineered. After cases of Creutzfeldt-Jakob disease discovered, biosynthetic human growth hormone only was licensed (1985).

Space shuttle *Columbia* makes its maiden voyage. 1986 shuttle *Challenger* breaks up on launch killing all seven crew. Final shuttle flight in 2011.

1982: First artificial heart (Jarvik-7) transplant into a human conducted, the patient survives 112 days.

Recombinant DNA technology (combining DNA from two different sources to produce a DNA form not otherwise found in biological organisms) used to create non-animal-sourced insulin.

1983: Polymerase Chain Reaction (PCR) invented, a technique that uses enzymes to make millions of copies of a piece of DNA quickly and cheaply. PCR allows for genetic codes in illness to be detected, notably HIV, facilitating earlier diagnosis.

1984: DNA profiling (using PCR) made possible by Alec Jeffreys, UK. 1987 Colin Pitchfork was the first person to be convicted of murder using profiling.

1985: Hubble Space Telescope completed, launched on shuttle in 1990.

1986: High-temperature super-conductors discovered by Georg Bednorz and Alex Müller for IBM (Nobel Prize for Physics 1987). These are solids that conduct electricity with practically no loss of energy at temperatures above 30 Kelvin (–243 degrees Centigrade). Currently used in MRI scanners and the particle accelerator at CERN, further applications are still being explored in energy storage and radical improvement of national power grid.

Soviet Mir space station launched.

1988: The RU-486, the morning-after pill available (invented by Georges Teutsch 1980).

Prozac (fluoxetine hydrochloride) a selective serotonin re-uptake inhibitor, arrived on the market. Now the most prescribed antidepressant.

The first patent for a genetically engineered animal is issued to Harvard University researchers Philip Leder and Timothy Stewart.

1989: Unmanned *Voyager* spacecraft reaches Neptune, two billion miles from Earth, and sends back images. *Voyager 1* and *2* are still going strong heading for the heliopause (extent of the Sun's influence) as this book is published.

Technology

1980: Nintendo release LCD handheld electronic Game & Watch games.

1981: MS-DOS (Microsoft Disk Operating System) for IBM home computers invented.

1982: Audio CDs became commercially available, although cassette tape recorders were still necessary to tape illegally from the radio. CD-ROM (Read-Only Memory) technology was available from 1984, to store computer data and visual data.

1983: Programmer Jaron Lanier first coins the term 'virtual reality'.

Cellular mobile phone technology had been developing since the 1960s; the Swedes had car phones. Handheld mobile phones are first created in 1973, in 1979 Tokyo has first cell phone coverage. In 1981 Denmark, Finland, Norway and Sweden have coverage. In 1983 after the British Telecom sell-off, two licences for UK mobile phone coverage were sold – one to Cellnet, created by BT and Securicor, the other to Vodafone, created by Racal Electronics and Millicom.

The Motorola DynaTAC 8000X mobile phone cost over £3,000, weighed 800 grams and had a battery life of thirty minutes of call time.

1984: Apple Macintosh commercially available.

Inspired by the Strategic Defense Initiative, ground-based missile interceptors were developed as 'hit to kill' technology. Laser technology as imagined by SDI only developed in actuality in 2011.

1985: Windows, the graphical user interface for Microsoft programmes, was introduced.

By the mid-1980s, the fax machine (invented in analogue form in 1843) becomes an essential piece of office equipment.

1989: High-definition television invented.

Tim Berners-Lee proposes a database and software project called ENQUIRE. By 1990, the project is called the World Wide Web. It allows Hypertext documents to be read by different browsers connected through a client-server architecture. This emerges from needs at the CERN (European Organisation for Nuclear Research) particle physics laboratory in Europe.

Industry

1980–93: Six Employment Acts restrict industrial action by requiring pre-strike ballots, outlawing secondary action, restricting picketing and giving employers the right to seek injunctions where there is doubt about the legality of action.

1984: British Telecom privatised by Telecommunications Act. Two million initial shareholders. Telecommunications was decoupled from the General Post Office in 1981, prior to privatisation.

US firm Union Carbide's badly maintained plant in Bhopal leaked methyl isocyanate gas from an underground storage tank. It hovered over an urban area, home to around a million people. Three thousand people died immediately, 8,000 from related illness, 50,000 were treated for blindness, liver failure, etc. with an ongoing legacy of congenital deformity. One of the world's worst industrial accidents.

1986: British Gas privatised. Saturation advertising campaign 'If you see Sid . . . Tell him'. Produces a monopoly private supplier. Four and a half million initial shareholders.

Building Society Act (1986) allows them to demutualise, becoming banks: TSB is privatised with three million initial shareholders.

1986 Financial Services Act deregulates financial services industry: all firms can combine previously separate roles of dealer (who trades shares on others' behalf), with jobber (who makes markets); derivative contracts are removed from court oversight; outside corporations can own London Stock Exchange firms; face-to-face trading disappears as trading floors are computerised. Financial Services industry increases its significant role in UK economy.[16] Dubbed the 'Big Bang' because of the amount of trading the day of change over permitted, the Act also permitted companies to be Self-Regulating Organisations, removing layers of oversight.

Defence Secretary Michael Heseltine resigns over Thatcher's refusal to back European recovery deal for British Westland Helicopter manufacturers.

Guinness chief executive and other businessmen arrested for 'insider dealing', trading shares with advanced knowledge of the takeover of Distillers, the Scottish whisky group, which had earned them personal fortunes.

1987: British Airways privatised, after reducing staff and loss-making routes, and having a brand overhaul prior to sale, at taxpayers' expense.

1988: Abbey Building Society demutualised.

1989: Electricity Act begins privatisation into three companies: Powergen and National Power, intended to be competing suppliers, and the National Grid Company, responsible for transmission. National Power was intended to include nuclear provision, but this was too financially draining and was retained in government ownership as Nuclear Electric.

6. Political events

1980:

May Iranian embassy siege by Khomeini loyalists ended by SAS.

June Defence Secretary Francis Pym announces US Cruise missiles will be housed at RAF Greenham Common, Berkshire.

July Moscow Olympics are boycotted by US and West Germany because of the Russian presence in Afghanistan. US arm Afghanistan's Mujahideen as anti-communist force – a playing out of Cold War enmities.

August First free Polish union, Solidarity, formed at Gdansk during a shipyard strike led by Lech Walesa.

September Tension between Iran and Iraq becomes war. Sensing Iran is destabilised after the Shia revolution of 1979 which ousted the Shah and brought Ayatollah Khomeini to power, Iraq invades. The conflict is fought as trench warfare, with chemical weapons used by both sides, and lasts until 1988. Iran estimated it lost a million military and civilian lives, and half a million Iraqis die. The UN ceasefire brings no change to borders. Iraqi Kurdistan supports the Iranians, and 'Chemical' Ali Hassan al-Majid was held responsible for the chemical attacks on Kurdish Halabja, killing 5,000 civilians in 1988.

November Ronald Reagan, Republican and ex-movie star, elected US President.

December John Lennon shot.

1981:

January Tehran frees the US Embassy hostages it has been holding since November 1979.

March New UK political party the Social Democrats (SDP) formed by dissident Labour politicians, led by David Owen, Shirley Williams, Roy Jenkins and Bill Rodgers. Merges with Liberal Party in 1988 to form Liberal Democrats.

April Unrest in Brixton, the Brixton 'riots', tension between police and young black men in the Brixton area tension is exacerbated by 'sus' laws (stop and search) for which the police do not need to give a reason. A young man is arrested outside a minicab office and the confrontation escalates.

May IRA hunger striker Bobby Sands starves to death in attempt to be recognised as political prisoner not a criminal; 100,000 attend his funeral. In wake of this Sinn Féin, seen as the political wing of IRA, begins to participate in elections.

July Tension between police and black residents of Toxteth, Liverpool erupts into 'riots'. The later Scarman Report noted that here and in Brixton poverty and deprivation were main drivers of unrest. Other inner-city areas with high unemployment had disturbances, including Handsworth Birmingham, Chapeltown Leeds.

Prince Charles and Diana married in Westminster Abbey.

December A mystery disease, which came to be known as Acquired Immune Deficiency Syndrome or AIDS, is identified in US.

1982:

February Freddie Laker's first attempt at a low-cost, no-frills airline, SkyTrain, goes bankrupt. The firm was both significantly undercapitalised during the recession, and had been aggressively price matched by bigger carriers, who could carry the loss.

London International Financial Futures Exchange introduced – a new trading floor in futures at the London Stock Market.

April Argentina reclaims the Falkland Islands (population 1,800) and lands a small force. The UK government sends a task force and declares war. Suspected oil reserves make the islands valuable. Nine hundred combatants are killed, mostly Argentine conscripts. The defeat of Argentine forces in June precipitates the fall of the Argentine military junta, and in 1983 Argentina elects a democratic government and ends the junta's 'dirty war' against left-wing sympathisers.

July IRA bombs ceremonial displays of Household Guards in Hyde Park and Regent's Park, killing eleven and injuring fifty soldiers.

August Israeli Prime Minister Menachem Begin invades Lebanon as far as Beirut, to force Yasser Arafat, leader of the Palestine Liberation Organisation (PLO), out of country. Syrian militant assassinates Bachir Gemayel, Israeli-supported Lebanese president elect. Israeli-backed Christian militia massacres hundreds of Palestinians in two Beirut refugee camps in reprisal. US troops go into Beirut as peacekeepers. PLO establishes HQ in Tunis. Partial autonomy for Gaza and West Bank agreed at Oslo 1993, and Palestinian National Authority created to administer areas.

1983:

March US President Reagan unveils plans for a space-based laser shield to destroy incoming nuclear missiles, the Strategic Defense Initiative, as alternative to Mutually Assured Destruction. This initiative has never proved technically feasible.

April Campaign for Nuclear Disarmament protesters form a fourteen-mile human chain from Greenham Common, Berkshire to Aldermaston Atomic Weapons Establishment.

African National Congress (outlawed Black Rights movement committed to overthrow the white minority rule of the apartheid regime) plants car bomb outside the South African Air Force HQ in Pretoria, South Africa, kills seventeen, injures 200.

June Margaret Thatcher defeats Labour under Michael Foot, with 140-seat majority in UK elections.

1984:

March Coal industry was nationally owned. Several mines were considered uneconomic, but government threatened closure of twenty mines before viability reports were received, producing 20,000 job losses. Miners' unions, most notably the federated National Union of Mineworkers led by Arthur Scargill, came out in regional strikes amounting to a national stoppage. There are bitter encounters between police and striking miners, particularly at Orgreave, where mounted police charge strikers, injuring fifty-one. Thatcher calls the miners 'the enemy within'. 1980 Social Security Act banned dependants of strikers from claiming welfare benefits; extreme hardship experienced in many areas of northern England, Scotland and Wales.

June Indira Gandhi orders Indian army to retake the Golden Temple of Amritsar where Sikh separatists were besieged. This raised Hindu–Sikh tensions. In October Gandhi was assassinated by two Sikh bodyguards, prompting anti-Sikh riots that killed around 500.

October IRA bomb Tory conference hotel in Brighton, in part as reprisal for hunger-strikers' deaths. Five people killed and many injured. Patrick Magee jailed 1986.

Emergency aid for famine in Ethiopia agreed by EEC.

November Pound notes withdrawn, replaced with coins.

Bhopal chemical disaster kills 11,000.

1985:

March Miners' strike ends in defeat for miners. Most UK pits closed.

Mikhail Gorbachev becomes general secretary of Russian Communist Party. *Glasnost* (openness) begins, and *perestroika* (economic restructuring) for Russia's flagging economy.

July Live Aid concert for Ethiopian relief effort facilitates first global live twenty-four-hour broadcast.

Unrest in Brixton after police shoot and paralyse a black woman, Cherry Groce, in her bed while searching for her son. Toxteth and Peckham experience violent protest initiated by incidents between the police and young black men. Unrest in Birmingham, Coventry, Bristol and Wolverhampton. Later that week, in Tottenham, black woman Cynthia Jarrett dies as police search her home for stolen goods following the arrest of her son. Violent protests follow and policeman Keith Blakelock is killed.

Anglo-Irish Agreement gave Irish government a 'consultative' role in Northern Ireland. Immediate increased response from loyalist forces Ulster Volunteer Force (UVF), Ulster Defence Association (UDA) and Ulster Resistance.

1986:

March Greater London Council disbanded, considered left-wing threat by government.

US Navy undertakes exercises in contested waters off Libya in the Mediterranean, fire on and destroy Libyan vessels. In April, Libyan involvement is suspected when a West German disco used by US marines is bombed, killing three and injuring 200. Regan orders the bombing of Tripoli and Benghazi and uses UK bases to coordinate the attack. International criticism of Colonel Gaddafi grows stronger. British hostages are taken in Beirut, Lebanon and shot, and journalist John McCarthy is kidnapped.

April The Chernobyl nuclear reactor in Ukraine, USSR, explodes and goes into meltdown. A wide area of Europe is affected by radioactive fallout blown on the wind.

October Mordechai Vanunu, Israeli nuclear technician, kidnapped by Mossad, Israeli secret service, for revealing that Israel had nuclear weapons.

1987:
June Conservatives win third term in government.

August Michael Ryan shoots fourteen in Hungerford in a random attack.

October Freak hurricane in southern England closes London Stock Exchange.

> The stock market crash. Fall in value of shares on Wall Street by 22 per cent. Dubbed 'Black Monday', the London Stock Exchange (LSE) experiences a loss of £50.6 billion in the value of shares. Economists have been unable to identify reasons for the crash, although it may have been linked to US retaliatory bombing of an Iranian oil platform in the Gulf and suspended trading on the LSE due to the hurricane. Apparent rebound proves illusory and long recession begins in 1990.

November Eleven killed and sixty-three injured by IRA bomb at Remembrance Day parade in Enniskillen, County Fermanagh.

December US and USSR sign Intermediate-Range Nuclear Forces Treaty.

1988:
January Piper Alpha oil rig explosion due to poor maintenance, 167 of the 226 men on the rig died.

March Three unarmed IRA members shot dead on Gibraltar. At the IRA funeral, Ulster Freedom Fighter member Michael Stone shoots three mourners. At funeral of one of those shot, two plainclothes soldiers accidentally drive towards funeral cortege; they are dragged from their car and killed by crowd.

July US warship shoots down an Iranian passenger jet in error, killing 300 passengers, most of them on the way to Mecca.

October 'Right to silence' withdrawn in Northern Ireland; judges and jury can 'interpret' refusal to answer questions.

December Pan Am flight 103 explodes over Scottish town of Lockerbie, killing all 259 people on board and eleven on the ground. Libya accused of involvement, Iran also suspected for reprisal for US shooting down of passenger jet.

1989:

February Ayatollah Khomeini issues fatwa against author Salman Rushdie for his allegedly blasphemous novel *The Satanic Verses*.
   Soviet forces leave Afghanistan, where civil war continues.

March Exxon Valdez tanker runs aground, forty-two million litres of crude oil spill off the Alaskan coastline.

April Polish union Solidarity, outlawed since 1981, is recognised by President General Jaruzelski and ruling Communist Party. First partly free elections. 1990 Lech Walesa first freely elected President of Poland.

April The Tiananmen Square protests, Beijing, China. Students and workers gather to mourn the death of a liberal Communist Party reformer. This develops into protest for economic and political reform, including the publication of leaders' incomes, freedom of the press, increased funding for education and some democratic elections. The enduring image is of a lone protester in front of a tank, but many protesters are beaten. Figures are contested, but at the time (later officially retracted) the Chinese Red Cross estimated that around 2,400 protesters had been killed in Beijing during disturbances.

June Austrian foreign minister and Hungarian foreign minister cut through the barbed wire at the border. In August a pan-European picnic was held and several hundred East Germans entered Austria. In September Hungary opened its borders and 70,000 exited to the West.
   Ayatollah Khomeini dies.

September IRA bomb at Deal Barracks, Kent, kills eleven Royal Marines.

October Gorbachev visits East Germany advising reform. Hungary adopts multi-party democracy. East German leader Erich Honecker steps down. On 9 November, a spokesperson for the East German Politburo announces free movement from East Berlin to West Berlin with immediate effect. East Berliners immediately congregated at the Wall and were allowed to cross without papers. Throughout next few weeks the wall was demolished piecemeal by citizens and the authorities opened several significant crossings. Led to German reunification in October 1990.

November The Velvet Revolution in Czechoslovakia begins with protests in Prague and a general strike on 27 November. Borders with West Germany and Austria were demilitarised. On 10 December, President Husak resigned and in first free presidential elections playwright Václav Havel is elected president on 29 December.

December In Romania, a Roman Catholic priest is placed under house arrest after calling for reform. Protests develop into a national strike, further fuelled by widespread poverty and frustration at military control. A rally on 20 December in Bucharest addressed by Nicolae Ceauşescu was broadcast live. When the crowd unexpectedly jeer they are fired upon, and a full-blown battle begins between unarmed protesters and the military. The Ceauşescus escape to the countryside, but are captured, tried and executed on 25 December.

CHAPTER 1
THEATRE IN THE 1980S

'always historicize'

Fredric Jameson[1]

'Most of my heroes don't appear on no stamps
Sample a look back you look and find
Nothing but rednecks for 400 years if you check'

Public Enemy[2]

'Can we not have before again, can we not?'

Valerie in *Road*[3]

This chapter sets out to examine playwriting in the theatrical culture of the 1980s. The institutional structures of theatre making and theatregoing were placed under considerable strain during the period, as indeed were all aspects of British economic and institutional life. Theatrical events, plays and performances were engaged with the political realities of their day and many were imbued with the competing political discourses of the time. This chapter looks at the way we might approach the recent past and considers the impact of political and economic shifts upon cultural life in the 1980s. It is within this cultural context that playwrights' careers, and the plays they wrote, were forged.

Thinking about the recent past

There is a curious paradox at work in writing a history of the recent past. On the one hand, this past is still very present in the economic, legal and political structures of our contemporary experience. For example, the 2008 recession in the West, still being played out as this book is written, could not have happened without the deregulation of financial institutions, and the drive towards home-ownership, introduced by the monetarist policies of 'Reaganomics' and 'Thatcherism'. On the other hand, at the same moment, the 1980s seem a distant and alienated past, and the processes of 'historification' have been at work, making a period of lived experience into history.[4] The BBC took a nostalgic look back, in January 2001, with the nine-part series *I Love the '80s*: a bricolage of interviews, news footage and cultural artefacts from each year of the 'decade of greed'.[5] *Electric Dreams* (September 2009), another BBC series, co-produced with the Open University, explored the impact of technology on the domestic environment and lifestyle. It followed a family whose house was appropriately redecorated and new technology introduced to mark the decades from the 1970s until they returned to the Wi-Fi, gadget-laden present. As the 1980s dawned, they celebrated the arrival of the microwave, video recorder, synthpop and early home computers, and judged it a time of optimal balance with the benefits of technology that reduced the burden of domestic chores, still primarily undertaken by the working mother, but that did not yet privilege individual entertainment over family communication. Required reading as an antidote to these gently celebratory, nostalgic returns to the decade is Jonathan Coe's extraordinary indictment of the period in his comic novel *What a Carve Up!* (1994). Coe refuses the consolations of the domestic in his family saga, and exposes the vested interests of an elite power group, figured in the novel as members of the Winshaw family, who control influence in the media, banking, the arms trade, agriculture, politics and the arts.

There are two very particular narrative forces at work when we attempt to construct a history of a period that we, or our personal circle of acquaintance, have lived through. The apparently cool objectivity of an idealised scientific, fact-filled history will always run alongside the warm recollection of an emotion-laden experience of personal relationship to social, economic and political structures and events. The narratives of history and memory co-exist. While memory might seem to offer a more authentic version of the past, Andreas

Huyssen reminds us that, rather than 'giving us verifiable access to the real, memory, even and especially in its belatedness, is itself based on representation. The past is not simply there in memory, but it must be articulated to become memory. The fissure that opens up between experiencing an event and remembering it in representation is unavoidable.'[6] Experiencing a theatrical event, being on a protest march, or a first kiss is one thing, but our memory of that experience is quite another, already translated into representation and given meaning and significance in our self-narrative. Huyssen suggests that from this unavoidable split between experience and remembering, 'cultural and artistic creativity' might spring. It is also within this gap that nostalgic desire emerges. One form of the nostalgic desire that emerges is the search for an idealised past as a coherent and authentic refuge from the difficulties of an uncomfortable present. As Susan Stewart suggests, 'nostalgia, like any form of narrative, is always ideological: the past it seeks has never existed, except as narrative'.[7] In this reading of nostalgic desire, its praxis is inherently 'conservative', and in the British cultural context any nostalgic search for a theatrical golden age inevitably leads us back to Shakespeare, as Susan Bennett has articulated.[8]

During the 1980s, theatrical culture was subjected to a range of policy, political and economic pressures that, as we shall see below, produced an enormous sense of dislocation and dissatisfaction with the present, and many of the most fêted theatre companies and directors of the decade turned to Shakespeare to provide a stable and reliably commercial foundation for their theatre work: Deborah Warner's Kick Theatre Company (founded 1980), Cheek by Jowl (1981), Michael Pennington and Michael Bogdanov's English Shakespeare Company (1986), Kenneth Branagh's Renaissance Theatre Company (1987) all achieved national touring success with versions of Shakespeare, and were leading British cultural exports internationally through the British Council. Some commentators, notably Robert Hewison,[9] have suggested that British culture itself was inherently nostalgic during the 1980s, and that in the face of declining investment in manufacturing industry, the heritage industry was born. For David Edgar this was an explicitly party political activity: 'popular in form, patrician in content, the heritage industry *is* cultural Thatcherism'.[10] Indeed, this reveals another nostalgia at work in the rhetoric of many theatre makers of the 1980s, not just for Shakespeare, but also for an idea of the lost radical, left-wing alternative theatre of the 1970s.

The style of 1980s culture in the broadest sense was laden with a cultivated nostalgia, produced by the economic logic of advanced capitalism's commercial life.[11] The attraction of the retro, the 'making-do', and the recycling of past objects as a statement of resistance or alternative values had been part of British cultural life since the 1950s, but by the 1980s retro was big business. The alternative, small-scale entrepreneurial ventures of the 1960s and 1970s, such as Laura Ashley with its Victorian-style cottagey prints or the Body Shop with its glass-bottled natural products reminiscent of Edwardian chemists, had been capitalised, floated on the stock market (the Body Shop 1984, Laura Ashley 1985) and brought to a mass market. The 1980s saw the gift shops of National Trust properties enlarged and filled with potpourri, and 'heritage' chic reached the high street in the form of Past Times (founded 1986), a chain selling gifts that referenced design from rousing moments of a British past characterised by a sentimental nationalism, with Second World War public information poster designs on mugs, tea towels, etc. This 'retrochic', as Raphael Samuel dubs it, was not driven by a revivalist or conservationist spirit. It preferred 'remakes to originals, cheerfully engaging in the manufacture of replicaware without any attempt to disguise the modernity of its provenance. When it imitates or cribs, it draws attention to its own piracies: [. . . it] involves not an obsession with the past but an indifference to it.'[12] The objects of retrochic were cheap and widely available. The increased discretionary spend of women in the workplace contributed in no small part to the feminisation of retrochic goods, from Crabtree & Evelyn's Victorian-look soaps to the 'hand-made' snacks of Phileas Fogg (launched 1982), that summon a manufacturing heritage of cottage industry, but can only be made affordable through the application of advanced industrial manufacture and distribution. From the late 1980s these manufacturing processes were increasingly likely to be based abroad, using cheaper labour, and shipped into UK distribution centres.

That nostalgia and versions of a national heritage might be used to serve contemporary political purposes was not lost on the Conservative government of the 1980s. It was Brian Walden who coined the phrase 'Victorian values' in a television interview with Margaret Thatcher prior to the general election of 1983, but Thatcher responded with enthusiastic endorsement that is worth quoting at length:

> Those were the values when our country became great, but not only did our country become great internationally, also so much advance was made in this country. Colossal advance, as people prospered themselves so they gave great voluntary things to the State. So many of the schools we replace now were voluntary schools, so many of the hospitals we replace were hospitals given by this great benefaction feeling that we have in Britain, even some of the prisons, the Town Halls. As our people prospered, so they used their independence and initiative to prosper others, not compulsion by the State. Yes, I want to see one nation, as you go back to Victorian times, but I want everyone to have their own personal property stake. Property, every single one in this country, that's why we go so hard for owner-occupation, this is where we're going to get one nation. I want them to have their own savings which retain their value, so they can pass things on to their children, so you get again a people, everyone strong and independent of Government, as well as a fundamental safety net below which no one can fall. Winston [Churchill] put it best. You want a ladder, upwards, anyone, no matter what their background, can climb, but a fundamental safety net below which no one can fall. That's the British character.[13]

This is a nostalgic summoning of a mythic past, rather than any specific historical moment: Victorian imperial greatness is conflated with the Second World War, through the reference to Churchillian resilience. The idea that the Victorian era was one of social unity, implied by the phrase 'one nation', is hardly a vision that a Chartist or suffragist would recognise.[14] Indeed, 'one-nation conservatism', with its conciliatory desire for social and political consensus embodied by Edward Heath, was precisely that kind of 'wet' Toryism that Margaret Thatcher had sought to drive out of her cabinet. The political rhetoric of 'return' to greatness in this interview is undercut by the necessity of addressing all the differences of the current moment of 1983 from that mythic past. In particular, property-ownership as a capital, heritable investment was largely the preserve of the upper middle and upper classes in Victorian Britain, and the aspiration of the Conservative government for a much broader expansion of house-ownership was indeed a critical distinction from both the myth and actuality of the Victorian past.

The political use made of nostalgia and heritage, and the relation of this nostalgia to the forces of multinational capitalism, was key to a fundamental debate in intellectual history during the 1980s, about postmodernism. Within UK, US and European university humanities departments where theatre, literature and culture were studied and taught, the dispute about postmodernity[15] was dubbed the 'theory wars'. Until the 1970s the dominant modes of literary and cultural analysis had been focused either on the literary text, in the formalist or structuralist New Criticism, or on the production of art within its cultural, economic and political context, as in the Cultural Materialism of critics such as Raymond Williams. With the increased translation of post-Second World War European philosophy into English, ideas that critiqued the nature of language, thought and Being began to inflect critical approaches more fully. Great excitement was caused by the English translation of the first volume of Michel Foucault's *The History of Sexuality* (1978).[16] Bitter feuds were fought about the relative place of theory and literary text, and much ink was spilled from a range of ideological positions. The theory wars were played out less aggressively in theatre departments, but the same impetus led to the rise of Performance Studies. A significant moment of emergence came in 1980 when the Drama Department at New York University was renamed Performance Studies.[17] Initially a subsection of the discipline, Performance Studies has become increasingly voracious in its appetite for subject matter and address. While the study of theatre and drama had always, at its most enlightened, involved questions of the nature of performance, the 1980s saw a broadening out of analysis to the performance of all events, behaviours and actions, far beyond the theatrical. All subsequent histories and analyses since the 1980s have been coloured by these intellectual trends.

So, our approach to any period of history and the organising structures of thought we bring to the enterprise will condition our interpretative possibilities. In thinking about theatre in the 1980s, the history that follows will examine three areas. First, this chapter will chart shifts in the structural modes of production of theatre, notably in its institutions, the cultural policies applied to it and the mechanisms that funded it. Second, new writing during the 1980s will be reconsidered and the range of playwrights writing for all kinds of theatrical performance. Finally, plays written during the 1980s and their engagement with the issues of the day will be explored, reflecting on the relationship between content, form and audience.

Institutions, policies and funding

Theatre and crisis?

The language of arts workers, artists and academics during the 1980s was the language of crisis. As Catherine Itzin notes, when the first Conservative budget of June 1979 announced public spending cuts and the Arts Council responded by naming a swathe of arts companies it proposed to axe, theatre workers joined a mass demonstration in July to 'save our stages'.[18] At the other end of the decade, in December 1988, a conference of academics and leading theatre workers was entitled 'British Theatre in Crisis'.[19] Hewison and Peacock both record that Margaret Thatcher appears bemused by the furore in her memoirs, remarking that spending on the arts 'rose sharply in real terms while I was in Downing Street. Though from the chorus of complaints about the "cuts" you would not have known it.'[20] The increased spend on the arts that Thatcher is recalling was predominantly accounted for by large-scale *capital* projects in the museum and libraries sector, such as the building of the new British Library at St Pancras, London. After a bumpy start, with a £1 million cut in 1980, *revenue funding* for performance arts and museums was maintained at about standstill levels through the 1980s.[21] Yet a pervading sense of anxiety about funding was produced. For individual theatre companies, playwrights and theatre venues, this average figure of sustained funding was experienced differentially – some companies saw an increase in their subsidy over the decade, while other companies disappeared from the Arts Council's books.[22] The Arts Council's publications themselves were frequently gloomy in their financial prognoses, and the realities of economic life in the 1980s could not be avoided. The impact of inflation on 'standstill funding' produced a real-terms cut, and the broader economic background to theatre funding was the two major recessions of 1980–83, and in the second half of 1990. In fact Britain had felt unsettled since 1987 and the 'Black Monday' stock market crash. Inflation rose to 7.7 per cent in 1989, and produced a crash in house prices in the same year. These economic realities encouraged a powerful nostalgia for the 1970s, which had seen modest increases in arts funding, the building of civic regional theatres and a proliferation of small-scale, alternative companies, all in the face of even more startling inflation rates.

Beyond the economic difficulties, the language of crisis characterised a perception that the 1980s was a decade of philistine governmental attack on the arts. First and foremost, anxiety was induced because the very principle of government subsidy for the arts was brought into question. A host of government pronouncements raised the spectre that the Arts Council, as central dispenser of government subsidy, and arts subsidy itself, might be ended.[23] After all, state subsidy through the Arts Council was a new-fangled creation, available only since the Second World War. Before that the performance arts had earned from all kinds of audience receipts, patronage, subscription series, commercial imports and cross-subsidy from property income, food and drink franchises. During the 1980s, in actuality financial support as state subsidy continued unabated, but, tellingly, it was increasingly rebranded as 'investment'. Michael Billington considered that this change in nomenclature 'debased' the arts.[24] John Pick warned that the 'habitual use of the language of the bucket shop in the Arts Council's reports for example may have had some of its origins in the desire for self-preservation ("talking to the government in the only language that it understands"), but it has now become ingrained in all that Arts Councils think, say and do.'[25] The Arts Council did participate in this shift in rhetoric as self-preservation. Most obviously, in 1985 it co-commissioned with the Gulbenkian Foundation, the Office of Arts and Libraries, the Museums and Galleries Commission and the Crafts Council – all those direct and indirect dispensers of government subsidy to the arts – an audit of arts funding in the UK. *The Economic Importance of the Arts*, produced by John Myerscough and his team, had a radical impact on the perception of arts funding, firmly establishing the idea of the 'cultural industries' and evidencing their contribution to the real economy in terms of employment, invisible export and the production of goods and services.[26] The principal objection to this way of viewing the arts was that it reduced art to its economic or instrumental value alone.[27] Without irony, the initially critical term 'culture industry', coined by philosophers of the 1950s Frankfurt School to describe a totalising force that reduced art to mass consumption controlled by market interests, became part of a lexicon of defence for government subsidy for the arts during the 1980s.[28] The rhetoric of the 'cultural industries' as reframed by Myerscough remains dominant in descriptions of the value of the arts today.

The second key issue that produced the perception of crisis in theatre during the 1980s was the party politicisation of the institutions of arts subsidy and administration. Robert Hewison, John Bull, D. Keith Peacock and Vera Gottlieb have all noted the increase of party political influence in the running of the Arts Council in the early 1980s, both in the appointment of key personnel and in the rhetoric employed in policy and strategy documents. Richard Hoggart, a broadly left-wing academic and founder of Cultural Studies at Birmingham University, was elbowed out of his role as Vice Chairman of the Arts Council Board in 1981, because 'Number 10 did not like him'. This despite his having been the member who communicated the Council's decision to translate its £1 million budget cut into the withdrawal of funding for forty-one companies, although his clear articulation that responsibility for this lay with the government cuts, not with the Arts Council, was seen as incendiary.[29] For Hoggart, his removal 'confirmed that governmental intervention in the work of such bodies started very early in the Eighties [. . . with f]iats from Number 10 and compliance from some of her ministers'.[30] Hoggart's exit was followed by the appointment of Conservative sympathiser William Rees-Mogg, ex-editor of *The Times* (1967–81), as Chairman of the Arts Council in 1982.[31] The installation of Luke Rittner, founder-director of the Association for Business Sponsorship of the Arts (ABSA), as Secretary-General of the Arts Council in 1983 seemed to confirm that the direction of the Arts Council would be in line with that set by the Conservative government, rather than representing cross-party interests as had been the established practice before the 1980s. Many commentators noted the erosion of the 'arm's length' principle under the guise of increased 'accountability' of public funding.[32] Party political influence was most evident in rhetoric of Arts Council annual reports that celebrated and urged increased 'partnership' between public subsidy and private sponsorship, and the diversification of income streams to arts organisations – an explicitly Conservative idea.[33]

The 1980s also saw the return to prominence of the theatre manager. The earlier twentieth century had seen the emergence of the theatre *director* as the dominant figure in the running of theatre companies, superseding the earlier roles of actor-manager or impresario. Vera Gottlieb suggests that the significance of 'management' to theatre organisations was an inevitable outcome of the introduction of monetarist policies of the Conservative government in the wider economy. She cites Adrian Ellis's definition of monetarism as 'a managerial philosophy introduced during a period of retrenchment rather than growth, creating an umbilical link in most people's minds between cuts in available funding and the introduction of private sector management tools and language'.[34] Most commentators consider the increased layer of management that theatre companies were obliged to introduce during the 1980s as a negative innovation, although some cultural policy academics have considered it produced an 'upgrade in management techniques'.[35] The government's call for increased 'accountability' for public spending led to the increased presence of accountants in theatre institutions. The role of the executive director, a companion role to the artistic director, with responsibility for financial planning, the search for sponsorship and partnership funding, managing resources and producing, emerged as an expected figure in theatre companies and venues of all sizes.[36] This level of management intrusion was more marked in the later 1980s and for building-based companies, but the case of 7:84 Scotland is an illuminating example of the ways in which this managerial influence might fundamentally alter a company's ethos and working methods. Discussed in some detail by John McGrath himself in *The Bone Won't Break* (London: Methuen, 1990) and by Keith Peacock, the Scottish Arts Council withdrew funding for 7:84, insisting that the company change its flat management structure and principle of equal wages for all company workers into a traditional management hierarchy, introducing a highly paid general manager. John McGrath, director of this community-based, actively political company, resigned; the new artistic directors secured funding by promising not to be 'concerned with politics with a capital P'.[37]

Linked to the question of accountability and financial management, the 1986 Insolvency Act had unintended but wide-ranging implications for theatre managers, trustees and advisory boards. Under this act, directors and trustees of a company were made personally liable to contribute to the assets of a company and help meet the deficits to creditors, if the company traded while insolvent. This applied to charitable bodies such as arts organisations, as well as commercial companies. Although in practice prosecutions of arts boards were vanishingly rare, trustees were urged to have more careful oversight of the financial operations of the theatres they supported. The extent to which this financial regulation increased the pressure that theatre boards placed on artistic teams to produce reliable, financially successful seasons of work, in other words more cautious, mainstream programming, is difficult to assess. Ironically, as recently as 2011, Colin Tweedy of Arts & Business (the new incarnation of ABSA) noted the way in which this legislation was causing some regional theatre boards to declare bankruptcy against the advice of the Arts Council. Tweedy suggested that arts organisations would be safer operating as cooperatives or social enterprises, and thus falling under a different legal framework.[38]

Issues of scale

If the 1970s had been the decade of the small-scale alternative theatre company, the 1980s were primarily concerned with the large-scale. The two theatre companies in receipt of the largest proportion of Arts Council funding were the Royal Shakespeare Company and the National Theatre. The RSC expanded its operations in 1982, finally moving into its London base at the Barbican, where it leased the mainstage and the small Pit. In 1986, it opened the Swan auditorium in Stratford with its fantasy creation of a covered inn-yard structure, an intimate and theatrically exciting space it considered more authentic than the main stage's proscenium arch. With regular visits to Newcastle Theatre Royal, and occasional small-scale regional tours, the RSC resources were sometimes split over seven stages. The National split its attention across three stages, and in 1984, Peter Gill established National Studio to develop experimental work and new writing, without the pressure (or some might bitterly say, the promise) of mainhouse production. Across their multiple stages, the National and RSC were funded at standstill rates from the mid-1980s, and in 1985 an exasperated Peter Hall, director of the National, closed the Cottesloe for six months in protest. The Greater London Council (GLC) stepped in, with a grand gesture and £375,000.[39] Both the RSC and the National produced new writing alongside international classics and modern adaptations, in the short-run repertory system that had become the mainstay of British producing houses since the early twentieth century. However, it became clear that the most commercially successful mode of theatrical production for the 1980s was the large-scale extravaganza, with long runs and the possibility of franchised worldwide reproduction. This was only possible in the commercial theatres of the West End.

The West End had a particularly difficult time in the recession from 1979 to 1981, but by 1982 there had been a turn in its fortunes. It made some steps towards improving its own lot when the Society of West End Theatres opened a half-price ticket booth in Leicester Square in 1980 – it sold 350,000 tickets in its first year. The real resurrection for the West End came in two ways, through governmental support for cultural tourism to the UK as a 'heritage' destination, and through the transfer of successful shows from the large subsidised theatres. The West End had rarely opened new plays, with the exception of the likes of Harold Pinter, Alan Ayckbourn and Tom Stoppard, but regularly adopted proven successes. A notable model for transfer came in 1980 with David Edgar's adaptation of *Nicholas Nickleby* for the RSC. Some more adventurous producers, such as Ian Albery, transferred less mainstream work such as left-wing alternative theatre company Belt and Braces' version of Dario Fo's satire *Accidental Death of an Anarchist* to Wyndham's Theatre (1980). Although this was admittedly in a version that Fo disliked for its ready use of comic Italian stereotypes at the expense of its biting critique of state power.

Two leading entrepreneurs spearheaded the development of musical theatre, always a lively component of West End theatres, as that rare phenomenon – financially profitable theatre. Andrew Lloyd Webber and Cameron Mackintosh collaborated to establish the form of the global musical with *Cats*, which opened in the poorly regarded New Theatre in 1981. The musical, based very loosely on T. S. Eliot's poetic collection *Old Possum's Book of Practical Cats*, would run for twenty-one years and 8,949 performances. The show, with its simple poster, expensive memorabilia and soundtrack in tape, vinyl and the new CD form, was essentially plotless, highly physical and able to transcend language barriers. In similar form, Lloyd Webber developed *Starlight Express*, which opened in 1984 at the Apollo. More successfully, *Phantom of the Opera* (1986), developed as a vehicle for Sarah Brightman, then Lloyd Webber's wife, opened at Her Majesty's Theatre. Andrew Lloyd Webber musicals tended to begin life in the West End, whereas Cameron Macintosh developed a range of projects from the subsidised sector, most famously the musical adaptation of

Victor Hugo's *Les Misérables*, which transferred from the RSC Barbican to the West End in 1985. The *Les Misérables* team followed that success with a West End creation *Miss Saigon* in 1989, and *Buddy – The Buddy Holly Story* opened in 1989 at Victoria Palace Theatre.

Not all West End musical transfers came from the major London companies: Willy Russell's *Blood Brothers*, originally written as a Theatre-in-Education piece in 1981 for Merseyside Young People's Theatre, was developed as a musical for the Liverpool Playhouse in 1983. Its transfer to the Lyric in 1983 began its West End career – it is still running as this book is written. *Me and My Girl* was resurrected in 1984 at the Leicester Haymarket, transferring to the London Adelphi. There was undoubtedly a chemistry between musical extravaganza and 'literary heritage' that generated a draw for tourists to the UK in the 1980s. The lure of basing musicals on older literary works continues today, with all the dated female, black and Asian stereotypes such works might contain: for example *Blood Brothers* is based on Dumas's *The Corsican Brothers*, *Miss Saigon* on *Madame Butterfly*, *Cats* on Eliot's 1930s poetry and *Phantom* on Leroux's 1911 novel. The West End's repertoire has remained remarkably stable since the mid-twentieth century, consisting of literary musical adaptations, coupled with musical adaptations of films, and compilation musicals of popular musical trends, sometimes centred around biography. As John Bull recounts, the rise of American musical imports in the 1980s was also directly linked to tourist spend, and large initial investment with long runs maximised profits: *Les Mis* earned £1.8 million profit in its first five years, and *Cats* made £15.7 million in ten years. The importance of this tourist spend to the UK economy became obvious when, in 1986, in the wake of the Libyan bombing of a US marine base in Germany, and the Chernobyl nuclear reactor meltdown, American tourists stayed away.[40] The West End's mode of production became the model for 'success' in politicians' eyes, as an obvious demonstration of the 'industrial' elements of the cultural industries. The musical could tour commercially to large theatres in the US and Far East, acting as British cultural export, and with its lavish sets, spectacle and music, language was relatively unimportant.

There has always been an international export of British culture: it acted as a crucial component of British imperialism, justifying the civilising nature of British colonial control wherever British garrisons were established, or large flows of migrants settled. Tracy C. Davis has charted the economic innovations of nineteenth-century West End theatre industry, franchising successful shows abroad. 'By exporting theatre to the empire as an intellectual product, the original producer's utilization of a wholesaling phase improved the cost–benefit ratio. This caps a series of such innovations through the nineteenth century: circuits of real property, long runs, and horizontal integration, keeping credit markets tight amongst cooperating capitalists.'[41] So the export of large-scale, lavish theatrical spectacle was not an innovation of the 1980s, but a well-established theatrical structure that found itself in tune with government policy. The global market for British heritage tourism, most notably the musical and Shakespeare, was revalidated during the 1980s. In the global development of British cultural export, the performing arts of diasporic communities, notably British Asian and black British, in the UK were not as visible in this celebration of cultural heritage. This was in contrast to the field of literature, for example, where Salman Rushdie (whose *Midnight's Children* won the Booker Prize in 1981), Ben Okri, Caryl Phillips (as novelist rather than playwright), or Joan Riley were all British Council-sponsored exports.

Size also mattered, or seemed to, to the 'political' playwrights of the 1980s. In the 1950s, as Simon Shepherd has noted, playwrights identified themselves as 'serious' dramatists by having their work produced on the 'small Royal Court stage', in resistance to the commercial, entertainment-centred theatres. By the late 1970s, Shepherd notes, the 'serious place to be is in the National or Aldwych'.[42] Indeed, playwright David Edgar argued in 1979 that plays about public subjects could not take place in little rooms, and that political playwrights needed to reclaim the mainstages of British theatre.[43] Alan Plater agreed that the 'core of it is that you don't prove yourself a proper, grown-up playwright until you've written a big play with a big cast for a big theatre, with a proscenium arch'.[44] Certainly large-scale production offered a playwright increased cultural capital, both in terms of the visibility of the work, where a play is more likely to have an extended run, national reviews and an afterlife in publication. Writing for a sizeable cast and production budget meant limiting the available venues for staging to the larger producing theatres. In terms of economic capital, the financial return through royalties from larger audiences might mark a play as 'successful'. While in the early 1980s there is a paradoxical desire for a politicised 'new writing' within the bastions of large-scale, state-sponsored cultural institutions, as a maker of cultural significance and success, by the end of the 1980s, the very idea of 'success' itself has been monetised by the discourses of the cultural industries, privatisation and the free market. Thus, whether any large-scale production of new writing at the end of the 1980s could consider itself a 'success' in terms of its political impact, rather than its economic return, is a moot question.

Regional identity

Much of the attention and energy of the Arts Council, if not its funding, was expended on regional theatres during the 1980s. At the end of a long period of building and development of civic theatres in the 1960s and 1970s, regional theatre was still trying to offer a diverse repertoire and local community-related activity, entertainment, cultural improvement and tourist lure – a complex 'cultural offer' in today's language. A Policy Studies Institute report in 1982, *A Hard Fact to Swallow*, highlighted the disparity in Arts Council expenditure between the regions and London, across all art forms. This was in part inherent in the impossible agenda the Arts Council had had from its inception in 1945 as an institution designed to develop high-quality arts across the country, *and* to sustain London as a centre of particular excellence. In 1984 the Arts Council produced a reflective document, *The Glory of the Garden*, which suggested the devolution of Arts Council funding for regional and touring theatre companies to the Regional Arts Associations (RAA), a search for increased local government funding, and threatened to cut more companies. The Arts Council report of 1985 asserted there would be increased funding to the RAAs as 'a genuine shift of resources away from London, and towards the regions',[45] yet few regions felt the benefit. In response to pressure from the Drama Panel, the Arts Council commissioned an enquiry into the state of all professional theatre in England, the 1986 Cork Report *Theatre IS for All*. This revealed the parlous state of some building-based regional theatre, and suggested that local authority income was needed.[46] The following year the Arts Council gave the national companies standstill funding to enhance funds to the regional theatres. Local authorities took up the challenge of funding and several regional building-based theatres saw more stability in their financial situation.

With statuary authority conferred only by Parliament, structurally the regions have always been considered *in relation* to the centre, rather than as autonomous spaces. The local regions in Britain were particularly tied to the centre in political terms, unable to spend on *capital* projects without central government's approval. Indeed revenue arts spending itself was a relatively novel power for local authorities, who had only been granted discretionary spending on arts since the 1972 Local Government Act. Financial pressures on local authorities in the late 1980s were intense, and the increased support for the arts that many councils provided was a result of creative budget balancing. Local councils answered to their local electorate, and that produced a different level of attention to the provision of art and amenities, proudly claimed as defining local or regional identity in resistance to national government agendas. Local council money for the arts was not as centrally controlled as government departments, and perhaps the Arts Council, would have liked. While the rhetoric of the Conservative government throughout the 1980s was about 'rolling back the state' and decentralisation, in actuality several centralising mechanisms were enforced. In 1984 the government introduced the Rates Act that prevented local authorities from raising income through the rates system to support local activities and initiatives: a system of rate-capping. The explicitly party political outcome of this legislation was that only Labour-led local authorities were capped. This produced huge de facto cuts for many local authority budgets, yet even rate-capped councils continued to try to fund regional theatres, arts centres and touring companies. A second piece of legislation, the Local Government Act (1985), brought about the abolition in 1986 of six large metropolitan, Labour-controlled councils and the Greater London Council (GLC), again an expressly party political manoeuvre. The way in which local authorities might use funding to enhance their relationship with particular electoral communities within their constituency, or to serve regional priorities, is well illustrated by the example of the GLC. Although not strictly regional, the Greater London Council had operated as an important funder of suburban theatre, offering key financial support for gay and lesbian activist art initiatives and developing funding for black arts from £400,000 in 1982 to £2 million by 1985, for the work of black and Asian theatre groups like Temba, Tara Arts, the Black Theatre Co-operative and Talawa.[47]

The impact of these funding battles on the repertoires of regional theatres was complex. Brown and Brannen's research for the Cork Report in 1986 found a diverse picture of large and small theatre provision outside London, where the repertoires of regional theatres that produced work (rather than simply receiving it), comprised 45 per cent post-war drama, with Shakespeare, Alan Ayckbourn and new writing occupying around 6 per cent of the repertoire apiece. Regional producing theatres still acted as regional bases for touring, as well as providing local-flavoured performance. Indeed, regionality and regional identity could provide a vital audience base for a theatre, as John Godber and Hull Truck discovered, or as Willy Russell's work for the Liverpool Everyman illustrates. However, the need to balance the books and sustain very strong box-office figures meant that the regional reps had to balance popular mainstream work drawn from contemporary national fashions and trends, with locally inflected performances. Baz Kershaw has argued that the resistance to homogeneous mainstream performance sustains democracy and a regional theatre's connection to its local constituency. For Kershaw, theatre is a barometer of a democratic society: 'as an institution it has to conform more or less to the disciplines of the market in order to survive, but as an arena for creative performance it always offers the potential for radical critique of the social (and its economics) as a disciplinary apparatus'.[48] Kershaw concluded that the marketisation of theatre resulted in the atomisation of theatre audiences into 'customers', where the theatre building becomes a 'classy cultural drop-in centre

[. . .] theatre-going was gradually transformed into an "experience" to be consumed',[49] rather than an act of nurturing community identity. Yet Michael Billington had hoped for just this kind of experience to become more widespread in 1981. He hoped to see 'theatre happening more and more in the suburbs where people actually live'. And he expected to see a growing popularity for 'big arts centres like the National and the forthcoming Barbican where you can eat and drink as well as go to a play or concert'.[50] Billington's predictions for the 1980s pointedly included a warning that there would be a decline in 'those repertory companies that fail to find a policy, a style, an identity that is peculiar to them'.[51]

Regional identity as a distinctive cultural force was, if anything, enhanced during the 1980s, in response to the legislative changes that continually drew power back to Westminster. Economic restructuring saw the financial services and banking sector in central London make exceptional gains, while broad swathes of the country were living with the outsourcing of large-scale industrial manufacturing overseas, and sudden absence of demand for all kinds of industrial skills. The north–south divide was an economic truth revealed by the disparity in house prices as the housing boom gripped the country in the late 1980s. Regional life, cultures and accents were present in everyday popular culture: television still had regionally produced drama and series which represented regional diversity and interests. When Channel 4 launched in 1982, its soap opera, *Brookside*, was set in Liverpool. *Coronation Street*, set in a fictional town in Greater Manchester, had been going strong since 1960. In 1981 Ken Barlow's marriage to Deirdre was watched by twenty-four million households, almost double the number that watched the Royal Wedding two days later. The rise of British new wave music and electronica in the 1980s saw regional identity as a badge of honour, and suburban pop often carried 'a kind of rueful complaint that the lyricist was not born in Liverpool or Manchester but in a London dormer town. [. . .] The North/South divide is as much a feature of English pop as of postwar UK economics.'[52] Indeed the representation of regionality, particularly of 'northern' identity, increasingly came to register as political resistance. The Royal Court Theatre fêted regionally based writers such as Andrea Dunbar and Jim Cartwright for their working-class grit, but also their non-metropolitan exoticism, read as politically oppositional.

Although regional theatres' funding for locally addressed new writing was squeezed in the late 1980s, there was some sustaining of a regional perspective because it drew local audiences. These regional or suburban theatres very often ran playwriting competitions expressly to capture local potential. The Second Wave Young Women's Project at the Albany, Deptford in south London drew both a high number of black participants and good audiences from the predominantly Afro-Caribbean community, by promising mainstage productions of the winning scripts. April De Angelis won in 1986 with *Breathless*, and Judith Johnson with *Working Away*.[53] There was rash of playwriting competitions set up by regional theatre companies to meet their commitment to 'new writing support': the biennial Mobil Playwriting Competition with the Royal Exchange Manchester was established in 1985, producing winners such as Robin Glendinning, with his study of sectarianism in a Belfast grammar school *Mumbo Jumbo* (produced 1986), Iain Heggie's *A Wholly Healthy Glasgow* (1987) and Michael Wall's *Amongst Barbarians* (1989). The Warehouse, Croydon, established the International Playwriting Competition in 1986, staging the winning entry and providing an international profile for the author. Not all playwriting competitions offered full productions: Nottingham and Derby Playhouses collaborated to run *Write '87*, which Jenny McLeod won with her satiric *Cricket at Camp David* (1987), which was given a rehearsed reading. Whether they offered a rehearsed reading or a full production, such competitions promised the chance for a script to move quickly into a director's hands, and attempted to draw on a more diverse pool of writers with regional interests.

Other formulas for regional participation and the expression of regional identity came through the surviving community theatres, both those attached to regional building-based theatres and small-scale touring theatre companies. In Dorset, Ann Jellicoe developed an independent version of the work that the Victoria Theatre, Newcastle-under-Lyme, had pioneered. Jellicoe set up the Colway Theatre Trust

(1978), where the community of a small town participates in order to stage a play written for them by well-known writers. Jellicoe had been Literary Manager of the Royal Court Theatre and attracted writers such as David Edgar and Howard Barker to the projects. Whatever the perceived weaknesses or strengths of this kind participatory theatre,[54] it produced theatre performances grounded in the specificities of a place. However, one set of local theatre companies which practically disappeared in the regions in the late 1980s was the Theatre-in-Education (TIE) companies. Many regional theatres had supported their own TIE companies since the 1970s, often offering oppositional and sometimes politically radical material. David Holman wrote for Belgrade Theatre, Coventry's early Theatre-in-Education work and became resident at the Theatre Centre in the 1980s. Theatre Centre was a children's theatre company which commissioned new writing, and which saw its place as blending 'the highly politicised content of the best TIE companies like Coventry and the early Cockpit TIE Company, with the undoubted theatrical strengths of the established Children's Theatre Companies, and the burgeoning new wave of "alternative theatre"'.[55] Holman wrote a peace trilogy for schools and small-scale touring: *Peacemaker* (1982), about two people resolving their differences on either side of a wall; *Susummu's Story*, about families dealing with the aftermath of Hiroshima (1983); and *1983* (1983) about Cruise missiles. Although the plays were circulating mainly in schools, they came to the attention of the *Daily Mail* and *Daily Express*, and drove Home Secretary Norman Tebbit to urge children in his constituency to stay away from school to avoid the 'anti-nuclear propaganda' of *1983*. Other writers who worked for the Theatre Centre included Bryony Lavery and Noel Greig. Theatre-in-Education companies and young people's theatre continued to provide an alternative source of commissions for playwrights until the 1988 Education Act, which devolved budgets from the local education authority to schools themselves, cut funding and brought about the radical reduction in the number of regional Theatre-in-Education companies.[56]

Over the 1980s local authority funding for the arts, and theatre in particular, grew as a proportion of arts subsidy, in the teeth of centralising economic and political forces. Local and regional identity in the repertoire of these theatres and companies continued to be an important way of attracting local audiences for producing theatres, and co-production with London subsidised venues remained a significant way of winning regionally based playwrights access to national audiences. As the Conservative government attempted to control regional power and identity through its rate-capping and administrative legislation, the very representation of regionality and regional identity came increasingly to stand as a symbol of political opposition.

Funding

Debates about theatre financing, and the ideological and party political implications of the sources of that financing, were unmissable during the 1980s. Of course, the language of value for money, and discussion of the commercial value of the arts was not one that began with the Thatcher administration. The 1976–77 Arts Council annual report was entitled 'Value for Money', and some commentators suggest that monetarist policies arrived under Dennis Healey, Labour Chancellor, as Britain accepted an International Monetary Fund Loan and the concomitant imposition of monetarism by that institution.[57] However, as we have seen, during the 1980s, the terminology of arts subsidy was translated into the language of 'partnership' and 'challenge funding' – the desire to see the private sector fund the arts alongside government. The Conservative government had an organisational body already at its disposal through which to channel private-sector involvement in the arts: the Association for Business Sponsorship of the Arts (ABSA). ABSA had been founded in 1976 by the Labour government, with a start-up budget of £15,000 of taxpayers' money and the support of six companies chaired by Imperial Tobacco (who, in the face of increasing legislation against direct cigarette advertising, had hit upon a mechanism for high-end brand promotion). ABSA came into its own under Thatcherism. The arts have always been deeply implicated in mechanisms of patronage and prestige, obligation and interest, and in the 1980s increased encouragement for corporate business to become involved in the arts produced some unique combinations. That the private sponsors receive no tax relief on their financial contributions to arts indicates a clear distinction in corporate thinking between philanthropic giving and sponsorship as advertising. In 1980, Peter Sanguinetti, external affairs spokesman for Imperial Tobacco, gave an interview about their sponsorship of the National Portrait Gallery Annual Portrait Award: 'We want the arts people we pick to work hard to give us publicity. We don't talk about "giving" money on sponsorship – the recipient gets the money, we get the publicity.'[58] ABSA emphasised its contribution to the arts not only in financial terms, but also in introducing business advice to arts organisations and helping them to conceive of themselves as producing a commodity like any other. What the corporations gain is airtime and public space for their name and logo, brand awareness, alignment between specific brand 'values' and artistic values from an apparently disinterested artistic milieu, the endorsement of shared agendas, access to a range of potential customers, clients and policy formers through invited galas, openings, private views and previews. From 1984, the government enhanced flagging business interest by offering match-funding for all donations from sponsors through the Business Sponsorship Incentive Scheme. In effect, therefore, a large amount of public subsidy was moving into private business advertising.[59] By 1994, the taxpayer offered £21 million of subsidy to private businesses' advertising sponsorship of £43 million, from 300 companies. The high-profile rewards for businesses included the ABSA/*Daily Telegraph* awards ceremony, which in 1987 hosted the Prince and Princess of Wales at the Victoria and Albert Museum.

Sponsorship was not always a comfortable route for arts companies to pursue, and businesses were primarily interested in high-profile arts organisations. Questions were asked in the House of Commons when sponsorship deals failed; for example, Sotherby's pulled out of fine art sponsorship in 1982 because of recessionary pressures, and the Nash Ensemble lost its funding when the sponsor's chairman left.[60] In the early 1980s the Arts Council had complained about the excessive publicity sponsors received, given their small contribution in comparison with the Council. By 1985, after Luke Rittner's appointment as

Secretary General in 1983, the Arts Council was urging reviewers of the Hayward Gallery's show to mention the sponsors more fully, and sponsors' names begin to be integrated into the title of competitions and awards – the BT New Contemporaries or Barclays Young Artist Award – to ensure that newspaper reviewers and commentators included the sponsor's moniker: a practice that has become ubiquitous.

The Conservative government's championing of the entrepreneurial principle for the arts, coupled with mechanisms they had put in place to attempt to reduce the official unemployment figures, had some consequences they certainly did not intend. The Manpower Services Commission (MSC), a body that should have been anathema to a Thatcherism intent on reducing state intervention and critical of Labour's full employment policies with its 'state-created jobs', actually expanded in the early 1980s. In 1981 Secretary of State for Employment Norman Tebbit introduced the Youth Training Scheme, a step on from the Youth Opportunity Programme, run by the MSC. The government was prepared to tolerate state-controlled employment programmes to counteract the crippling levels of youth unemployment (in 1980 half of the unemployed were young; by 1984 25 per cent of young people aged between sixteen and twenty-five had been unemployed for two years), and massage the headline unemployment figures. Unexpectedly, the MSC offered financial support for some artists.[61] This was how Richard Cole found the workers to build 'Windy Nook' (1986) commissioned by Gateshead Metropolitan Borough Council, a striking sculpture from natural stone high above a housing estate, and called 'the fortress' by locals. Owen Kelly argues that the MSC were increasingly interested in community arts training and projects in the early 1980s, as inner-city unrest and riots in Brixton, Toxteth, Handsworth, Chapeltown and elsewhere needed an immediate response.[62] Multiple kinds of arts projects had Manpower Services funding: Reminiscence Theatre projects based around Dartington; an adult education theatre workshop in Hull; Lucy Neal and Rose Fenton, programmers of the London International Festival of Theatre (LIFT) were able to pay themselves for a year; Greater Manchester council employed five mural artists to work across the county; Hijinx Theatre started on it in 1981. In addition, the Enterprise Allowance Scheme, established in 1982, paid theatre 'entrepreneurs' £40 a week to set up a company: Tic Toc Theatre Company Coventry, founded in 1983, set up through this scheme, as did the feminist company Red Stockings, and the all-women Hogwash Theatre in Sheffield. The system was still operative in 1990 when storytelling and physical theatre Rejects' Revenge set up in Liverpool.

Funding for individual playwrights and playwriting was largely untouched by the rise of corporate sponsorship. Playwriting remained an activity tied to public subsidy through the Arts Council. The number of Arts Council bursaries payable to companies and venues to commission new work ebbed and flowed over the decade. In 1987 Colin Chambers and Mike Prior suggest 'the indirect and uncertain nature of subsidy has continued to make a playwright's life both meagre and precarious',[63] meaning 'fine playwrights have been abandoned, have drifted grumpily away or have taken easier and financially more rewarding options in other media'.[64] The move some playwrights made into film and television was often construed as failure or compromise, 'the factory line production of scripts for a well established TV serial'.[65] There are two aspects to the suspicion about writing for the media: first, an ideological resistance to incorporation by mainstream, commercial hegemony from those writers who cut their teeth on the left-wing alternative scene of the 1970s, and indeed the mode of television production and the nature of its reception might prove this to be often the case. But, second, the descent into television imagines the playwright abandoning a particular kind of solo authorship and independent creative process. The recurring enlightenment myth of individual genius was rarely borne out in the process of playwriting for the theatre, and presupposes that one particular kind of playwriting process is more satisfying than any other, privileging the completed arc of a narrative journey or total control over characterisation. For Sarah Daniels, working on the BBC World Service soap opera *Westway*, with a team of writers, proved to be a stimulating creative writing process: 'I've never enjoyed anything so much. The producers nearly pulled their hair out, because if you get six writers in the room and you give them control – one of us had a magic marker and a board – and we just behaved like very, very naughty kids at a party.'[66] Many playwrights from the 1980s earned money writing for television serials like *The Bill* and *Grange Hill*, including Judith Johnson, Sarah Daniels, Tanika Gupta and Jim Cartwright. It is undoubtedly true that the macro-economic situation including recessions and inflation in the late 1980s meant that making a living from playwriting was increasingly difficult. Yet the idea that authors of any kind are able to make a reliable living remains broadly fantastical, as a recent study of UK and Germany author earnings found. Most authors, then and now, supplement their income through a wide variety of other jobs. Playwrights, like most artists, had 'portfolio careers', a phrase coined in Charles Handy's *The Future of Work* (1984), which warned of the end of full employment or jobs for life, and heralded an era of freelance working that the legislative and investment decisions of the Conservative government in the 1980s indeed produced.

Yet there were a number of ways that a playwright might be subsidised, for the production of a completed play or, more importantly, for time to write.[67] Theatre Writers' Bursaries were direct awards from the Arts Council to playwrights for specific projects. Bursaries were worth around £1,250 in 1980, and had risen to £3,000 by the end of the 1980s. These bursaries paid playwrights for a short period of time in order to write, without needing the commitment of a theatre company to produce the work that emerged; for example, Karim Alrawi won one to develop his one-act play *Before Dawn* into *Migrations*.[68] Overall the bursary scheme reveals the Arts Council's alertness to the diverse range of playwriting voices: in 1981–92 £46,450 was disbursed to thirty-seven playwrights including Michael Abbensetts; Iranian exile, poet and playwright Iraj Ataie; and Timberlake Wertenbaker.[69] While the bursary scheme offered support to playwrights from diverse backgrounds, it was not available for writers working non-traditionally, producing 'text' from or for devising or visual theatre rather than a playscript. The Thames Television Theatre Writers' Scheme (established in 1976) was a parallel scheme offering five bursaries to playwrights, and the resulting plays were entered in a competition, with additional prize money.

Hanif Kureishi's *Borderline* was written under this fund, and won the award in 1982; Debbie Horsfield won in 1983 with *True, Dare, Kiss* and Billy Roche for *Poor Beast in the Rain* (1989).[70] An alternative way for funding time to write was through the Arts Council's 'Resident Dramatist Attachments' or the Writer-in-Residence scheme, where writers were retained by a company and integrated into the life of the theatre; they were also paid a commission for a play which, if it was produced, paid royalties. Writers-in-Residence at the Royal Court Theatre illustrate some of the tasks of reading, advising, teaching and mentoring that were required during their stay, but they offered a playwright salaried writing time, an extraordinarily rare experience. Hanif Kureishi was Writer-in-Residence at the Royal Court Theatre in 1982, and Sarah Daniels was followed by Timberlake Wertenbaker in 1985. Nick Stafford (who went on to adapt the very successful *War Horse* in 2008) was Writer-in-Residence at the Half Moon Young People's Theatre in 1987. Residencies were worth around £2,400 in 1988.

A third way of earning money came through the commissioning or optioning process. Building-based and touring theatres in receipt of grant income could offer commissions, subsidised by additional Arts Council funding. In 1981–82, thirty-seven of these 'Contract Writers' Awards' were allocated, which varied in value from around £600 to £3,000. By the early 1990s it was the expectation that every building-based theatre with a certain level of subsidy should be commissioning new work in this way.[71] The Theatre Writers' Union (founded 1976) had established standardised fees, copyright agreements and royalties to protect a minimum package of remuneration for writers in their contracts with theatres and companies.[72] As a result of this the Arts Council also ran the 'Royalty Supplement Guarantee' scheme, which subsidised companies who staged named new plays to ensure that 'playwrights receive a reasonable reward from the first production of their plays'.[73] In 1981–82, £24,715 was disbursed to forty-eight plays under this scheme, including Barker's community play for the Colway Theatre Trust, *Poor Man's Friend*. By 1988 the Arts Council had also recognised the importance of revivals of new works to the reputation and careers of playwrights, and the Second

Production Scheme was introduced, offering a royalty guarantee for the revival of a play. One final source of financial income directly from playwriting came in the form of awards and prizes, which also offered the indirect economic rewards of acclaim and a raised profile; the accruing of cultural capital that was significant for a playwright in order to sustain a career.[74] As Simon Shepherd notes, the principles of copyright which changed in the mid-nineteenth century allowed playwrights to benefit from their ownership of the created artefact. Authors had always gleaned some benefit from a theatre company from the *performance* of their work, but by the late twentieth century this had been extended and codified, and the payment of royalties for print versions and subsequent performances and production added considerably to the earning potential of a written text, particularly one that might have an extended life.

New writing and playwrights in the 1980s

At the end of the 1980s theatre reviewers and cultural commentators reflected gloomily on a decade of new writing. Benedict Nightingale, critic for *The Times*, dubbed the period 'barren'[75] and Michael Billington of the *Guardian* suggested there was a 'crisis in new writing [. . .] new drama no longer occupies the central position it has in British theatre over the past 35 years', arguing that for financial and political reasons there had been 'manifest decline in big plays capable of addressing a large audience and tapping a vibrant community response'.[76] Christopher Innes concluded his study of *Modern British Drama 1890–1990* suggesting that British playwriting, in the mode of George Bernard Shaw, 'seems to be running out of steam [. . . Howard] Barker and [Howard] Brenton have ceased to develop, and their recent plays do not measure up to their previous achievements; [Peter] Shaffer has retreated into commercial entertainment. [. . . And] the most telling indicator of diminishing theatrical vitality is the comparative absence of new playwrights.'[77] Innes's eulogy for new writing prefaces the only female playwrights of his study, Caryl Churchill and Pam Gems, who are required to offset 'this bleak

picture'.[78] Such a picture is, of course, dependent upon your definition of 'new writing' and upon your perspective. It is undoubtedly
true, as we have seen, that the retrenchment of subsidy to regional and
large-scale theatres in the late 1980s reduced the number of productions those venues could stage, and thus the opportunities for new
'big' plays. However, it is less obvious that the imaginative invention
or ambition of playwrights was vitiated, as Nightingale and Innes
seem to imply.

A vibrant debate still continues around what counts as 'new
writing' for performance. A recent Arts Council report *New Writing in
Theatre 2003–2008* considers new writing as both individually
authored playwriting and as a writer collaborating with other artists,
including in devising processes.[79] This inclusiveness has not always
been obvious in policy terms. The Arts Council New Drama
Committee responsible for playwriting may have briefly changed its
name to the New Writing Committee in 1975, before being restruc-
tured as a subcommittee on Theatre Writing and Bursaries in 1980,
but it was always concerned with facilitating solo playwrights. So, at
the beginning of the 1980s the term 'new writing' usually implied an
individual playwright crafting a playscript for traditional theatrical
production, in a process modelled by the Royal Court Theatre since
the 1950s. Indeed, as late as 1995 the Arts Council was carefully
distinguishing 'new writing' (playwrights) from 'experimental
theatre'.[80] So, however partial its description of the actual new plays
written, in the late 1970s and early 1980s the term 'new writing' was
used to suggest a certain kind of state-of-the-nation play, employing
realism, from a leftist political perspective, and addressed to a middle-
class, liberal audience. Speaking in the early 1990s, Dominic
Dromgoole, Artistic Director of the Bush (1990–96), celebrated the
decline of this mode of 'new writing', which he dubbed the
'Miserabilist Tendency [. . .] state-of-the-nation plays rehearsing arguments already settled long before the audience arrived; journalistic
plays on single issues; [. . .] the odd twentieth-century idea that argument is at the centre of theatre'.[81] Even the incoming Artistic Director
of the Royal Court Theatre in 1993, Stephen Daldry, noted the
danger of 'the New Writing Aesthetic (capital N, capital W) [. . .]

pseudo-televisual terrible seventies naturalism'.[82] Yet this sense of ennui with new writing was the result of a particular perspective, as Timberlake Wertenbaker warned:

> When lazy commentators say there was no theatre in the 1980s, they mean there was very little male theatre. In fact, the 1980s saw an explosion of writing from women, first in small theatres, often in all-women companies, and later on the bigger stages. This writing was often blatantly feminist and by defini-tion made men uncomfortable. Sarah Daniels's blisteringly funny first play at the Royal Court caused as much discomfort as Sarah Kane's.[83]

These contesting voices reveal that the decade saw a significant shift in the development of 'new writing' on the ground – by the end of the 1980s *who* was writing, as much as *what* was being written, was chal-lenging the accepted definition of 'new writing'. The decade saw the increased popularity and significance of live and performance art, physical theatre and dance theatre, all of which used text or what we might now call 'performance writing'. 'New writing' could have broadened in definition to account for the creative processes, perform-ance modes and spaces of the alternative theatre scene of the 1970s, as much as for the large-scale, social realist play. Yet, during the 1980s 'new writing' was not used to refer to the diversity of texts for performance produced in non-traditional spaces or forms.

It is this very limited view of new writing that produces the elegiac tone in the commentators above. Yet, if one examines the rich actu-ality of playwriting and playwrights in practice during the decade, it is clear that in both form and subject matter playwrights were facing square-on the challenge of a politics fragmenting beyond class into the complexities of identity politics, as national identities were hollowed out from within by a government 'rolling back the state', and from without by global economic forces. Often central to new plays of the decade was a concern to reach different, perhaps even new, audiences.

Venues for new writing

The largest of London venues, in terms of auditorium and of subsidy, expressly for new writing was the Royal Court. The other large-scale subsidised institutions which produced new writing alongside a classic repertoire were the National, where new writing was usually commissioned from established writers and produced in the small Cottesloe space, and the Royal Shakespeare Company. The RSC's Warehouse (now the Donmar) 250-seat venue was its London partner to The Other Place in Stratford. Walter Donohue, Literary Manager for these two venues in 1978, articulated the Warehouse's new writing policy:

> to be responsive to whatever is being written at the moment in British theatre, not only among established writers, but we try to do plays by people who have had only one play or two or three. We commission a number each year, and then the space is open within the season for plays [. . .] which just come in without me asking.[84]

Although new writing often began in the smaller subsidised spaces at the National or RSC, the boundary with the commercial West End theatres was very porous in the early 1980s. In 1980 the RSC commissioned the two-hander *Educating Rita* from Willy Russell for the Warehouse, because the rest of the company was engaged in David Edgar's eight-and-a-half-hour spectacular *The Life and Adventures of Nicholas Nickleby*, at the West End's Aldwych, which later transferred to Broadway.[85] *Educating Rita* itself transferred to the West End's Piccadilly Theatre in September, then went into production at the Liverpool Playhouse in 1981, was made into a film in 1983 and has been regularly in production internationally since then. This kind of trajectory allows a playwright to earn a living wage from one piece of creative writing, and demonstrates the pragmatic mechanisms that permitted subsidised new writing to become part of the commercial mainstream.[86] So while practically no new writing was directly premiered by West End venues, these theatres became increasingly significant as transfer venues, with the attendant financial rewards available. While this did allow playwrights to make a living from work, it had unintended consequences for writers, as Sarah Daniels pithily points out, encouraging a 'lottery mentality: you are writing this play which you really hope hits the jackpot. [. . .] Thatcher killed off theatres in this country in that everything had to make money, everything had to be a money-making product.'[87]

A number of smaller-scale London venues committed to new writing included the Bush (founded in 1972) and the Soho Poly (founded 1969), which presented almost exclusively new plays or contemporary plays in translation. They formed a de facto circuit with the larger subsidised theatres, certainly in the minds of writers' agents, attracting a similar range of playwrights and playwriting. Peter Wilson, Literary Manager of the Bush in the 1980s, noted that scripts 'often had the rejection notes still inside them from the Royal Court Theatre (where David Leveaux was Literary Manager) or the National, or the RSC or Hampstead or the Riverside'.[88] Several small- to medium-scale theatres in the London boroughs, which had been founded in the 1970s with broadly left-wing agendas and a commitment to serving their local communities, also presented new writing. The Half Moon (founded 1972, moved to Stepney 1979) was one such theatre, premiering Steven Berkoff's *Greek*, which transferred to the West End's Arts Theatre in 1980. Other premieres the Half Moon staged included Berkoff's anti-Thatcher *Sink the Belgrano* (1986) and Winsome Pinnock's story of a Jamaican woman's journey to England to train as a nurse in the 1950s, in *The Winds of Change* (1987).[89] In the 1980s, these smaller-scale theatres inhabited a cross-over world between the 'alternative' theatre circuit and the mainstream, in terms of the content of the work they produced and the audiences they addressed. Mike Bradwell, Artistic Director at the Bush (1996–2007), challenged the idea that the Bush could be dismissed as 'fringe', and by implication, marginal:

> we do New Writing and New Writers move on, it's easy to think that the Bush is some kind of halfway house or a stepping stone to greater glories in the more obviously commercial or more conspicuously subsidised sector, but it's simply not true. [. . .W]e are as important to the cultural health of the nation as the Royal National Theatre.[90]

Writers whose work was produced at the Bush and Soho Poly valued the intensity of audience experience that these small venues offered. Yet it is also true that productions from these venues were indeed readily picked up and taken to larger audiences through the BBC's 'Play for Today' (Dusty Hughes's *Commitments*, 1980; Doug Lucie's *Hard Feelings*, 1983) or transfers to the West End, such as Sharman Macdonald's *When I was a Girl I Used to Scream and Shout* (1984, Whitehall Theatre 1986).

Although not centrally concerned with new writing, a number of other venues in the London boroughs included new writing in their repertoire, but for different reasons – to attempt to serve their local communities more fully. Theatre Royal, Stratford East, once home to Joan Littlewood's radical experiments, had the largest black audience in the UK, its Artistic Director Philip Hedley asserted.[91] Among a programme of music and variety, Stratford East premiered Howard Brenton and Tony Howard's satiric *A Short Sharp Shock* (1980) before its move to the Royal Court; Nell Dunn's all-women reverie about a public bathhouse *Steaming* (1981); Karim Alrawi's *Migrations* (1982); and later in the 1980s it developed young playwrights' showcases and black playwrights such as Trevor Rhone. The Albany Empire, Deptford, had a history of supporting alternative theatre and had housed alternative theatre company The Combination in 1970s, and spearheaded the Rock against Racism concerts. The Albany retained an activist agenda and a strong community focus during the 1980s, and set up the Second Wave Young Women Playwrights project, aimed at young black women, in 1986.[92] In 1984 the Drill Hall formally developed a theatre programme with a commitment to gay and lesbian playwrights and performances.[93] New writing in these locations, inflected by the oppositional or radical alternative histories of the theatres, was reconfigured most often as an investigation of identity politics, rather than sharing a party political or class point of view. The artistic directors tended to see the role of new writing as developing new audiences and cementing the theatre's centrality within the community's culture.

The focus on London has skewed our histories of British theatre and in fact many new playwrights in the early 1980s had their work produced by the subsidised regional theatres, most of which commissioned new writing for their studio or mainstages, ran writing workshops, and developed local playwriting ability. Regional theatres that had developed a reputation for supporting new writing were the Birmingham Rep and Drum Arts Centre Birmingham, Contact Manchester, Royal Exchange Manchester, Nottingham Playhouse, Leicester Haymarket, Bolton Octagon, Sheffield Crucible Studio and the Liverpool Playhouse Studio. As Rowell and Jackson have argued, new writing and innovative programming had been the hallmark of many of these theatres during the 1970s.[94] These theatres often worked in collaboration with London venues such as the Royal Court Theatre to build a tour for new plays. For example, the Drum Arts Centre collaborated with Riverside Studios and the Black Theatre Co-operative in 1980 to commission five new plays to tour between venues: Mustapha Matura's *A Dying Business*, Hanif Kureishi's *The Mother Country*, Michael O'Neill and Jeremy Seabrook's *Black Man's Burden*, Nicholas Wright's *One Fine Day* and Tunde Ikoli's *Scrape off the Black*. During the 1980s, there were two approaches taken by regional companies in response to financial pressure.[95] Some regional programming became more conventional, increasingly mounting musicals, adaptations and familiar theatrical fare in order to secure their traditional and loyal audience base, as the Cork Report revealed.[96] However, a number of regional theatres saw their future in building a sense of locality, particularly through links with the diverse communities in their region, and this led to a range of new regional playwriting opportunities. Annie Castledine's directorship of the Derby Playhouse (1987–90) exemplified this approach: 'I hadn't realised regional rep was about money. I thought it was about encouraging the young and being radical,' she noted playfully.[97]

Companies

Alongside the *venues* staging new writing, and often working in co-production with them to produce tours or to co-fund production, were theatre *companies* with a specific brief to produce new writing. Paines Plough (founded 1974) was one of the most established. In the 1980s Paines Plough staged new work such as Terry Johnson's *Days*

Here So Dark (1981), Tony Marchant's *Welcome Home* (1983) about soldiers returning from the Falklands, Louise Page's nuclear satire *Goat* (1985), Christina Reid's *Joyriders* (1986) about Belfast teenagers on the Youth Training Programme in the middle of sectarian violence and Kate Adshead's dark study *Thatcher's Women* (1987) about factory workers forced into prostitution by their economic circumstances. Looking at this list of significant plays written for relatively small casts and touring arts centres, it is difficult to sustain the argument that only large-cast plays in large-scale venues tackled urgent political themes in the 1980s. The ambition of the plays produced by Paines Plough offered a significant cultural contribution to the regional theatres they visited. The recognition of this contribution by the Arts Council resulted in a 19 per cent upgrade in Paines Plough's funding in 1988 – no small feat in the straitened funding rounds of the late 1980s.[98] Another new writing company, Joint Stock (founded 1973), was closely linked to the Royal Court Theatre during the early 1980s through Max Stafford-Clark's directorship. Joint Stock co-produced Hanif Kureishi's *Borderline* (1981), Howard Barker's *Victory* (1983) and Sue Townsend's *The Great Celestial Cow* (1984). The company increasingly developed as an integrated multi-racial collective during the 1980s, producing more of Karim Alrawi's work. Like Joint Stock, Foco Novo (founded 1971) tended to commission writers on specific topics, working regularly in the 1980s with Howard Brenton and Tunde Ikoli. The story of these smaller-scale new writing companies, often regionally based like Annie Castledine's Nothern Studio Theatre in York, has not yet been told. Yet, access not only to regional *venues*, but also to regionally based *theatre companies* interested in writing, was often a formative part of a playwright's development, and was a key feature of the landscape of British new writing in the 1980s.

It is important to think about new writing as encompassing a broad range of forms, voices, genres and perspectives in order to see the richness of new writing in the theatre culture of the 1980s. Many of the theatre companies who facilitated new writing were expressly interested in writing from particular political perspectives, or in working in a more collaborative manner than appeared possible in the mainstream new writing venues (although this was often a misperception), or who felt their work would not find an appropriate audience in those venues. Either one could be disappointed, with David Edgar, that a Theatre Union survey in the mid-1980s found 'eight out of nine of the new plays presented by funded small-scale companies in the West Midlands were either devised or written by a company member', or one can view this as a way of facilitating new writers to develop their work into performance with a creative team committed to communicating to audiences.[99] Theatre companies indeed worked with writers within their own creative team, although in fact many touring theatre groups also commissioned writing from those outside their core group. The Women's Theatre Group (founded 1973, now Sphinx) commissioned work from Byrony Lavery, Deborah Levy, Jackie Kay and Amrit Wilson; the Women's Playhouse Trust (founded 1981) reclaimed neglected women's playwriting of the past and commissioned new work; the Black Theatre Co-operative (now Nitro) founded in 1978 by Mustapha Matura and Charlie Hanson, staged the work of established US and UK black playwrights, and in the 1980s they performed work from women playwrights including Trish Cooke and Maria Oshodi. Temba (founded 1974) further developed Trish Cooke's talents, under the artistic directorship of Alby James (1984) staging her *Back Street Mammy* (1989) about teenage pregnancy and Barbara Glouden's *The Pirate Princess* (1986), a Jamaican pantomime. The Theatre of Black Women (founded 1982) developed Jacqueline Rudet's *Basin* (1985) and Jackie Kay's *Chiaroscuro* (1986). Graeae (founded 1980) by Nabil Shaban and Richard Tomlinson, showcased the work of disabled performers and writers. *M3 Junction 4* (1982), devised and written by Richard Tomlinson and the company, imagined disabled citizens interned in Aldershot army barracks, as the most economically efficient outcome of the government's planned cuts to disability attendance and mobility allowances (forerunners of the Disability Living Allowance). These companies were politically engaged in the theatrical economy in two ways, first through creating opportunities for, and developing careers with, playwrights who were under-represented in the more main-stream venues. Second, the plays developed by these groups were often formally innovative, concentrated on the status, conditions and experiences of citizens not often represented in 'state-of-the-nation' plays, and as a consequence they found new audiences.

What is often missing from the usual accounts of new writing during the 1980s is the development of text and writing for theatre companies who were devising work, drawing on installation or visual art, or writing for and with dancers in cross-disciplinary forms of experimental theatre. Forced Entertainment's performances (founded 1984) had text and textual structures scripted from devising by Tim Etchells and the company. Built from improvisation and rule structures, early Forced Entertainment performances were games with film or popular culture genres. *200% and Bloody Thirsty* (1987) or *Some Confusions in the Law about Love* (1989) circled increasingly self-reflexively around questions of death and the value of performance, using a mix of gibberish, slang, narrative, question and answer in texts by Tim Etchells. Impact Theatre (founded 1979), another important group of the 1980s with a strongly physical element to their performance, worked with writer Claire D. MacDonald. Their best-known work, *The Carrier Frequency* (1984), used text from a collaboration with novelist Russell Hoban, to depict a post-nuclear wasteland of water and metal towers, where six performers wrestle to the point of real physical exhaustion to sustain the rituals of their lost civilisation. As Claire Macdonald points out, the work of many solo artists 'combines the roles of writer, performer, designer and director', so that the performance artists that flourished in the 1980s such as Claire Dowie, Rose English or Bobby Baker, should be considered new writers too.[100]

While small-scale touring theatre companies might not seem as significant as the large subsidised venues, in terms of the development and evolution of a playwright's career these companies were a vital mechanism of support. Several companies in the 1980s centred their work on a particular playwright's oeuvre. Hull Truck (founded 1971) produced devised and improvised work initially, before Artistic Director John Godber took over in 1983 and developed several trademark comedies that addressed local communities, as well as finding national success, with *Up 'n' Under* (1984), *Bouncers* (1983) and *Teechers* (1987). Red Stockings, a female agitprop group founded in

1988 by Helen Edmundson, produced her early work. Field Day Theatre Company (founded in 1980 by Brian Friel and Stephen Rea in Derry) has produced most of Friel's plays. Charabanc, founded in 1983 by five Irish actresses in Belfast, evolved a workshopping process around devising, drawing on archives and interviews with local people that were crafted into plays by Marie Jones. Jones and company produced six new plays between 1983 and 1989 on issues in Northern Irish life, including the comedy *Somewhere Over the Balcony* (1987), which follows the lives of three Catholic women in the Belfast's run-down Divis flats, surrounded by British army patrols. From these collaborative and co-devised projects, Marie Jones's independent play-writing continued in the 1990s with her best-known play being the West End hit *Stones in His Pockets* (1996).[101] Although emerging from a slightly different impetus, the Wrestling School, established in 1988 by Kenny Ireland and Hugh Fraser to stage Howard Barker's work, was akin to these companies.

The relationship between the small-scale touring theatre companies, often identified within an alternative scene of arts centres and regional studios, and the mainstream, commercial or subsidised, metropolitan theatres is a complex one. Many of the playwrights who emerged from these small-scale touring theatres have had their work picked up by commercial venues and have developed a strong mainstream presence: Godber, Edmundson, Friel and Jones have all had West End production and have seen their plays and adaptations in print and on school curricula. Yet for other playwrights the transition from small-scale company to mainstream acceptance was not so straightforward. In 1983 a group of black British and British Asian theatre companies created the Black Theatre Season to make explicit the dual theatrical cultures, and to stimulate theatre making from Afro-Caribbean and British Asian playwrights. Taking over the Arts Theatre in the West End, the premise of the Black Theatre Season was to bring black playwrights into mainstream theatre venues. It presented work from experienced black playwrights as well as Paulette Randall's first play *Fishing* (1983). The difficulty of building an audience for black work in a predominantly white, middle-class demographic location, and the difficulty of transferring existing audiences for black playwriting to new locations in commercial theatre's heartland, meant that the first couple of seasons struggled to fill the theatre.[102] In contrast, small-scale touring took playwrights' work to a wide range of audiences across the nation, often to more diverse communities and audiences because of the location and programming of the small-scale network. This scale of touring undoubtedly imposed limitations on cast size and scenographic experimentation. However, as the examples above indicate, small-scale production need *not* imply limitations on the visibility of the work, publication of the text, the chance for transfer to the mainstream, international touring, or revival – all those elements that earn a playwright ongoing royalties and income from a piece of creative intellectual property. The small-scale theatre companies were a vibrant seedbed for new writing. They showcased and facilitated the work of many black British, British Asian, women, disabled, gay and lesbian writers whose urgent and innovative political writing was less readily picked up by the large-scale London-based theatres, and who have, until recently, dropped out of our narratives about 'new writing' during the 1980s.

Cultures of protest: issue as subject matter

The cry went up throughout the 1980s and beyond: what has happened to political theatre? In 1976 when the National staged his *Weapons of Happiness* Howard Brenton talked of the play as 'an armoured charabanc' within the National's walls, and at the end of the 1970s David Edgar talked of the need to have big plays on 'national stages', but a key question for oppositional theatre is whether it can remain transgressive 'political theatre' from within the theatrical estate. Undoubtedly, the public debate about socialism was undergoing a crisis of confidence in the early 1980s, as the Labour Party and the unions recovered from a decade of turbulent industrial relations. This was coupled with the rise of broadly right-wing theories of postmodernism, which challenged political binaries. Baz Kershaw suggests that mainstream theatre in the 1980s was not able to provide a home for transformative theatre, but that 'more fruitful domains for both the practice and analysis of the radical in performance might be found in areas of culture that are crucial to the control exerted by the dominant formations, but which may also be more pervious to ideologically transgressive action.'[103] This for him means the streets, community-level production, and non-standard theatre spaces.

During the 1970s, *Guardian* theatre critic Michael Billington coined an adjectival phrase 'state-of-the-nation' to describe Howard Brenton's *The Churchill Play* at Nottingham Playhouse (1974).[104] John Elsom in *Post War British Theatre* picked it up and used it of John Osborne's work, particularly *A Sense of Detachment* (1972), in which '"State of the Nation" attacks' became too broad to retain their political piquancy.[105] Catherine Itzin employs the phrase in her study of the rise of alternative theatre in the 1960s and 1970s, *Stages in the Revolution* (1980), to describe Howard Barker's plays on the state of England in decline.[106] John Bull uses it of David Hare's writing in the 1970s, in *New Political Dramatists* (1984). Billington entitles his collected reflections on post-war mainstream British theatre *State of the Nation: British Theatre Since 1945*,[107] and in this he mourns the loss of large-scale, party political, discursive plays written by men and staged on the larger stages at the National, RSC or in the West End. For him, the absence of these types of plays in the 1980s marked a decline in public culture in England, encapsulated by the rise of the large-scale musical. Dan Rebellato suggests that the 'state-of-the-nation' plays are outmoded in the globalised world of the 1990s.[108] There are limitations in determining one mode of writing, and an ill-defined one at that, as *the* political writing of a decade. As Simon Shepherd caustically observes, 'the explanatory interlocking of private behaviours and larger social changes was associated with unfashionable philosophies such as Marxism, now [apparently] proved ineffectual by the overthrow of Communist regimes in Eastern Europe. State-of-the-nation dramaturgy no longer seemed credible' in the 1980s, yet political dramaturgy did not come to an end.[109] As Timberlake Wertenbaker pointed out above, if you want to find state-of-the-nation plays during the 1980s you will find them, just not written by the usual suspects, and not only concerned with the personal crises of a particular professional political class.

Janelle Reinelt usefully illustrates the flexibility of political writing: there is neither one form of politics (left/right), nor political expression, nor political style, and to limit the work of those 1970s playwrights to a strict conception of what state-of-the-nation might mean limits our reading of their political force.[110] Indeed the perception of the death of the political play during the 1980s is very closely related to a trammelled idea of an appropriate political stylistic, and a proscribed idea of what counts as political – one which chooses not to note the outdated gendered and racial limitations of many earlier plays dubbed state-of-the-nation. Such a limited perspective on the political serves neither the established playwrights, nor those who, during the 1980s, wrote explicitly political plays about the nation, the global, and the personal as interlocking. Reinelt broadens the definition of state-of-the-nation to comprise: '[the] condition of collective life in the *dēmos*, where there is a doubleness of the United Kingdom as *dēmos* on the one hand, but the global surround as *dēmos* on the other, and where the 'people' are both configured as (through language, British casting, venue, etc.) British *ethnos*, but also citizens of the world'.[111] Reinelt is talking of Caryl Churchill's plays here, but the political perspective is more broadly applicable. As May Joseph asserts, black women's playwriting 1980s was 'an evocative site of citizenship'.[112]

In fact, many plays of the 1980s dealt directly with political issues of the day in a recognisably explicit way – as personal satire of parliamentary and leading establishment figures, in all kinds of dramaturgical form. In a rough theatrical protest over the government's mantra of individualist aspiration, Howard Brenton and Tony Howard's *A Short Sharp Shock* (1980, Theatre Royal Stratford East; Royal Court) was a scatological caricature of the Thatcher government's dismantling of the welfare state and the imposition of monetarist policies. At one point the economist Milton Friedman explodes from Industry Secretary Keith Joseph's chest, in a parody from the scene in *Alien*; later Jim Prior, 'wet' Employment Secretary, is required to drink Friedman's sperm. To add to the play's sense of heightened carnivalesque, all of the cabinet ministers were played by women. The play's title (originally from a song in Gilbert and Sullivan's 1885 operetta *The Mikado* to describe execution) had been used by the Home Secretary Willie Whitelaw at the Conservative Party conference in October 1979 to describe the fate awaiting young offenders. Garnering enormous publicity for the play, two Tory MPs denounced it on television and Arts Minister Norman St John Stevas apologised in the House of Commons for the misuse of public funds. More conventionally, Peter Flannery's epic *Our Friends in the North* (1982, RSC Pit; Newcastle), with seventy characters played by sixteen actors, followed the shifting political lives of a group of friends, including an MP, through local and central government corruption and the political landscape from the 1964 Labour election victory to the eve of Thatcher's election in 1979. Edgar's *Maydays* (1983, RSC) charted the disillusionment and drift to the right of Martin, erstwhile socialist, in a meditation on the failure of the left, and the lurch to the right that saw the Conservative government re-elected in 1983. Despite its somewhat limited creation of female types, David Hare's *Secret Rapture* (1988, National) centred on a woman Conservative minister who transfers her asset-stripping economic policies to her sister's business, ignoring the personal cost that this must incur. So, here we have the representation of the political parliamentary class on national stages.

Beyond the political class, there were plays that ran close to the wind by representing thinly veiled versions of contemporary establishment individuals on stage. The Royal Court Theatre ran into legal trouble with G. F. Newman's *Operation Bad Apple* (1981), dealing with corruption in the Metropolitan Police Force, as it was staged during the trial of those policemen, while the jury were deliberating.[113] Brenton and Hare's *Pravda* (1985, National) offered a tragicomedy about a South African newspaper magnate's megalomaniac control of his paper's representation of the truth. The object of the satire was taken to be Rupert Murdoch, who had taken over *The Times* in 1981, and included lightly disguised versions of past editors, including William Rees-Mogg, who had quickly moved from editor to Chairman of the Arts Council.[114] There were also political plays that picked up topical debates on aspects of the establishment practice: Howard Brenton and activist, novelist and playwright Tariq Ali wrote *Iranian Nights* in five days, in response to the fatwa (February 1989) issued by Iranian Supreme Leader Ayatollah Khomeini against Salman Rushdie for blasphemy in his novel *The Satanic Verses*. Rushdie was a leading figure of the British literary establishment, and Brenton and Ali's short play works as an allegory, paralleling Scheherazade's storytelling under condition of death in *One Thousand and One Nights* with the death threat issued against Rushdie. The short run at the Royal Court Theatre (April 1989) caught the spirit of immediate response to events, and ended with the emotional reading of a list of writers and artists who had been persecuted and censored, broadening out the political point from a specific individual to the wider issue of censorship and free speech.[115] Yet this play also revealed some of the pitfalls of immediacy and topicality. From another perspective, in defending Rushdie, and even though Tariq Ali had written extensively on the relationship between Pakistan and India and very thoughtfully on migrant experience and fundamentalism, the Muslim figures in the play were predominantly depicted as stereotypes of fanaticism.[116] While indeed Brenton and Ali's point was to parody fanaticism, in the context of its time the media furore that surrounded the Rushdie affair too often slid into stereotyping of Islam.

Other plays of the 1980s chose to deal with broader political themes, concerning power, surveillance and control on an international scale, through a more oblique dramaturgy. Churchill's *SoftCops* (written 1978, staged 1984 at the RSC), was a response to Michel Foucault's *Discipline and Punish*, a reflection on the way regulations are internalised. Reinelt reads it as one of Churchill's most feminist plays, despite the absence of any female characters, demonstrating 'how the dominant hegemony represses certain meanings and naturalises others through the manipulation of spectacle and the selection of social gests for public consumption'.[117] Harold Pinter's one-act play *Mountain Language* (October 1988, National) centres on the fates of the Elderly Woman, the Hooded Man and the Prisoner, whose nationality, subjecthood, individuality and power of expression are incrementally silenced by military power. Parallels were inevitably drawn in an international context with the genocide of Kurds in the mountainous regions of northern Iraq, in 1988.[118] Parallels were also drawn with the national conflict in Northern Ireland, as on 19 October 1988 the Conservative government had ruled that the demo-cratically elected representatives of Sinn Féin could not be granted 'the oxygen of publicity' by having their words broadcast – that led to the surreal phenomenon of actors lip-synching television and radio interviews with politicians, until the ban was lifted in 1994. Timberlake Wertenbaker's *The Love of the Nightingale* (1989), discussed later in this volume, likewise meditates on the power of conquest imposed through control of language and silence, as well as the more explicit modes of rape and torture.

Nor was the stage slow to mount reflections, meditation and inter-ventions on the major events and issues of the day. The idea of 'issues' in a play has often carried pejorative overtones, and such work has been tarred as simplistic agitprop, or too narrow in its focus or mono-chrome in its perspective to be considered 'political' drama in the fullest sense of a 'state-of-the-nation' play. To be described as issue-based can be the kiss of death to a play's commercial success, as Sarah Daniels reflects below. Yet, much political writing of the 1980s centred on issues, exploring the ways in which legislative, economic and executive decisions impact on the social worlds of characters. These political plays were not confined to London mainstages, many originated on regional stages and toured widely beyond theatres into community halls and spaces. Leading concerns were with unemploy-ment, women's rights, racism and black British and British Asian identity, gay and lesbian rights, financial deregulation, the Cold War and the nuclear arms race, and Britain's armed presence in Northern Ireland.

Unemployment

Some commentators have suggested that one of the novel aspects of playwriting in the 1990s was its focus on a crisis of masculinity.[119] Yet much of the playwriting of the 1980s, from both male and female writers, was centrally concerned with a crisis in masculinity in context. When George Michael sang 'Wham Rap', 'I am a man/Job or no job you can't tell me that I'm not' (1982)[120] or Heaven 17 urged the nation 'Crushed by the Wheels of Industry' to dance (1983), the emasculating force of unemployment was played out in nightclubs and on tape recorders across the UK. In the light of the 1981 riots in inner cities ravaged by unemployment, Norman Tebbit rebuked the almost three million unemployed with a personal anecdote: 'I grew up in the 1930s with an unemployed father. He didn't riot. He got on his bike and looked for work.'[121] This was a surprisingly frank acknowledgement that the Conservative policy of using unemployment to control wages and inflation was producing circumstances that mirrored the 1930s. The significant distinction was that the de-industrialisation of the north of England, in train since the 1950s, had exacerbated the north–south divide to such an extent that there were no jobs to be had within cycling distance. Characters in Alan Bleasdale's TV series *Boys from the Blackstuff* (1982) followed the mixed fortunes of a group of unemployed road-builders from Liverpool, who travel across the country to find whatever work they can. Unemployment and temporary contract work challenge the masculinity of one of the lead characters Yosser, whose aggressive catchphrase 'Gizza job' became a byword for an unemployed generation of sixteen- to twenty-five-year olds. Bleasdale offers a picture of working-class community as a group of once-workmates support each other out of, and into, employment. Valerie in Jim Cartwright's *Road* (1988) reflects on the emasculation of her husband:

> **Valerie**   It's not his fault there's no work. He's such a big man, he's nowhere to put himself. He looks so awkward and sad at the sink, the vacuum's a toy in his hand. [. . .] Like a big wounded animal, moving about, trying to find his slippers.[. . .] Can we not have before again, can we not?[122]

The character's elegiac nostalgia for a past of full, male employment, and the repercussions of male unemployment for women's lives, echoes through a great many plays of the period. Unemployment was not only represented as producing a crisis in masculinity; a series of plays in the 1980s looked at employment and unemployment from women's perspective, particularly working-class women: from the limited choices of Joyce in Churchill's *Top Girls* (1982), the four teenagers of Debbie Horsfield's *Red Devils* (1983, Liverpool Playhouse Studio), to Kay Adshead's *Thatcher's Women* (1987, Tricycle and tour), which follows working-class women from Manchester forced to travel to London to work as prostitutes to support their families.

The Conservative government perceived the trade unions as a hindrance to commercial success for private companies, and introduced a series of Employment Acts that removed worker protection and made trade union representation more difficult. Rights of protest and picket were removed incrementally – the Employment Act of 1980 recommended that numbers of pickets at any workplace be limited to six. The 1986 Public Order Act gave the police powers to break up public assemblies of twenty or more people, where the police judged the assembly 'likely to result in serious public disorder'.[123] The 1982 Employment Act permitted employers to sack all striking workers at one location on one day, and for employers to claim damages against a union for stoppages. Employees were permitted to take action only against their immediate employer – workers employed elsewhere by the same employer were not permitted to participate – secondary or 'flying pickets' were not allowed. The 1984 Trade Unions Act further atomised union organisation by requiring secret balloting of members before any industrial action. This is the legislation that the National Union of Mineworkers, headed up by Arthur Scargill, fell foul of in 1984. Increasingly restrictive conditions on strike ballots have been imposed, requiring given percentages of participation that few general elections could hope to achieve, for example. These trends continue today as employers increasingly use injunctions to delay or prevent strikes on the grounds of questioning the mechanisms of a ballot's conduct.

Plays which explicitly dealt with unemployment and the erosion of employment and trade union rights were legion in the early 1980s. They form a central part of the work of John McGrath's 7:84 (England) company. John Burrows's play *One Big Blow* (1980) presented the fortunes of a group of miners and the fate of their colliery brass band, and toured community venues for two years, also playing at the Half Moon, London.[124] Peter Cox's monologue play *Jimmy Riddle* (1983), about a sacked union organiser at British Leyland's closed Liverpool plant in 1981, looked at the personal repercussions of redundancy and long-term unemployment, playing in working men's clubs and local theatres in Liverpool and beyond. *The Garden of England* (1984), about the experience and consequences of the miners' strike, toured civic halls, particularly in areas affected by the strike, and was supported by both the unions and the Labour Party. McGrath wrote about the kind of theatre that 7:84 pursued: 'Any theatre that concentrates on "emotional" plots and does not question the structures that underlie its characters' lives is being political by default. We choose to examine the political issues openly because they shape the reality we live in.'[125] The miners' strike and the interconnection between political structure and the personal are entertainingly evident in Cordelia Ditton and Maggie Ford's *About Face* (1985), a satiric one-woman analysis of working-class women from Nottinghamshire, with Ditton playing thirty-five characters include The Thatcher, an Oil Sheik and a Rubbish Tip.[126] Beyond the mode of performances geared for non-theatregoing community venues, plays about the 1984–85 miners' strike reached mainstages, such as John Godber's bittersweet comedy *Salt of the Earth* (1988, Wakefield Opera House and tour with Hull Truck) about its impact on West Yorkshire families, and David Edgar's *That Summer* (1987, Hampstead) which analyses the inadequacy of middle-class socialism's response to the strike.

Women's rights

The rise of women's theatre groups and women playwrights was a significant aspect of the late 1970s and early 1980s, and Lizbeth Goodman has detailed the emergence of explicitly feminist work. During the early 1980s, women's presence was unmissable on the small-scale touring circuit and among small-scale companies, some of whom were all-female, some explicitly feminist, including Black Mime Theatre Women's Troupe, Clean Break, Imani-Faith, Monstrous Regiment, Mrs Worthington's Daughters, Red Ladder, Siren, Talawa, Theatre of Black Women, Women's Playhouse Trust,

Women's Theatre Group. Often supported initially by these groups, a series of women dramatists became canonical during the 1980s, evolving writing from a wide range of perspectives and forms, from the experimental work of Caryl Churchill, Sarah Daniels or Bryony Lavery; the biographical and elegiac focus of Pam Gems echoed in younger writers such as Charlotte Keatley and Sharman Macdonald; and the social realism of Andrea Dunbar. Black women dramatists have made slower progress into regular revival and on to school syllabi but include Winsome Pinnock and Meera Syal. The absence of black women dramatists on most stages was one addressed actively by small-scale women's companies, regional theatres and the Arts Council during the 1980s, with playwriting initiatives from regional and suburban theatres, as we have seen; for example, at the Drill Hall Cheryl Robson set up a Women Writers Workshop for black women writers, and Aurora Metro Press in order to publish their work.[127]

As the 1980s wore on, several women playwrights found the sobriquet 'feminist' a difficult one, and for some it was more pigeonholing than helpful.[128] And indeed, by the mid-1980s feminism was rarely the only focus of feminist works. Jane Thornton's *Amid the Standing Corn* (1985) follows the fates of four miners' wives, connected by the strike, drawing on Thornton's personal experience of the frontline strike in Yorkshire. Thornton, who had written and performed regularly with Hull Truck, developed the play with Joint Stock for Soho Poly, locating women's challenges to socially restricted gender roles in traditionally tight-knit communities within a broader class critique on the power struggle that the miners' strike represented. Caryl Churchill's *Top Girls*, now one of the most canonical works of the 1980s, explicitly wrestles with the limiting impositions of class for feminism – Joyce's role as adoptive mother to Marlene's daughter is one circumscribed more firmly by class than gender – at the moment that class was supposedly becoming irrelevant.

Racism and black British and British Asian identity

The rise of racism in post-war Britain was variously tackled by anti-racist movements, including, in the late 1970s, Rock Against Racism. In 1978, in the run-up to election, Margaret Thatcher said in an interview that 'people are really rather afraid that this country might be rather swamped by people with a different culture'.[129] The unfortunate choice of the word 'swamped' overshadowed her other comments on the need to resist the National Front's extremism and to treat all citizens equally under the law, 'once they are here'. In 1981 and again in 1985 there was protest and civil unrest in a number of inner cities, in 1981 in Toxteth (Liverpool), Handsworth (Birmingham), Chapeltown (Leeds) and Brixton (London), attributed to a mixture of rising and systemic unemployment, particularly among young people, the obvious decay of urban areas as a result of de-industrialisation, disproportionate police activity around black and Asian people – the 'sus' laws[130] and police reluctance to investigate anti-black crime, notably an arson attack in New Cross in January 1981 that killed thirteen young black people. The 'sus' laws were particularly loathed. Two white playwrights engaged with the anti-racist movement. Barrie Keeffe's *Sus* (May 1979, Soho Poly; Royal Court; community venues tour; Theatre Royal Stratford East) laid bare the iniquitous manner of the 'sus' laws' application. The music scene was trying to resist the rise of skinhead culture in the form of two-tone ska revival groups such as The Specials, Bad Manners, The Selecter and The Beat. Trevor Griffiths's *Oi for England*, about the rise of skinhead racism after the 1981 riots, had a life at the Royal Court Theatre Upstairs in 1981 and toured community halls and schools in Birmingham and Greater London, and was filmed in 1982.[131] Black playwright Don Webb's *Black Ball Game* (Sheffield Crucible and Tricycle, 1981) tackled upwardly mobile racism in a comedy about two racist businessmen.

Part of the context for the experience of black racism was the international pressure of the South African regime, where apartheid was still fully in force, and the white government under P. B. Botha established some autonomies for designated tribal 'homeland' areas and forcibly 'resettled' many people according to their 'group identity'. Nelson Mandela, titular head of the African National Congress, was still imprisoned and anti-apartheid movements in Europe and the US were boycotting companies who supported or traded with the regime. Musicians were particularly outspoken, and in the UK two-tone ska bands made an explicit link between international racism and the black British and British Asian experience, and The Special AKA wrote the anti-apartheid anthem of the 1980s, 'Free Nelson Mandela' (1984). National trade sanctions were imposed in the mid-1980s, but most commentators consider that an end to apartheid was produced by shifts in the Cold War in 1989. New South African president F. W. de Klerk argued that the communist threat, reified in the Marxist discourse of many of the African independence movements of the 1950s and in the ongoing funding from the USSR for several African regimes, was lifted with the fall of the Iron Curtain. De Klerk permitted a more libertarian approach, and apartheid was ended and Mandela released in February 1990.

Black and Asian playwrights were exploring the question of identity and heritage in Britain, and part of the formal attention paid to black arts during the early 1980s was a result of an important report commissioned by the Community Relations Commission, *The Art Britain Ignores* (1976), in which Naseem Khan studied the wealth of artistic activity in diverse ethnic communities. The 1980s saw more formal interest in funding art for and by 'minority communities' not least as part of the state's response to race-related urban upheaval. The Greater London Council funded a wide number of black, Asian and other 'ethnic' arts events, groups, community artists and festivals in the early 1980s. Channel 4 (started 1982) had a specific remit for inclusive programming for 'minority interests', and drew on black and Asian theatre practitioners. Among Channel 4's commissions was a sit-com *No Problem!* (1983–85) written by Trinidadian-born Mustapha Matura and British-Asian writer Farrukh Dhondy, developed from characters and storylines from the Black Theatre Co-operative. Dhondy was Channel 4's commissioning editor for multicultural programming (1984–97) and wrote his own comedy series, *Tandoori Nights* (1985–87). Black and Asian filmmakers and film production companies began to emerge during the early 1980s, often supported by Channel 4's Film Four wing.

In 1986 Kwesi Osuwu's *The Struggle for Black Arts in Britain: What Can We Consider Better than Freedom* (London: Comedia, 1986), argued for the building of a black aesthetic that resisted Western theatre traditions, but one of the characteristics of black and Asian writing during the 1980s was its diversity. Indeed, part of the extensive debate during the 1980s was about whether the phrase 'black', which had worked as a political term of solidarity for earlier generations of people with Indian, Pakistani and Asian, Afro-Caribbean and African origins, had become a homogenising term that effaced specific experiences. The work that playwrights produced during the 1980s was multifarious, ranging from searching for a distinctive black aesthetic to demanding colour-blind casting in Western classics, drawing on multiple backgrounds and disparate experiences of migration, and representing considerable differences in experience and in relation to their 'heritage' between first-generation migrants and their British-born children.

The questions of migration, arrival, belonging, national and cultural identity run through much of the writing of the 1980s. Hanif Kureishi's *Borderline* (1981, Royal Court) represented multiple perspectives through realistically drawn characters from the British Asian community, wrestling with issues of family structures and pressures, housing, racism, exploitation from both white and Asian characters, and citizenship. Anglo-Canadian-Egyptian writer Karim Alrawi's first play *Migrations* (1982) won the John Whiting Award, and Alrawi became Literary Manager of the Theatre Royal Stratford East. Alrawi commissioned white writer Barrie Keeffe, whose *King of England* (1988, Theatre Royal Stratford East) reconfigured King Lear as a tube driver, who after thirty-five years of service is ready to split his hard-earned wealth between his three daughters before his return to Trinidad.[132] Neil Bartlett's review for *Time Out* reveals that the playwright's white background did not deter local audiences: 'animated and argued by an ensemble of careful committed performers, these crucial hours in the life of one angry, confused black family, have the audience buzzing with comment and unexpected laughter'.[133] Winsome Pinnock's *Leave Taking* (1988, Liverpool Playhouse) was likewise about the conflict between first- and second-generation members of a black British family, who churn over and over their cultural identity and location – Del, a second-generation woman, describes her life as 'running around trying to find a place to fit in'.[134]

The role of small-scale black and Asian theatre companies was crucial in the development of a black presence in British culture, and three of the longest-lived were Temba (1972–92), Talawa (1986–) and Tara Arts (1977–), alongside Carib Theatre, Tamasha Theatre and Hounslow Arts Co-operative. The companies took very different approaches: Talawa choosing from the mid-1980s to cast all-black versions of Western classic plays; Temba taking a more spectacular route and seeking to integrate black cultural traditions; and Tara, moving from community-centred realist work with second-generation citizens towards Binglish, which integrated Indian classical forms and acting traditions into more epic stories. These companies were commissioning routes for playwrights such as Rukhsana Ahmad, Paulette Randall, Jacqueline Rudet, Maya Chowdhry and Parv Bancil.[135] Yet the route to performance was not always straightforward, as Caryl Phillips, in a tellingly entitled essay 'I Could Have Been a Playwright', illustrates. After initial stagings of his first three plays, *Strange Fruit* (1980, Sheffield Crucible), *Where There is Darkness* (1982, Lyric Studio) and *The Shelter* (1983, Lyric Studio), he was commissioned by the Royal Court Theatre for a larger-scale work, but it 'was ultimately deemed too difficult to stage and I was told that it was too much of a financial risk'.[136] This raises the spectre that theatres did not trust that there was a large enough black audience, or one that they could attract, nor that their current audience constituency would find black playwrights' work 'accessible' or a reflection of 'universal' human experience. Lynnette Goddard notes the transition from the pump-priming of black theatre at the beginning of the 1980s, to a policy of encouraging all theatre companies to engage with issues of cultural diversity. This is not a positive step for Goddard: 'The shift from "black theatre" to "cultural diversity" epitomises the new right discourses on British identity that effectively endorses the decline of a sustained black theatre movement and the dispersal of practitioners as individuals throughout the industry.'[137]

Gay rights

Several lesbian theatre groups had emerged in the 1970s, including Character Ladies, Gay Sweatshop, Female Trouble and Siren, who raised the profile of lesbian playwrights. At the same time the Drill

Hall and the Oval House Theatre housed a lively cabaret and comedy scene that celebrated lesbian and gay identity and community, and highlighted injustices and discrimination with irony and pastiche. Many gay and lesbian playwrights found a staging through these venues and companies, including Tasha Fairbanks, Bryony Lavery, Jackie Kay, Sarah Daniels, Maya Chowdhry, Nina Rapi and Noel Greig. Greig's writing covers very diverse topics from *Poppies* (1983), a futuristic view of the world on the brink of nuclear annihilation, to *Plague of Innocence* (1988), on the press hysteria and bigotry that surrounded the arrival of AIDS, and he was a key writer for Gay Sweatshop for many years. Much of the work that Gay Sweatshop developed and commissioned from playwrights dealt with the actively discriminatory language and legislation of the era. Despite a Home Office policy recommendation in 1979 that the age of consent for homosexual partners should be reduced from twenty-one years to eighteen years, legislative equality between same-sex and heterosexual consenting partners was not achieved in England until the *Sexual Offences (Amendment) Act* of 2000. Public figures were 'outed' in tabloid newspapers, which went on to call for their resignation. The language of the tabloid press was at odds with a variety of campaigning gains made by gay and lesbian activists such as Peter Tatchell, who stood as Labour candidate for Bermondsey in 1981.

One of the central issues on which Gay Sweatshop commissioned plays was the introduction of the Local Government Act 1988 that included a homophobic Section 28, which prohibited local authorities from the 'intentional promotion' of homosexual equality or the 'teaching in any maintained school of the acceptability of homosexuality as a pretended family relationship'. This was a direct challenge to much mainstream local educational authority policy, which had been trying to develop *anti*-discriminatory literature for schools, and to counter bigotry focused on 'sexual orientation'. Stonewall in the UK was established to combat Section 28's discriminatory legislation, uniting gay and lesbian men and women. Gay Sweatshop headed up a response in a variety of theatrical ways, including producing Philip Osment's *This Island's Mine* (1988), which drew attention to the personal costs of discrimination. The play follows the stories of four characters who experience queer-bashing, and the complicity of the homophobic police, a miner made redundant on the grounds of his sexuality, and an elderly Jewish lesbian refugee living in fear. Section 28 was not repealed in England until the Local Government Act of 2003.

Cold War and arms race

The nuclear arms race and the global instability produced by the Cold War had a significant impact on playwriting during the 1980s, not least because nuclear weapons became linked to party political agendas when, in 1982, the Labour Party adopted a policy of unilateral nuclear disarmament. This was in response to the agreement of the Conservative government to host American Cruise missiles, aimed at the USSR, in the UK (1982). The bases for these weapons at Greenham Common became the site of an ongoing women-only protest movement, but also produced many marches from the Campaign for Nuclear Disarmament. The Labour Party abandoned its unilateral disarmament stance after its 1987 electoral defeat. The Greenham Common protest became a much-used image in theatre pieces of the time, and one piece of performance, *The Fence* (1984, St Paul's Church, Hammersmith and Greenham), emerged from women protesters at the site.[138]

The 1980s saw numerous plays that dealt with the nuclear threat, or which depicted the potential aftermath of the policy of Mutually Assured Destruction, from Theatre-in-Education pieces such as David Holman's *1983*, to Brenton's *The Genius* (1983), Edgar's *Maydays* (1983) and Daniels's *The Devil's Gateway* (1983). The tone and approach of the plays about nuclear annihilation range from darkly comic, such as Nick Darke's *The Body* (1983, RSC) to the relentlessly bleak in Edward Bond's trilogy of War Plays (1985, RSC), particularly the second play, *Tin Can People*, which depicts the power struggles of a small group of post-apocalypse survivors and echoed Barry Hinds's *Threads* (1984, BBC), which imagined life in Sheffield after a nuclear attack. Robert Holman's *The Overgrown Path* (1985, Royal Court) returns to the experience of actual nuclear destruction at Nagasaki, and pictures the hydrogen bomb's creator reflecting on his life's work.

The most moving section of the play is its opening, where children enact Etsuko's story of survival of the moment of the H-bomb's explosion. During the 1980s, the reality and imminent threat of nuclear destruction was emphasised by government information broadcasts and the distribution of leaflets, *Protect and Survive* (1980). The pressure of Cold War antagonism was played out in proxy wars across the globe, notably in Afghanistan, where the repercussions of the US arming the Mujahideen to resist communist encroachment produced the context for more recent Western intervention in that country. The paranoid rhetoric of the Cold War was parodied in much popular music during the 1980s, from Frankie Goes to Hollywood's 'Two Tribes' (1981), Nena's '99 Luft Ballons' (1982), Heaven 17's 'Let's All Make a Bomb' (1983), Prince's '1999' (1985), to the elegiac Ultravox song 'Dancing with Tears in My Eyes' (1984) or Sting's solo 'Russians' (1985) with its much-mocked rhyming couplets, 'We share the same biology/Regardless of ideology'. While post-nuclear holocaust fiction had been an evolving genre since the 1940s, the arrival of Cruise missiles on British soil in 1982 undoubtedly focused the attention of dramatists back to the potential local repercussions of Cold War brinkmanship.

Financial deregulation

One of the most significant legacies of the 1980s, politically and economically, has been the deregulation of the financial institutions. The old-style City of London as a bastion of the old-boys' club peopled by a privileged class in bowler hats gave way to new-style Americanised trading, and most crucially it saw the compression of the competing roles of stockbroker with market-maker and dealer. A series of corporate takeovers produced macro-financial organisations that were predominantly foreign-owned. The disproportionate bonus unconnected to productivity, and the long-hour, hyper-macho trading environment were born. Producing the conditions for an over-inflated bubble in the financial markets, banks were deregulated at the same time – the amount of capital banks need to carry was radically reduced, capital could leave the country without the approval of the Bank of England, the distinction between retail banking and investment banking was eroded, and the role of banks in the retail and personal banking sector was greatly increased. High-street banks were permitted and encouraged to move into the mortgage business, and consumer credit became far more available than ever before.[139]

One of the few plays to directly challenge the phenomenon was Caryl Churchill's *Serious Money* (1987, Royal Court) – a response that used some of the plot line of Thomas Shadwell's late-seventeenth-century comedy *The Volunteers: or, the Stockjobbers* (1696), written just after the formation of the Bank of England, the national debt and the explosion of speculative trading in futures in the late 1690s. Shadwell's comedy is not written in rhyming couplets, but Churchill uses the form as a distancing device to encourage the audience to remain in critical dialogue with the piece. The personalities of many of the unremarkable jobbers who pass through the play are barely sketched, reducing any realist response. Yet when the play transferred to the West End much of its audience was made up of those City traders, who took the satire on the chin and relished seeing themselves represented. In its use of satire, the play keyed into the rising culture of alternative comedy that had become commercially successful at the Comedy Store (opened 1979), and which was further popularised through the television broadcast of *Saturday Live*, hosted and led by Ben Elton, and featuring a youthful Harry Enfield in a short mono-logue skit, developed by Paul Whitehouse, as Loadsamoney (1987): 'You know what this is? *(waving wad of paper money)* it's loadsamoney.' The Loadsamoney character was a builder in a shellsuit, with a broad estuary accent, who announced his wealth in an ostentatious and 'tasteless' way. Enfield launched a single as Loadsamoney in 1988, and toured off the back of the character, despite having only five outings on *Saturday Live*. The figure operated as a satirical jibe at the nouveau riche jobbers making huge salaries in the financial sector, the yuppies – young upwardly mobile professionals – who aspired to conspicuous consumption. In May 1988 Neil Kinnock accused Margaret Thatcher at Prime Minister's Question Time of encouraging a 'loadsamoney mentality'. Yet, as several commentators pointed out at the time, there were many viewers who did not see the character as parodic exposure, but instead as positive role model or validation of their 'kind' on stage and television. The disproportionate unbalancing of the UK economy in favour of financial services and banking, as opposed to manufacturing, was established during the 1980s. The UK has run a manufacturing trade deficit since 1983, becoming a net importer of electronic goods in particular, from South Korea, Hong Kong, Taiwan and Singapore – in the era before China had established itself as the manufacturing centre of the globe.[140] George Soros has argued recently that the financial collapse of 2008 and the resultant Western recession was a direct result of a financial bubble that began in the 1980s with deregulation. When this arch-speculator and financier, whose attack on sterling precipitated its exit from the Exchange Rate Mechanism in 1992, suggests the need for increased regulation of the financial markets, it is clear that the current deregulated system has become too unstable.[141]

Northern Ireland

The silent war that England was fighting during the 1980s was that in Northern Ireland. In 1981 Bobby Sands, an IRA member and an elected Westminster MP, died after a hunger strike in the Maze prison, attempting to have his status changed to that of political prisoner. Nine other hunger strikers died that year. Over 100,000 people attended Sands's funeral. While the Conservative government asserted these hunger strike deaths were wasted lives, they did quietly change the prison regime for Republican prisoners to reflect their status as quasi-political, as they had been demanding. A mainland bombing campaign followed the hunger strikers' deaths, with eight British soldiers on ceremonial duty killed in Hyde Park and Regent's Park in 1982; in 1983 a car bomb exploded outside Harrods; in 1984 the IRA bombed the Brighton hotel where all the Conservative cabinet were staying during the party conference, killing five; and in 1989, a bomb at the Royal Marines Deal barracks in Kent killed eleven soldiers.

In 1982 the Northern Ireland Assembly was set up as an appointed assembly from Westminster with some independent powers, but the moderate SDLP and the more extreme Sinn Féin boycotted the assembly from the start and it came to an end in 1986. In part the

Assembly's end was precipitated by the July 1985 Anglo-Irish Agreement, which gave the Irish government a 'consultative' role in Northern Ireland. This produced an immediate increase in attacks from loyalist forces, the Ulster Volunteer Force (UVF), Ulster Defence Association (UDA) and Ulster Resistance. The Agreement laid out the basis upon which devolved government in Northern Ireland, which had been revoked since 1972, might be revived. Stewart Parker's *Pentecost* (1987), produced by Field Day, examines the Ulster Workers' Strike and the ending of the Sunningdale Agreement of 1974 (the last time some kind of power-sharing arrangement had been mooted), at the moment that protests over the Anglo-Irish Agreement were growing.

Then, in 1987, an IRA bomb in Enniskillen on Remembrance Sunday killed eleven people. Despite the progress made through the Assembly, in October 1988 government legislation revoked a suspect's right to silence in Northern Ireland, and judges and juries were able to 'interpret' a refusal to answer questions. In March 1988 SAS members shot three unarmed IRA members dead in Gibraltar, revealing the government's explicit 'shoot to kill' policy for IRA suspects. As the three were buried back in Ireland at Milltown Cemetery, loyalist Michael Stone opened fire on mourners, killing three. He was captured by Royal Ulster Constabulary (RUC) officers before the crowd could reach him. At the funeral for those three mourners, two off-duty British soldiers drove into the funeral cortege, were mistakenly thought to be loyalist gunmen, and were lynched by the crowd. The lawyer Pat Finucane, who defended the men prosecuted for those lynchings, was shot in his home in February 1989 by the Ulster Defence Association. It was also clear at this point that the British Intelligence forces had infiltrated all major terrorist organisations, often at a high level, and were thus colluding with some of the violent actions occurring in Northern Ireland. While this violence seemed to point to an endless spiral of aggression, the transformations in Eastern Europe in 1989 and the release of Nelson Mandela from prison in apartheid South Africa demonstrated that seemingly intransigent political stalemates might change, and by 1991 secret talks began the slow road to a peace process.

The pop music of the 1980s addressed the ongoing engagement with Northern Ireland, as in The Police's 'Invisible Sun' (1981) and U2's anthem 'Sunday Bloody Sunday' (1983) which reflected on the ignominious shooting of unarmed civilians by British armed forces in Derry. Playwrights based in Northern Ireland were centrally concerned with this conflict, its history and with possible reconciliation, yet there was surprisingly little address to Northern Ireland in plays from England, with the notable exception of Howard Brenton's *The Romans in Britain* (1980). *Romans* opened at the National and immediately caused a furore with its frank representation of an attempted male rape, as part of Brenton's biting critique of British imperialism and of England's involvement in Northern Ireland. The parallel that Brenton was hoping his audiences might draw between Roman and British imperialism was largely lost on the broader public, as the issue quickly became one of the play's attempted censorship and suppression by Mary Whitehouse.[142] More straightforwardly, Ron Hutchinson's *Rat in the Skull* (1985, Royal Court) replays an interrogation between a suspected IRA bomber and an RUC officer in a London police cell, where all kinds of bigotry and violent intimidation are applied. Anne Devlin's *Ourselves Alone* (1985, Royal Court) studies the impact of the Troubles on the lives of three women, whose choices to stay in support of 'their men' Devlin critiques. Stewart Parker's oeuvre follows the questioning place of theatre in a time of extreme turmoil. His *Northern Star* (1984, Lyric, Belfast) replays the life of eighteenth-century Ulster rebel Henry Joy McCracken, dealing with each stage of his life in the form of a different Irish playwright from Boucicault to Beckett. Christina Reid's writing is explicitly about class, and although set in the Northern Irish context of the Troubles, she continually returns to the intersections of gender and class in her plays. Her earlier play *Tea in a China Cup* (1982, Lyric, Belfast) charts in flashback the lives of three Protestant working-class women. Her *Joyriders* (1986, Tricycle Theatre, London), commissioned by Paines Plough, is drawn from research on the lives of women on the notorious Divis estate, Belfast, like Marie Jones's writing with the collective Charabanc, and their first play *Somewhere Over the Balcony* (1987). Reid's most controversial play, *The Belle of*

Belfast City (1989), examines female characters who wrestle with the constrictions of the roles of wife, mother or daughter to which both sides of the religious divide condemn them. More tellingly, it explores the links between right-wing English movements such as the National Front and the loyalist Democratic Unionist Party, a particular issue for Belle, who is of mixed-race heritage. Frank McGuinness's *Observe the Sons of Ulster Marching Towards the Somme* (1986) covers some of the same territory as Reid's plays, exploring the interrelationship between masculinity, violence and the myths of heroism in the identity of Ulster men.

Present pasts

The nostalgic desire that underpinned much of the rhetoric around theatre during the 1980s was allied to a sense of loss of the momentum of the 1970s when radical, politically oppositional theatre had aligned with centralised funding agendas and facilitated an explosion of committed, 'authentic' playwriting and theatre making. This, of course, was a fantasy of a coherent, political past that occluded many of the omissions and silences of the 1970s, and devalued those voices that were heard more insistently during the 1980s, in spite of a conservative and Conservative funding regime. Despite the language of crisis in theatre, there was much to be celebrated in the political value of the many women, black and Asian, gay and lesbian playwrights who found regular public expression of their perspectives and theatrical skill during the 1980s.

The enduring significance of regional theatre and small-scale touring theatre to new writing during the 1980s has been greatly underestimated, particularly by versions of theatre history that want to consider leftist male-authored drama as the marker of true political art. Kershaw's explication of the complex negotiations between communities, audiences, participants and makers that produces a performance to support democratic engagement is one part of an alternative story. Another strand to an alternative history is to follow regional theatre's and regional theatre directors' commitment to new writing and the facilitation of the introduction of new voices to the stage. Most of the authors looked at briefly in this chapter have had one or more plays staged in a regional theatre – and this during a decade when both regional theatre and new writing itself were supposedly in abeyance.

The 1980s seems an era so distant that its style can be reclaimed by contemporary designers as 'retro'. Yet some elements of cultural life have endured into the present, most significantly shifts in the defence of the role of government subsidy for the arts. Conservative government policy centred on the extraction of the state from manufacturing and service industries and national industries were privatised, although this is not to say that government subsidy ceased. The logical corollary was the removal of state subsidy for the arts. While that did not occur, there was an ineluctable move towards privatising arts funding, attempting to produce a mixed economy of private sponsorship and government subsidy. The rhetoric of arts funding at all levels of policy, institutional and administrative life changed, and that impact endures to the present. The language of the 'cultural industries' had been generated much earlier in the twentieth century; since the 1940s, Cultural Materialism as a critical mode had concerned itself with industrial elements of culture in terms of the production of art, artistic labour, and the distribution of symbolic and cultural capital. However, during the 1980s cultural policy and Britain's cultural institutions, under the economic logic of monetarism, recast artistic activity as part of the cultural or creative industries. These cultural industries were defined primarily in terms of the markets for artistic goods, and by economic measures that equate profit with success. In these ways, the 1980s posed a series of challenges to the fraught question of the cultural 'value' of the arts that resonate to this day in British cultural life.

CHAPTER 2
INTRODUCING THE PLAYWRIGHTS

Crafting careers

During the 1980s there were a few innovations in the way in which playwrights might begin their careers, in terms of training, mentoring and finding a way to convey their scripts into the hands of directors or to companies that might bring them to the stage. The idea that a playwright might be specifically trained in playwriting was a relatively alien one in the early 1980s. Writers might have attended ad hoc courses at centres such as the Arvon Foundation, City Literature Institute or the Actors Centre, London, where stand-up comic Julie Balloo, for example, developed her playwriting through a two-year playwriting course run by playwright David Mowat.[1] As we have seen, theatre companies often ran workshops or short writers' programmes to develop new voices. There were one or two longer-term writer support groups, as at the Royal Court, but for the most part playwrights trained on the job. It was not until 1989 that David Edgar initiated the first MA in Playwriting at the University of Birmingham. The rhetorical construction of the arts as an industry and debates around the economic value of culture had increased a sense of the professionalisation of playwriting. Coupled with this, higher education had expanded exponentially in 1988 and 1989, opening up possibilities for new courses to attract new students.[2]

Once a play was written, a playwright might send it to a venue or company, where it landed on the desk of that much-maligned figure – the literary manager. Until the early 1980s most literary managers were writers themselves, were part-time, and concerned with reading the unsolicited manuscripts received, as well as developing and commissioning plays alongside their artistic directors. A gradual shift in status began to happen with the appointment of the first full-time, non-writer literary manager at the Royal Court, Rob Ritchie in 1977, and Colin Chambers in 1981 at the RSC. As the intervention of government within the arts grew, and with it pressure on the Arts Council, more and more attention was paid to the 'management' of theatres and their diminished resources. This led to a round of appointments of executive directors, as opposed to responsibility lying with artistic directors, and by the end of the 1980s literary management was caught up in the same rhetoric. Playwright Robert Holman, reflecting in the 2000s, decried the rise of the influence of literary managers: 'At one time artistic directors used to commission and receive scripts, and put them on if they thought they were good enough. They learnt about the plays along with the writers. [. . . Now w]riters have begun to deliver unfinished scripts, since they know they will be interfered with.'[3] Yet literary managers might also be a source of support. Timberlake Wertenbaker reflects on the significance of literary manager Rob Ritchie to the trajectory of the Royal Court in the 1980s:

> he was terribly influential. [. . .] Rob read every script, and he did see that it was time for some women writers. I was part of the Writers' Union, and there was a lot of bad feeling among women at that time, that they were being dismissed by the Court. [. . . Change] came from Rob taking the trouble to go and see plays written by women, instead of saying, 'Oh, I'm not going to see that, I'm not interested,' which had been the attitude before, it really had been. [4]

Once a playwright had written something and submitted it to a theatre or company there were a number of routes offering professional mentoring. The Royal Court had had a Writers' Group since its inception in 1955 and, in a natural extension of their policy, started its Young Writers' Group from the Young People's Theatre Scheme in 1979. Mentors on the scheme were often writers in residence; Hanif Kureishi returned in 1985 to be Writer-in-Residence at the Young People Theatre, then run by Elyse Dodgson. Other venues and companies mentored and supported writers in a variety of ways from commenting on drafts to rehearsed readings or workshopping plays in the studio. Time and space for developmental support was key for many writers, such as Jackie Kay, Scottish poet and novelist. She worked on her first half-hour play for the Theatre of Black Women, a group of performer/writers who had themselves been through the Royal Court Writers Workshops.[5] They commissioned her to extend it, and as *The Meeting Place* it was given a performed reading at the Gay Sweatshop Times Ten festival of new writing in 1985. Gay Sweatshop workshopped it for four weeks, and Kay revised it as *Chiaroscuro*. Further writerly revisions continued before it went into its full production premiere at Soho Poly in 1986.[6] After yet more revision it was published in Jill Davis's collection of *Lesbian Plays* for Methuen in 1987. Fractured poetic monologue and choric text is interspersed with more naturalistic scenes. The play follows the stories of four women who are negotiating their black heritage in an African diaspora, while also negotiating their sexuality within contemporary England. Kay reflected on how she retained the core of her creative interest through the process of refinement: 'in all the drafts of this play I have been obsessed with naming. What do we call ourselves as lesbians and black women?'[7] This kind of mentoring and workshopping allowed for a sense of a play as a working text, evolving in response to input from others and multiple voices. This mode of work was enshrined in many alternative companies' processes, not least that of Joint Stock. Thus, through Max Stafford-Clark's involvement with the Royal Court, qualities such as flexibility, the integration of others' voices, factual subject matter and research, and the input of the actors and director into the script as performance text, became increasingly valorised.

The 1980s also saw the emergence of new peer-support institutions for playwrights. Although, the Writers' Guild has existed since 1958, representing authors of all genres, to advise on legal and employment matters, it was clear that the very wide range of emerging playwrights, often from alternative companies and from groups under-represented in theatre, was not finding adequate support to develop their craft, to move on from a first play into a career, and to negotiate the networks of patronage that surrounded the leading theatre venues. In 1986 Susan Croft founded the New Playwrights' Trust (NPT) to provide a network of peer-support, shared experience and a script-reading service for these new writers.[8] Particularly important projects included Blackwright, which set out to support, document and archive the work of black and Asian playwrights, run collaboratively by the NPT and Black Audio Film Collective (founded 1982).[9] North West Playwrights (founded 1982) began as a series of workshops run by playwrights who had met through the Theatre Writers' Union. There was little regional investment for playwrights in the north-west, so with a small grant (£6,000) from North West Arts, they started a script-reading scheme, selected six of the best plays and staged script-in-hand performances at the Contact Theatre, Manchester, in 1983. This became an annual event, and funds were used to pay playwrights to develop their scripts towards professional production.[10] North West Playwrights was a forerunner of the writer-development agencies now sustained by the Arts Council.

This is the context for writing, training, mentoring, getting a first play read and establishing a career, in which the four playwrights who are the central study of this volume were at work. The careers of the four writers considered below, Howard Barker, Jim Cartwright, Sarah Daniels and Timberlake Wertenbaker, characterise aspects of the mainstream in playwriting practice in the 1980s. They are all writers whose work was staged at the Royal Court and on other leading national stages, and who have become part of the canon of British theatrical playwriting. The previous chapter has tried to give a sense of the rich context of playwriting within which they were working, and the alternative trajectories that these writers interact with at times in their careers. Like most other playwrights at work in the 1980s, these authors work with small-scale touring companies, as well as national stages, they have their work championed and produced by regional theatres in both studios and on mainstages, and they forge occasional links with community-centred groups which were focused on specific audiences. Some of these playwrights worked with devised processes, physical theatre or site-related work, and the pressure of other genres of writing for performance from experimental, live art, alternative theatre, as well as writing for media such as radio, television and film, is occasionally apparent in their experimentation with genre or form.

Howard Barker

Howard Barker, born 1946, began writing novels while studying history at Sussex University. One of his first theatrical experiences was seeing Edward Bond's *Saved* (1965), directed by Bill Gaskill at the Royal Court, which represented south London working-class young people trapped by their grim economic and social circumstances:

> I suppose that seeing the life of my own class and background could be represented on the stage made me want to write a play – and, perhaps, write it better. I do remember feeling that Bond's presentation of the South London working class was abominable and contemptuous. The inarticulacy, the grunting and the monosyllabics being accepted as a portrayal of working-class people did offend me and may have inspired me to write *Cheek*, which did lend articulacy to the characters.[11]

This gave Barker both the context and an obvious venue to receive his first stage play. He posted *Cheek* to the Royal Court and, in a very rare move, Gaskill directed it almost unaltered Upstairs in September 1970. *Cheek* follows the fortunes of school leaver Laurie, who resists work and becomes a property landlord. It opens in a domestic setting, but employs a heightened speech of poetic naturalism, and by its third and final act the style of the play becomes a metaphorical exploration of what Barker characterised as working-class experience: 'It annoys me when socialists glorify work, when all the work available is of a soul-destroying nature and always likely to be.'[12] Barker's entry into playwriting through the auspices of the Royal Court Upstairs is a model that holds true for many new playwrights of the 1970s and 1980s, although few saw their first submitted plays staged directly. In writing *Cheek*, Barker was following traditional advice offered to new authors: 'In order to enter the stage, I was either encouraged or decided to write about something I knew about, something literally almost autobiographical.'[13] Barker has not returned to this autobiographical mode in realist form, but many early plays follow working-class protagonists who are written with a poetic articulacy. His early work in the 1970s was characterised by a bitter, satiric vision of power and history exemplified in his second play, *One Afternoon on the Sixty-Third Level of the North Face of the Pyramid of Cheops the Great,* broadcast by BBC Radio 3 (1970), which Barker dubbed 'a half-hour comedy about a slaves' strike during the building of the pyramids'.[14] The play meditates on the futility of revolt and the power of charismatic leadership, when Cerebes, the mythologised leader of the slave revolt, is revealed to the audience as Cheops the Great himself. Barker wrote two more radio plays, a reworking of *Henry V* (1971) and *Herman, with Millie and Mick* (1972), but probably his best-known work for radio is *Scenes from an Execution* (1984), in which Glenda Jackson played Galactia. Indeed, Barker considers that the BBC Radio Drama department nurtured him, through commissions. Barker's practice of writing is quite different to most of the playwrights considered in this chapter, one much closer to the idealised view of the solo authorial voice:

> I've never been advised or told or been able to rewrite. My whole practice is at the typewriter. I do a first draft, then I produce a second clean copy which varies very little from the first draft. That's the draft that is offered to the theatres. Thereafter the only changes are cutting to reduce the length of scenes or speeches. I've never rewritten in rehearsal.[15]

During the 1970s, Barker produced at least two plays a year, which were staged at the Open Space, the King's Head and the Bush, as well as the Royal Court Theatre, and in the late 1970s and early 1980s the RSC Warehouse space produced *That Good Between Us* (1977), *The Hang of the Gaol* (1978) and *The Loud Boy's Life* (1980). His first three-act play was *Claw* (1975), which was staged at Charles Marowitz's Open Space, having been turned down by the Half Moon Theatre as too pessimistic. In his critical reflection on his style of writing, *Arguments for a Theatre*, Barker comments that he 'regarded this play at the time as a didactic play of politics demonstrating false consciousness, the futility of individualism and the myth of social mobility'.[16] The play characterises a number of elements of Barker's playwriting, charting the rise of working-class protagonist Noel Biledew, who rejects his father's communist rhetoric, and makes an entrepreneurial living as a pimp and blackmailer. Noel's fatal flaw is to be seduced by the wife of his ultimate client, Tory Home Secretary Clapcott. When Noel's attempts at blackmailing Clapcott fail, Noel is dramatically arrested by the Flying Squad and state power is reasserted. The final act is quite different in tone, set in an unidentified prison, and consisting of three long poetic monologues by Noel and his two guards, before he is executed – drowned in a bath.[17] Much of Barker's work in the 1970s had a black humour running through it, exemplified by the casting of music-hall comedian Max Wall as Old Gocher in the Royal Court production of *Fair Slaughter* (1977). During the 1980s, as we shall see in the chapter on his work in this volume, Barker moved from realistic or domestic settings and the depiction of recognisable politicians, towards the tragic, and settings and characterisation that mythologised power struggles – prison cells, wasteland, battlefields, castles. In an interview given in 1980, Barker announced a shift in his work from what might be called socialist realism to what he dubbed a 'theatre of catastrophe'. The relation between content, intention and form is explicitly laid out in his response to an invitation to reflect on ten years of writing:

> *Downchild* [written 1980, produced 1985] is my final play on English society and politics. I hope I've made a significant contribution in describing a society and a time. [. . .] I feel, too, a move away from the 'populist' figures who have dominated my work, characters like Gocher in *Fair Slaughter*, Hacker in *That Good*, towards more intellectual heroes. I also feel the stirrings of some change in form, which cannot be thrust on a play, but comes out of failures. Every play is a failure on which you aim to build. If the form cannot contain your intention, you must break it.[18]

Barker has only once accepted a commission, an uncharacteristic foray into the world of community theatre – 'anathema to him and explicable only by his passion for a woman who was resident in the distant town'[19] – when he wrote *The Poor Man's Friend* (opened 1 December 1981) for the Colway Theatre Trust run by Ann Jellicoe (playwright, director and Literary Manager of the Royal Court Theatre in the 1970s).

During the 1980s, Barker's work found production in a series of leading venues. Two Barker plays of the 1980s were co-produced by Joint Stock, *Victory* (1983) with the Royal Court and *The Power of the Dog* (1984) with Hampstead Theatre; neither was written through the Joint Stock collaborative mode, and raised some difficulties for the company because of this. In 1985, the RSC staged three Barker premieres in the Pit, *Crimes in Hot Countries*, *The Castle* and *Downchild*. Growing increasingly critical of the large-scale institutions for new writing, and in the face of falling revenue for premieres in large-scale venues, in 1988 Barker accepted a collaboration with Kenny Ireland, director and actor, and actor Hugh Fraser, both of whom were familiar with Barker's work, to form the Wrestling School as a production company to produce his work. The company won Arts Council funding[20] and has been the primary production vehicle for Barker's work, employing a relatively stable group of performers and, since the 1990s, with Barker increasingly in control of direction and design of the *mise en scène*. From the late 1980s, then, Barker's entrepreneurial company has allowed Barker to craft himself as an outsider to the modes of production and concerns of the large-scale venues for new writing, particularly the National.

> [T]hey and their *dramaturgy* (Barker consciously misappropriated the word, making a collective noun out of a function . . . he thought the professional dramaturgs an obstacle to significant movement in theatre) entertained a spectrum of writers as if to demonstrate their catholicity of taste, but their political prejudice and its aesthetic consequences could only have one outcome . . .[21]

Jim Cartwright

Jim Cartwright was born in 1958 and grew up in Farnworth, Bolton, Lancashire. From a working-class background, Cartwright developed an initial interest in writing despite the low aspiration of much of his school environment: 'There were a few teachers there who'd come from the Sixties and would encourage us, tell us we could do other things and there was the feeling, "Yeah, I can go out there and change the world".'[22] His school drama included improvisation work and he was involved in a youth theatre, but these arenas centred on performing, rather than creative writing. Having left school at sixteen and worked in a factory, Cartwright earned his way to study acting at Central School of Speech and Drama, pursuing the more acceptable route into theatre. However, his experience of drama school was not as he had hoped, 'it was real establishment and old-fashioned, all to do with cutting down your eccentricities instead of expressing them. It was just awful.'[23] He dropped out of drama school and joined a site-specific theatre company, Acme Acting, with friends Tim Potter, Louis Miller and Jim Herb, 'a takeaway-style theatre company: you could ring Acme to order the home performance of a potted play, a peripatetic audience following the action from kitchen to shower room to coal hole'.[24] The group took cut-down versions of classics such as *Psycho*, *A Streetcar Named Desire* or *Apocalypse Now* into people's homes, leaving fake blood in the shower. In January 1981 Cartwright acted in a more traditional context, playing Bob in Shaun Lawton's *Desperado Corner* at the Glasgow Citizens Theatre, directed by Di Trevis. This poetic depiction of street life in the northern seaside resort of Redcar had a cast of performers who would go on to be shakers and movers in British theatrical culture, including Mark Rylance and Gary Oldman.[25]

By 1982 Cartwright was back in a recession-decimated Lancashire dealing with the full force of Conservative economic policies. He worked only intermittently, 'There were no jobs. I used to spend hours walking around the industrial estates – "Any jobs, mate?" "No, sorry, try again next week." It was like the bloody '30s.'[26] Cartwright had sent some monologues and scenes from what was to become

Road, to the Royal Court, and they commissioned a full play from him: 'It took them a while but eventually they did a reading and it went down really well. They were just bits of scenes. They commissioned me to do a play and it took me a while to get it together – not to write it but to get round to doing it.'[27] David Lane's chapter on Cartwright in this volume follows the development of the play to its premiere in the Royal Court Upstairs on 22 March 1986, moving downstairs in June and returning the following season in January. It was considered a 'State of the Nation piece with a vengeance'.[28]

Cartwright exemplifies the working-class tradition of autodidacticism, a route into literature and into the cultural institutions taken by many others:

> I'm just discovering writers, just started to read Dickens and he's brilliant. Where I come from you hear people say Shakespeare is boring and you think, 'how can you say that?' [. . .] In a working-class environment creativity is not really expected or encouraged. I always thought it was clever people, upper-class people who wrote.[29]

Like many writers in the working-class tradition, Cartwright's writing is far from gritty naturalism or social realism: 'it's not overheard speech; they're not based on particular people'.[30] Cartwright peoples a poetic landscape with emotionally open characters, with plenty to say about their analysis of their circumstances. In his writing process there are traces of improvisatory theatre and his personal experience of performance that addresses its audience directly and intimately. Of his writing practice Cartwright suggests, 'I don't think about the process too much because I just like to let it happen.'[31]

Sarah Daniels

Sarah Daniels was born in London in 1957. She describes her limited exposure to theatre through her schooling, but at sixteen she was persuaded by a friend to attend a regional theatre where, after discovering the theatre bar and the repertory system that meant new possibilities kept arriving, 'sort of by osmosis' she developed an interest in drama.[32] On leaving school Daniels worked as a clerical assistant, moved to central London, and became increasingly interested in fringe theatre, particularly the feminist and political theatre groups of the late 1970s. Daniels sent her first playscript off in 1978, prompted by an article in the arts listing magazine *Time Out*, which 'said if you wrote a play the Royal Court reads it. And they did read it, and they sent me a really, really nice rejection letter. But it gave a little bit of the Reader's Report, which encouraged me because I thought: someone has taken this seriously.'[33] The report was double-edged, rejecting the play for hovering on 'the edge of melodrama', a style not associated with the gritty realism of the Royal Court of the time, but recognising, '[n]ot many people are writing like this for women – casual, angry talk, shrewd, bitter, violent, witty, etc.'.[34] This dichotomy has characterised much of the response to her writing over the years.

Although they rejected her first attempt, the Royal Court commissioned a play from Daniels, for £2,500 she recalls, and in 1981 she was attached to the English Department at Sheffield University, where the first full production of her work was of *Penumbra*, in the summer of 1981 at the university studio theatre. During this time Daniels was reworking her first script into *Ripen Our Darkness*, accepted by the Royal Court and opening Upstairs on 7 September 1981. In November 1981 *Ma's Flesh is Grass* was staged by the Sheffield Crucible Studio Theatre. Following this first flush of work, the Royal Court commissioned *Masterpieces*, which opened in co-production at the Royal Exchange Manchester in May 1983, before moving to the Royal Court. In the same season her satiric *The Devil's Gateway* was produced at the Royal Court Upstairs (August 1983).

Becoming an associate Writer-in-Residence at the Court in 1984, Daniels has acted as mentor to other playwrights, and acknowledges the value of collaborative comment on a script. John Burgess, reader of her first submission to the Royal Court, co-founder of the National Theatre Studio and Head of New Writing at the National from 1989 to 1994, has acted as occasional mentor for her. Daniels has described the evolution of the writing from the page into production as a difficult but valuable transition:

The playwright has to learn to 'let go' to enable the process to happen. There will always be things in a production that were not how I saw them in my head. The skills and imagination which directors and actors bring can enhance a play greatly. (Although, I am sometimes left [. . .] dangerously on the edge of wanting to shout 'No, I didn't mean it like that at all.')[35]

Daniels has worked with a variety of directors – in 1984, in line with her feminist principles, she aspired to 'only work with women directors', and she has formed ongoing writer–director relationships with Annie Castledine, Carole Hayman, Jules Wright and radio producer Sally Avens. Daniels has always written about issues that concern her, 'while I realize that even the most banal story told well is more satisfying than a profound one told badly, do people really want drama that is unworthy, i.e. empty, pointless, and irrelevant?'[36] This desire to write about ideas and to 'challenge assumptions, and encourage audiences to examine the way they think or feel about certain issues, and indeed about other people',[37] has also led her to write for young people, both for the stage and, from 1989, for *Grange Hill*, a TV series set in a North London school, which she wrote for twenty years. Characteristically, Daniels is comically frank about the difficulties she encounters in her writing process:

I still find it very difficult to start a play and I have a terrible tendency to rely on deadlines to force me into doing things. Weeks tick by and I find myself thinking I'll manage to draw some inspiration from morning television – which is a very big mistake, believe me.[38]

Timberlake Wertenbaker

[I draw on] the messy material of life. Nothing will come of nothing: inspiration is not a flame from heaven, but an intuition into how to order the chaos before us.[39]

Wertenbaker was born in Canada and was raised in the Basque country in France, where she recalls 'a lot of street theatre, probably because it was a Catholic country, a lot of processions, a lot of public performances'.[40] Wertenbaker studied in the USA and at the Sorbonne. She is a polyglot, often working in translation from French, Greek, Italian and recently from the Czech for *Jenufa* (2007). She recalls her first theatrical experiences as a child seeing *The King and I* and Jean Genet's *Deathwatch*: 'extreme Genet – three men in prison. I remember it very well, because I was fascinated by it, by these three men very close – it was a studio theatre – absolutely fascinated. [. . .] In fact I think that it's what made me a playwright. Or I think the combination of the musical and that.'[41] After a peripatetic career, in Greece Wertenbaker began writing plays for children, with friends, 'then I did a couple of plays for grown-ups – I thought, well, I'm going to give this a year and see if I can get some plays on in London'.[42] In London she began with a lunchtime one-hour play *This is No Place for Tallulah Bankhead* (1978, King's Head) about a medium who summons the spirit of a woman to explain her suicide. Her next, *The Third* (1980), staged at the King's Head, won the Wandsworth All-London Literary Competition, and the princely sum of £750. This led to a productive relationship with the Women's Theatre Group (WTG), who staged her comedy *Breaking Through* (1980) about two aliens attempting to prevent nuclear disaster, complete with singing and dancing atoms, at the King's Head. The WTG also staged *Case to Answer* at Soho Poly later in the year 1980, where an ostensible battle between husband and wife stands as a metaphor for a debate about the control of indigenous language as a mechanism of cultural imperialism. The play makes explicit reference to the eradication of the Basque language, through violence or cultural manipulation, and models the reaction of the oppressed as the silenced wife Sylvia is driven to violence.[43] *Second Sentence*, commissioned by Brighton Actors Theatre, also in 1980, was about a young woman attempting to rehabilitate herself after a prison sentence. *New Anatomies* (1981) was commissioned by the Women's Theatre Group and staged at the Edinburgh Theatre Workshop, Edinburgh Festival, and at the Institute of Contemporary Arts (ICA), in September.[44]

This play centred on the life of explorer Isabelle Eberhardt (1877–1904) who lived as an Arab man, Si-Mahmoud. Five women played seventeen roles, each doubling as an Arab and Western man. The performance style of the Women's Theatre Group is reflected in the montage structure and diverse playing registers of the play – moving from realist dialogue to physical imagery, with performers changing costume in full view of the audience, and adopting quick physical and verbal characterisations in order to play multiple roles across nationality and gender. The play was mainly taken up as a comment on sexual politics. Susan Carlson noted Wertenbaker's disappointment in 'the current division of left-wing political drama from "sexualised" plays, having found that discussions of sexuality are often considered "anti-socialist"'.[45] More recent commentary has emphasised the play's representation of what is at stake in the control of historical narratives and the policing of national identities. Much of Wertenbaker's writing has been concerned with historical material and questions of history and identity, and she describes the impact that her subject matter produces on her writing process and her use of form – 'if you write things in the past you free them of people's prejudices. You can be more poetic.'[46]

Inside Out (1982) was a reworking of a story about a female Japanese poet, for the highly physical RAT (Ritual and Tribal) Theatre Company, based in Stoke-on-Trent, and *Home Leave* (1982), for the Wolsey Theatre in Ipswich, was set on VE Day in an aircraft factory in East Anglia. In 1983 Wertenbaker became Writer-in-Residence with Shared Experience, again a physical-performance-orientated theatre company under the directorship of Mike Alfreds, for whom she undertook translations of two Marivaux comedies *False Admissions* and *Successful Strategies*, staged at the Lyric Hammersmith and on tour. In 1984 Wertenbaker had her first production, *Abel's Sister*, at the Royal Court Upstairs.[47] The play had initially been intended as a mentoring project with disabled writer Yolande Bourcier, but developed into a play by Wertenbaker drawing on the experience and elements of writing from Bourcier. It centres on two women yearning for children; one is an idealist who made the decision to be sterilised but finds herself regretting it, the other is her disabled sister-in-law, who is facing internalised and external prejudice against disabled motherhood. The following season, Wertenbaker became Writer-in-Residence at the Royal Court, during which residency she wrote *The Grace of Mary Traverse* (1985). It was commissioned by Danny Boyle for the Upstairs space, but 'we had a reading there. Janet McTeer is very tall and everyone said "No. No. She's too tall for Upstairs. She'll have to go Downstairs." So that was my first play [downstairs].'[48]

Mentoring playwrights had been a component of Wertenbaker's activity for some time, and as Writer-in-Residence she was also expected to 'read scripts, and I sat in on script meetings, which I loved. [. . .] I felt I "discovered" an Irish writer, Anne Devlin. I loved her work.'[49] From the mid-1980s Wertenbaker found the Royal Court was a vibrant venue for women's writing: 'It was where I wanted to be. It was the first theatre to realise that there were women out there who could write and that there was an audience for those women.'[50] This element of the cultural history of new writing is one that she now feels is in danger of being forgotten, as 'writing by women has never fitted neatly into Aristotelian definitions, the dictatorship of current convention, and rather than deal with its complexities, commentators prefer to ignore it'.[51]

Wertenbaker talked frankly about her writing process to Harriet Devine:

> I do a lot of research, as we've said. Eventually I sit down and write it, and it's always very difficult. [. . .] I do a lot of rewriting. I think people write in different ways, but the way I write, between the first draft to the final draft you could hardly recognise it. [. . .] I'll go through about ten drafts, at least. [. . .] Cutting out and paring down, following different characters throughout the play.[52]

This mode of writing was useful in her second collaboration with the Royal Court in the 1980s. Following *The Grace of Mary Traverse* was *Our Country's Good* (1988), where she wrote alongside a more interventionist director in Max Stafford-Clark. Her final play of the 1980s was a huge cast interpretation of the myth of Philomela for the Other

Place, RSC in 1988, which won the Eileen Anderson Central Television Drama Award. *The Love of the Nightingale*, written as the apartheid regime in South Africa and the regimes of Eastern Europe were moving into crisis, reflects on the political role of theatre as an act of public witness and on the playwright's responsibility to imagine a future for humanity, in the face of our history of producing and accepting regimes of violence and oppression.

CHAPTER 3
PLAYWRIGHTS AND PLAYS

HOWARD BARKER
By Sarah Goldingay

> In reassembling the corpse of ideology she
> Dismantles her commitment to the past.[1]

The two lives of a play

The performance of a play is an expression of a complex set of social relations that surround a fixed object: the artefact of a playtext. As cultural objects, the enactments of these texts form the nexus of a network of meanings. Scholars adopt a number of approaches to better understand the influence of sociocultural surroundings on the creation and reception of these performances. One such approach sees plays described as having two lives, their life at the time of writing (and often first performance), and the life they develop in each new production. This process means that over time playtexts gather a series of cultural interpretations, and appear to develop a life of their own. Or more precisely, a series of lives created by their enactment for a new audience in a new place and at a new time. These lives do not stand alone, but often coalesce and a previous performance-life becomes a texture for the creation of a new performance-life. Thus, playtexts are not simply an inert collection of printed paper, but rather an object with agency.

To facilitate the analysis of these lives, they are usually segregated into past and present, an elegant binary, where the 'cultural life of the play is a double one' ripe for comparison and problematisation.[2] With this approach, we are able to clearly articulate two lives of the same playtext – a fixed, particular past life and a fluid, emerging present. Here, the past life is treated as stable and narrativised in terms of the psyche of the author (usually dead), and their culture and geographical location. While the present life of the play is richly embedded in the evolving life-experience of the individual carrying out the analysis. But this binary is problematic, particularly when considering plays written in the recent past.

The lives of plays of the recent past do not yet have the certainty of an agreed biography. Therefore, they are not a stable point of comparison for the present life of the play. As Shepherd and Womack point out, the culture in which the playtext was originally written and performed haunts all subsequent productions. This distorts a comparative analysis. It obscures the neat divisions between past and present because of the variable rates of change between cultural phenomena: some things change radically over time, while others hardly shift at all. The past and present do not sit still. Moreover, the challenge of identifying two distinct, but interconnected, lives is compounded in the case of plays written in the lifetime of the analyst. They do not experience two distinct and separate contexts that form the lives of the playtexts under consideration: they live in and through a continuous culture. In addition, as individuals in this changing culture, analysts themselves change: we are neither fixed nor stable in our understanding of the world. Some scholars argue that this instability is compounded by postmodernity: for Kenneth Gergen to live in postmodern times is to have our sense of self destabilised by an excess of information and plurality of meanings. He calls this state a 'multiphrenic condition [. . .] in which one begins to experience the vertigo of unlimited multiplicity'.[3] Consequently, a double-life distinction is more difficult to achieve than the past–present binary suggests. This separation is not just challenging in terms of teasing out past from present productions, but also on a personal level for the scholar attempting to create a sense of positionality and estrangement for themselves from the lives of the play.[4] In these cases, the life of the play is not so much double as multiphrenic.

Such is the case for this chapter, which considers the work of Howard Barker (1946–) in the 1980s. In 1983 when the first play under consideration was written, I was twelve years old and Michael Jackson's *Thriller* on cassette was my pride and joy. On a personal level, my understanding of my own experiences of this time is far from concrete, let alone my grasp of such a turbulent decade on a theoretical level. It is difficult for me to describe a fixed culture for the original life of the play to occupy. My critical examination of these plays then requires reflexivity: an awareness of the hobby-horses I ride and the baggage I carry. I cannot, after all, deny my own historicity, or the threat of nostalgic positioning. When the plays were first published, I was some distance from what Elisabeth Angel-Perez has termed 'Barkerland' in terms of class, culture and geography.[5] Now, I work as a scholar and Barker's executive producer: I am embedded in both the past and present lives of his work, the academic discourse surrounding them and his life as a practitioner. In order to consider the significance of the plays at their time of writing and look at them again now, I want to take another approach, and consider a range of playtexts and productions whose multiphrenic lives both confirm and challenge the double life model. In an attempt to account for the complexity of the relationship between playtexts and both their present and almost-present productions, we need to consider a range of factors. Factors which themselves are mutable. We need to consider the chaotic nature of culture moving behind the fixed artefact that creates a multiphrenic playtext in performance. In so doing, we recognise that culture is seldom linear, sometimes circular, and often erratic.

The slippery Howard Barker

Is he an effing (and blinding) genius, or an incurable logorrheoiac?[6]

Before examining these three plays, there is a further layer of complexity that requires our attention, the playwright himself – Howard Barker. For some, like Sarah Kane, he is 'the Shakespeare of our age',[7] for others, 'an adolescent [with a] reliance on four-letter expletives to make belligerent points'.[8] He has been writing plays for more than forty years, and directing them since 1992.[9] As I write, he is in his sixty-fifth year and at a moment in his life when cultural norms might suggest he should be retiring from work in order to take up some sort of 'hobby'. For others this might be writing poetry or painting, but Barker is already accomplished in both fields: his paintings are held in the national collection at the V&A museum in London, while his fifth volume of poetry *Sheer Detachment* was published in 2009.[10] He is an artistic polymath – a writer and director, theoretician and artist. He is an *auteur* with a clear, creative vision that is expressed in multiple forms, which coalesce around his staging of his own work with the Wrestling School. This company was established 'to act as a focus for the work of Howard Barker, whose highly distinctive style of writing and its poetic and tragic character requires the investment and continuity of an ensemble and a developing performance technique to realise its full potential'.[11] For some, however, such 'focus' and the apparent totality of power that Barker exerts over the delivery of his playtexts is problematic, limiting the capacity for external critical enquiry, audience engagement and even mitigating the work's capacity to challenge dominant forms. For them, as Robert Shaughnessy suggested at the end of the 1980s, his completist approach is, 'controlling, mediating, and ultimately explanatory'.[12]

Those in agreement with Shaughnessy would be dismayed at the interventions that Barker has made into the reception of his work in the last twenty years. Through further publications he has become a theoretician-historian: with *Arguments for a Theatre* (1997 [1989])[13] and *Death, the One and the Art of Theatre* (2004)[14] he has grown to be the foremost thinker on his own Theatre of Catastrophe; and with *A Style and Its Origins* (2007),[15] his own (auto)biographer. As these texts and other scholarly articles show, Barker shapes the discourse surrounding his work more directly than most other writers, and this adds to the multiphrenic complexity of the lives of his plays that we are considering: it is difficult to separate out his life, personal and professional, from the lives of his playtexts.

Arguments for a Theatre is an enduring work, which is about to be published in its fourth edition by Manchester University Press. It is a collection of essays, thoughts, fragments and poems: a 'manifesto' concerned with Barker's own style of theatre – a development of a tragic theatrical form – that he terms the 'Theatre of Catastrophe'.[16] At the end of the 1980s, just before its first publication, Shaughnessy made an astute observation of the critical work on Barker so far:

> It may be the case that the critical use of the term 'Howard Barker' is intended to be understood as designating the text rather than the author, but the cumulative effect of its repeated invocation is powerfully to suggest that the real subject of the critical discourse is the controlling intelligence and personality behind and revealed through the texts under discussion.[17]

It appears that, at least from the 1980s onwards, there is a tendency to conflate Barker the person with Barker the writer, and Barker the playtext. This fusion of identities was compounded with the constitution of the Wrestling School, established as a test bed for his writing and theory in 1989, which Barker came to design and direct for. It is at this point that Barker fully embodies his role as *auteur*, an unpopular position at a time when the authority of the author had been broadly rejected and the singularity of the director was giving way to collaborative and devising practices.

In an attempt to deflect some of the criticism of his excessive control of the interpretation of his written work, Barker has responded by adopting the 'strategic masks' of Tomas Leipzig (set), Billie Kaiser (costume) and Caroline Shentang (design) to become 'scenographic *personae*' for his design work with the Wrestling School.[18] All three are, however, Barker. He has also created a further mask, Chilean photographer Eduardo Houth, to be his (auto)biographer. Via Houth, Barker has become his own and the Wrestling School's historian with the publication of *A Style and Its Origins* (2007). Throughout, this alter ego describes Barker in the third person. Rabey observes that through this device, 'Barker dramatized *himself* against the crowd, as if reversing the telescope through which he usually scrutinized the outside world, training it inwards'.[19] Barker is placed as an individual in opposition to the crowd, thus confirming Shaughnessy's earlier criticisms of his insular approach. However, this is not the whole story. Although for some, Barker's theorisation of his work limits the inroads that scholars can make into a 'non-authorised' version of events, this is not an absolute. Barker himself challenges the ossification of discourses, although perhaps not his own personal narratives, and has a chameleon capacity to slip easily between roles and identities, to lever open spaces and challenge the dominant form. Barker is still living and his story is evolving. He is not just a playwright, or his plays, but an accomplished artistic polymath of rounded expression.

Barker contradicts his critics, and often contradicts himself. After forty years of work this is unsurprising. However, this causes particular difficulties for those writing about his work because he is still alive; he necessarily changes within his cultural landscapes. We are left then with a complex, conflicted landscape of multiphrenic plays written and staged by a multiphrenic playwright. One might suppose that, in a confirmation of postmodern uncertainty, any sort of fixity will be impossible to find, leaving any sort of analysis moot. Houth says of Barker, disorder is 'the essence of him and that to place order on it would be to do violence to it and in effect distort the character of this complex artist and his creations'.[20] But as we will see with our first playtext, *Victory: Choices in Reaction*, we are not only dealing with disorder, there is continuity too. Despite there being twenty-six years between the performances under consideration, the cultural backdrops for two separate productions, and consequently their lives, share striking similarities.

Victory: Choices in Reaction (1983)

Not an evening for the squeamish.[21]

Howard Barker's work is challenging at the best of times – but a recent production makes me wonder if enjoyment is actually the point.[22]

We begin this exploration of Barker's work in the 1980s with *Victory: Choices in Reaction*. It was first performed by Joint Stock in 1983, at the Gardner Centre in Brighton before going on to the Royal Court in London, with Danny Boyle as director. The revival of *Victory* that we will be considering here was created by ICENI Productions for the Arcola Theatre in 2009. This was the same year Danny Boyle won a BAFTA for *Slumdog Millionaire*. His acceptance speech ended with a line from *Victory*, 'there's nowhere to go in the end, but where you come from'. His use of the (slightly amended) line from the play was an expression of celebration, a recollection of his roots and those who helped him to his present success. The line's original purpose in the play is more ambiguous: perhaps an expression of relief, perhaps resignation. It is spoken in the closing scene by the play's heroine, Susan Bradshaw, returning home after a long journey. She says, 'I came here because – because there is nowhere to go in the end, but where you came from, is there?' [23] This process of returning to the same place, to find that things have moved on, is important when we consider the lives of *Victory*.

Victory opens at a point, just after the English Civil War, when the Commonwealth has collapsed and the monarchy has been restored. Susan Bradshaw's husband, John, is already dead and buried, but one of the conditions of King Charles II's return from France is that the bodies of his father's murderers should be displayed, and exhumed if necessary. Regicide John Bradshaw presided over the court which condemned Charles I. Susan is told that once he is displayed she cannot reinter him, or gather the 'bits' of his body as they rot and drop from public view to the gutter. In response, at the end of scene two she makes a promise to her husband:

> **Susan** I will bring you back. I will get your bits, your chops and scrag, your offal and your lean cuts, I will collect them. I will bring your poor bald head away that hurt me so much with its arguments . . . (p. 8)

Here the course of the play is set: Bradshaw's pilgrimage through a landscape littered with 'blood, gore, and the frankest sexual expletives'.[24]

The determined and resourceful Bradshaw is joined by the devoted

Scrope, her husband's secretary, and pursued by the randy and repugnant Cavalier, Ball, across an England filled with a 'banquet of bankers, a lewdery of courtiers, [and] a straggle of beggars', corruption and degradation.[25] Although Bradshaw's quest is successful and the pilgrimage for the relics of her husband is completed with her return home at the close of the play, Bradshaw herself is viscerally, morally and emotionally atomised. John is whole, Susan is not. Yet, although it is a different Bradshaw who returns, she comes back to her point of origin reminding us that 'there is nowhere to go in the end, but where you came from, is there?' (p. 63). The tension between change and circularity is at the core of the playtext's characterisation and narrative. But it is not change as a dramaturgical device in the structure of the play that I want to consider here, but rather the circularity of sociocultural and political-economic conditions across twenty-six years that forms the catalyst for the interpretation of the lives of the playtext in its present and almost-present forms, and how this repetition challenges the assumptions of the double life model.

Victory: Choices in Reaction's May 1983 review in *Plays and Players* follows those for two musicals: *Marilyn!*, 'a musical biography [. . .] of nonsense words and lugubrious music',[26] and *Call Me Madam*, which was for critic Charles Spencer 'a cloying, tasteless and utterly fatiguing evening'.[27] The publicity photographs accompanying these two reviews show a brightly sequined Stephanie Lawrence as Marilyn Monroe and satin-clad, soap opera star Noelle Gordon in ball gown and elbow-length gloves as Sally Adams the 'Hostess with the Mostes' (*sic*). They are in brittle contrast with the images provided for Barker's *Victory* at the Royal Court. We see Julie Covington as Susan Bradshaw, the widow of a 'polemicist' dressed as a puritan woman. She stares off into the middle distance, her hands clasped before her and her hair modestly covered by a starched white cap; 'all straight back and white linen' wearing a 'mask of honour' (pp. 3–4). In costume at least, Bradshaw, the apotheosis of Puritan womanhood, is in stark contrast to the glamorous excess of the musical, which was just beginning its journey to becoming the West End's dominant form.

This imagery harmonises with Barker's own stance on musicals, which he described in the *Guardian* in 1986 as the 'authoritarian art form', establishing an opposition between it and his own work, stating: 'You emerge from tragedy equipped against lies. After the musical you are anyone's fool.'[28] Twenty-six years on, in 2009, when *Victory* was revived by ICENI productions at the Arcola Theatre, musicals were still the financial powerhouse of West End theatre. And, although the musical had had a continuous run of economic success through the intervening years, the national's fiscal situation had gone full circle and Britain was in another deep recession.

Following the double-life model we would expect that during this time, while the playtext remained fixed, the cultural backdrop that provides the context for the lives of the plays would move relentlessly on. Meaning that, despite the inevitable haunting of the originating 1983 culture in the present 2009 production, it would be understood differently by the new audience of the new production. Yet, with these stagings of *Victory*, the socioeconomic cultures in which they were performed were not a matter of haunting, but rather déjà vu. The similarities are striking. Socioeconomic collapse and the fiscal incompetence of those in power dominated the national consciousness. In this environment the satirical scene that closes the first act of *Victory*, an 'Interlude' showing the foundation of the Bank of England, becomes particularly charged.

In the 2009 production the scene begins with voices off and we hear Hambro, the Banker, giving the password 'orange' to Gaukroger, a Captain, in exchange for the keys to the vaults of the Bank of England. This sets up two things. First, the password as the comic thread that connects the phases of this scene. And second, the complicity of financiers with the mechanisms for government enforcement. The narrative moves on, and the comic thread of the password is left hanging to be pulled again later. Hambro enters the vaults in search of Mobberley, a builder and key investor in the bank. Mobberley is a crude, self-made man with no interest in the mechanics of economics; his grasp is literal, he wants to 'feel the ingots'. Mobberley becomes the butt of much of the scene's satirical humour as the rest of the board explain rudimentary economics to him, where the gold is not real but represented in the world by 'bits of paper'. The password thread is tugged again and unravelled further with the arrival of Undy, who has been admitted despite not having the correct password. He is an exporter frustrated by the incompetence of the Captain, but transported by the opulence of the building. The rest of the board arrive; they decide to leave Mobberley placing his 'grubby paws' on the ingots of gold in the vault, and enact a pseudo-religious oath led by the stockbroker Parry. It begins, 'To those who God grants power grant honour, equity and conscience too'; the board respond with 'Semper fidelis, Semper honorabilis, Semper, Semper' (p. 30). It becomes clear that being always faithful and honourable is already something of a chore for the new board, an inconvenience to be completed quickly so that Street the Lawyer can return home to his wife ('more terrible than Louis le whatsname or the Tsar') who is expecting him (p. 31). In this first half of the scene honour, equality and conscience are understood to be a rather inconvenient necessity of power for a board so new it has not yet developed its rites and rituals that burnish its collective identity. Their slight incompetence at this point is still funny and non-threatening. However, as the morality and motivations of the scene shift, the mood darkens, and the scene enters a state of disequilibrium. The board contains archetypal representations of those in power; ones that Barker chooses to exploit through humour. His decision to make this scene 'funny' is an interesting one. Typically, he rejects humour, referring to satire as an exhausted form.[29] However, a bleak humour pervades the entire play, and perhaps what he is offering the audience is not so much an opportunity to 'bay [. . .] in pursuit of unity', but rather, 'in a bad time laugh [as] a rattle of fear'.[30] This fear is well placed, when as the scene turns on a political penny, the government Minister, Moncrieff, explains the real motivations for establishing the bank to Mobberley:

Before the war, the King told us to pay him money. Ordered us to, ye cud na argue with it. But we did na want to pay him money. He has to ha' the money from somewhere, it stands to reason. But noo, instead o' givin' it to him, we lend it to him instead. [. . .] An' ya' canna lend money if it's under the bed. (p. 32)

It seems, then, that the reason for the war was to give the bankers sovereign power over the funds of England, rather than that power continuing to reside with the monarch: the Civil War was never about empowering the people, but about giving the financiers control.[31]

As the scene develops it becomes clear that the residual effects of the war are far from over. Hambro argues that the violence and retribution of the royalist Cavaliers is 'getting out of hand' and is affecting his customers. Parry reminds them that the board benefited from the reallocation of wealth during the Commonwealth and warns them to move cautiously, because should the Cavaliers, 'sit about on doorsteps and start to think [. . .about w]hatever happened to their little estates, [. . .] they will look around and they will see who has 'em. [. . .] and we will be in deep shit I tell you' (p. 32). Clearly, it is in the board's interest to sustain the violence. Their incompetency is reframed: no longer benign and funny, but frightening because it exposes those in power as incompetent. No wonder that the laughter accompanying this scene is not a bay of unity, but rather 'a rattle of fear'.

From this moment of tension we tumble forth into the debauched world of Charles II's deliciously inviting court. In what Rosalind Carne described as 'a bizarre encounter [. . .] where a sex-mad monarch meets a new breed of low-libido capitalist',[32] the 'mad shagman' arrives at the bank (p. 33). He is accompanied by Nell Gwynn and the decaying head of John Bradshaw, which is treated 'like a much-loved pet',[33] the final piece of Susan Bradshaw's macabre jigsaw. The password thread is pulled again to comic effect: the fabric of the competency of the newly formed bank is unravelled further, while the royal party is reduced to a gang of attention-seeking teenagers. Nell Gwynn becomes the vessel for their bad behaviour as she takes the keys and asks, 'Can I 'ave one [. . .] A gold brick.' This request holds open a space through which the audience can see the residual, limited power of the monarch expressed though Hambro's desire to please: 'I should like nothing more, only – [. . .] it isn't that simple.' After the monarch's acknowledgement that, despite Nodd's goading of Charles to take one for himself, that 'I may not. Do you see Noddy? I may not' (p. 34); we are left with a powerless King, a figurehead with only contempt for himself and those who have restored him to his father's throne. The power lies with the bankers, and although the King has few redeeming qualities, his depleted exuberance at this moment wrings a drop of sympathy from an overriding sense of contempt. The King however is not yet impotent; he has one final gesture to remind the bankers that he does still hold some power, that he has sufficient clout to force people into repugnant acts.

While Nodd and Nell rummage around in a bag carried by the King, he extols her capacities as a lover, to 'stop their hearts' with a look. For the first time the audience understands that the contents of the bag is John Bradshaw's putrid and decayed head. On the King's instruction, Nell takes it between her hands and kisses the mouth. Against this grotesque act, the bankers watching horrified, the King reminds them of the events that brought Bradshaw to this state. Momentarily, the power is his. He dominates the bankers' space. He quotes from John Bradshaw's now banned treatise *The Harmonia Mundi*:

> And there were some called rich, who gathered to themselves the labour and the inventiveness of others, and kept them brutally in place, but these were like a nightmare of bad memory, for in Harmonia there was neither gold nor money, but such things were laughed at as superstition and a dead weight in the pocket. (p. 36)

The stage is in tension, the King chatting now, not to the bankers, but to Bradshaw's head. Then between syllables something changes, the King suddenly surrenders and he throws the head to Nodd and exits with a final pull on the password thread that unravels to the end of the scene. The residual tension holds open a space, in which the delinquent court departs and the silent bankers remain. Into the silence, Undy asks, 'Why in Christ's name did we bring that back?' Hambro replies, 'He knows. The rest is shrill and squealing. Never mind the squeal. I don't' (pp. 36–7). Here the power-play on the part of the King is shown to really be the power of the bankers giving permission for the King to play: money is no longer something to be laughed at, but is rather the deadly serious force behind a capitalist state.

The backdrop to both productions was one of international financial turmoil. In November 1983, eight months after *Victory*'s premiere, Nigel Lawson, Chancellor of the Exchequer, responded to a question on the international banking crisis:

> International debt problems were discussed at the annual meeting of the International Monetary Fund which I attended in Washington at the end of September. It is for each country to put its own house in order, but with the guidance and support of the fund. [. . .] As regards the world economic prospect, there is a clear expectation now of soundly based recovery, but the massive United States budget deficit continues to keep United States interest rates uncomfortably high.[34]

Thatcher was in power and was driving though a radical process of privatisation and deregulation in an attempt to turn the tide of a deepening recession and rising unemployment. Consequently, arts cuts were rife and the way that theatre was funded was changing drastically. This was the world that audiences brought with them into the newly vulnerable auditorium of *Victory*.

In these socioeconomic conditions, Barker's decision to include this Bank of England scene becomes particularly charged. Critic Benedict Nightingale suggests that this is personal and the vengeful character of the Cavalier Ball represents Barker:

> Barker, like Ball [the Cavalier], is looking for enemies, and like him, finds them in the money-men of the Bank of England. They would appear to have got rid of the fiscally importunate Charles I, brought about the Restoration when the commonwealth became unprofitable and are now the real rulers of the land, grudgingly recognized as such by their gaudy puppet on the British throne. For Ball, for Barker, some retribution is clearly necessary.[35]

This personification of the author is puzzling. Barker has repeatedly stated his work is 'without a message. [. . .] But not without meaning.

It is the audience who constructs the meaning.' [36] And yet here Nightingale suggests that Barker has a very personal agenda that he is attempting to communicate through his work. Is Nightingale correct, and if so can Barker really claim innocence?

A critic of the 2009 production recognised the socioeconomic similarities between the playtext's two lives but came to a different conclusion. The headlines that ran alongside the performance at the Arcola Theatre in London were of a failing economy personified by MPs exploiting their expenses and bankers almost bankrupting the Bank of England. Nigel Lawson's 1983 statement would not have been out of place in the House of Commons. This mirroring between the two lives of the play was not lost on critic Kevin Quarmby:

> Written [. . .] at a time when banking crashes had, like now, become headline news around the world, *Victory* [. . .] seems to be perfectly suited to our own uncomfortable times. When mention is made that the cavalier Ball has stabbed a banker, a collective ripple of existential applause becomes almost audible in the Arcola Studio space. [37]

With his identification of 'a collective ripple of existential applause' Quarmby challenges Barker's own theorisation of his work where he rejects the collectivism of an audience who 'bay [. . .] in pursuit of unity'. [38] The Theatre of Catastrophe does not offer reconciliation, so what is Quarmby's collective ripple of existential applause? Or Nightingale's suggestion of personal retribution? The play does not offer an intentional message from Barker, but through its productions the playtext gathers lives made via its audience who make meaning from their experiences. And these meanings will necessarily contain elements of collective understanding and individual comprehension. With this scene, intentionally or not, Barker is offering the audience a release of their frustration from the socioeconomic situation they are living in. He does not, however, offer them a moment of reassuring reconciliation.

One cannot suggest that Barker is innocent; he could not write plays without them expressing some particular of aspect of himself.

On the back cover of *Victory*'s first print, he alludes to this by pointing out the significance of the culture he was writing in. He explains that the play 'evades and exposes that nostalgia which languishes at the heart of an increasingly popular genre of our time, costume-drama, as well as pointing to the analogies between seventeenth century and contemporary political deception'. Yet, this was not just a play of the 1980s; in its present form something still resonated in the space between production, culture and audience to allow for 'a collective ripple of existential applause' – a moment when relentlessly moving culture fixes beneath a playtext to create a life of the play that resonates with its audience. I want to suggest, then, that at two locations in time and space, twenty-six years apart, *Victory: Choices in Reaction* became a state-of-the-nation play, not because that was Barker's intention at the time of his creation of the play, nor his prediction for the future, but rather a particular aspect of culture repeated itself, a background against the fixed point of a playtext, and was emphasised by the play. Here we might see Barker more as an exaggerator, as his 1984 poem 'Don't Exaggerate' explains, 'I am not here to tell you facts/ Only to exaggerate/Long live exaggeration/It brings you somewhere near the actual horror.' [39]

The Castle: A Triumph (1985)

> . . . a gripping feminist fable. [40]

By the mid-1980s we see Barker hitting the pinnacle of his mainstream success. Although the presentation of Barker as an outsider continued, this took a more positive turn and a common sentiment saw him as 'cutting a Byronic dash in British theatre – sardonic, detached, the insider's outsider'. [41] By 1985, the 'prodigal son' had returned, it seemed, to the bosom of the theatrical family. [42] The centrepiece of the year's success was a retrospective season by the Royal Shakespeare Company (RSC) in London – 'Barker at the Pit'. This consisted of work that spanned eight years: *Downchild* written in 1977, but not published or professionally produced until 1985,

Crimes in Hot Countries written in 1980, and *The Castle*, which was commissioned for the season. *The Castle* is the playtext that we will consider now through two productions, both created by the RSC. The 1985 production was commissioned for the Pit season, and its revival in 2009 was for the international one-day *21 for 21* festival that celebrated the Wrestling School's twenty-first birthday, for which I was executive producer. Unlike *Victory*, where there were strong points of similarity between the two lives of the play, direct comparisons between these performances of *The Castle* are harder to find. In the twenty-four years between productions some aspects of culture have changed significantly, others hardly at all. Here we are concerned with change, in particular the ways in which we understand the identity construction of marginalised groups in the playtext – women and British Muslims.

The play itself is multifaceted and slippery. Like *Victory*, it is a history, of sorts, but further fictionalised. It is not set in a real kingdom, but an imagined one beyond a specific place and time. This (mis)placing process is a useful dramaturgical device that allows a single span to include both medieval crusades and the jet engine. It begins with the men of a kingdom returning from a crusade to women who have created an alternative utopia: a landscape set apart, where they are the decision-makers. This is a happy, spiritually secure kingdom until the men come back and attempt to return it to their nostalgic imaginings of what it was before they left.

The play turns on two conflicts: gender and religio-cultural identity. The first is a battle of the sexes: a conflict between the men's recidivist desire, led by the King, Stucley, and the attempts of the women, led by the Queen, Ann, and her lover, the witch, Skinner, to protect what they have created. In their desire to return the kingdom to an idealised past of memory, the post-warfare men destroy what the women have created. However, in so doing they also destroy any possibility of a return to a cohesive community that operated before their departure. The second conflict intertwines with the castle; the physical manifestation of this wholesale control – a structure so vast it changes the kingdom's microclimate. It 'is not a house [. . .] it is a threat. [. . .] It will make enemies where there are none. [. . .] It makes war necessary.'[43] But, it is not the building that is the second focus of conflict under consideration here, rather the castle's engineer and architect, Krak. He is a prisoner-of-war whom Stucley has brought back from the crusades. He is an Arab and a Muslim living in an unstable Christian realm. The first conflict, between men and women, dominated the reception and reporting of the playtext's 1985 life. The second conflict, between Muslim and Christian sociocultural identities, dominated my own reception of it in its 2009 production. The next section explores the space and transition between these two.

The Castle's 1985 production received some of Barker's highest UK critical acclaim. The critics focused on its potential as a battleground for the sexes, describing it as 'a gripping feminist fable'[44] and, 'a political drama in the widest, most searching, and subversive sense. Its subject is sexual desire and its achievement is to show us how, in this field of behaviour, we are all fighting a kind of guerrilla war.'[45] This broad concept of men and women 'fighting a kind of guerrilla war' was narrowed, and culturally contextualised by Michael Billington in the *Guardian*. He saw

a complex battle between the male and female principle [. . .] a fascinating spiritual tussle in which competitive masculine destructiveness does battle with compassionate female creativity. [It] is far more than a simplistic championing of matriarchal values. Obviously it has strong parallels with Greenham Common and could be taken as the metaphorical Bomb play. [. . .] Barker through historical parable, is raising a vital moral question: how far could, and should, women go in order to change the values of society?[46]

In this review Barker is framed as a feminist champion asking 'how far could, and should women go'; he is a writer celebrating long-term, direct political actions like the Women's Peace Camp at Greenham Common airbase, and its signification of feminist opposition to the arms race. This is a significant and important theme that later scholars have continued to explore: for Dahl, for example, *The Castle*, along with *Terrible Mouth*, turns 'on a sexualized violation of a woman by men functioning as agents of military or state power'.[47] But Barker was not seen universally as a feminist champion. He was also criticized at the time for his attempt as a man to write a feminist play. Jim Hiley in the *Listener* pointed out that for all its feminist sensibilities, when writing *The Castle* Barker was 'caught in the very responses he seeks to dismantle'.[48] Both of these positions have validity: the play is both affirming feminisms and constructed by a man in and through a misogynist culture. How could it be anything other than 'caught' in that which it was challenging?

Barney Bardsley offers a subtly different reading that makes more sense of what is taking place if we remember that this is an expression of Barker's own style, Theatre of Catastrophe, where there are no winners or reconciliation. Bardsley explains, 'Barker denies the strength of women, but despises the tyranny of men, in what turns out to be a moving and eloquent admission of defeat.'[49] This returns us to Barker's admission that he does not intend for his work to have a 'message', but that the audience should give it meaning. In 1985, with the critics' reviews as the point of focus, the playtext's life resonated most strongly with questions of feminisms and the marginalisation of women. My own observations of the 2009 production fit with this notion that there have been no winners, particularly in the battle for women's equality. As a feminist watching the play, I expected to be fuelled by nostalgia for the 1980s and the Women's Movement through the representation of a female utopia – even though I already knew that it ended in failure. However, this did not take place. I was surprised that what was significant to me in this life of the playtext was not the strength and tenacity of the women, but rather the character of Krak.

Krak, the Castle's engineer, speaks as an intellectual of cool detachment. While Stucley rails against the betrayal of his disloyal subjects, the 'faithless bastards', because the kingdom has fallen into disrepair, Krak simply states, 'I am looking at this hill, which is an arc of pure limestone . . .' (pp. 11–12). This detachment is confirmed when Stucley's violent words escalate into violent actions with the attack on the woman villager, Cant. While Stucley attacks her with a knife, demanding, 'What's happened here, what! I slash your artery for you!'

Krak remains the voice of reason, reassurance and consolation. He offers: 'So much emotion is, I think, perfectly comprehensible, given the exertion of travelling, and all your exaggerated hopes. Some anti-climax is only to be expected. [. . .] Chaos is only apparent in my experience, like gravel shaken in water abhors the turbulence, and soon asserts itself in perfect order' (p. 13). This calm demeanour is what sets Krak apart from the rest of the King's entourage on stage: in this moment he is powerful. The scene then turns, and he is shown to be a vulnerable outsider. With a derisive verbal attack from Batter, the King's retainer, Krak's culture and position is marginalised.

Batter laughs at Krak's eloquence. He prods the prone Cant with his boot and instructs her to 'tell the oh-so-honest English Stucley's back with one mad retainer and a wog who can draw perfect circles with shut eyes' (p. 14). This one line gives us three striking points of information. First, Stucley is a 'devout [. . .] young English warrior' in England (p. 19). Krak is neither Christian nor English: the 'wog' is 'other'. Second, that in this kingdom, 'wog' is an acceptable term. And third, that even though this 'wog' is 'other', he is still exceptional, one might even suggest, romanticised, because he 'can draw perfect circles with shut eyes'. His characterisation is soon developed by another, small aside, that Stucley makes as he attempts to persuade the Queen, Ann, to put on a virginally white nightdress and have sex with him. He explains: 'coming back [. . .] I was saying to the Arab every hundred yards that I have this little paradise and he went mmm and mmm he knew the sardonic bastard, they are not romantic like us are they, Muslim, and they're right!' (p. 19). Krak is Muslim, and firmly located as one of 'them', against Stucley as one of 'us'. This marginali-sation of Arabs and Muslims may have been sufficiently naturalised in 1985 to not draw the attention, or challenge the audience to question if it is 'one of us' with Stucley. It certainly was not noted as significant by the critics of the time. However, for me, in 2009 it was problematic.

When I saw the production in Newcastle, this use of the word 'wog' was heightened further by the nuanced casting decisions made by the director Roxy Silbert. In this life, Batter, a servant with limited power, is played by a black actor. He calls Krak, an Arab Muslim, played by an actor of Middle Eastern appearance, a wog. This troubles not only the use of the word, but also a dominant assumption that it is white Christians who subjugate Middle Eastern Muslims. This was a moment of theatrical clarity, and a contentious one at that. Made all the more surprising given that, in years preceding the production, there had been a number of protests surrounding representations of race and religion in British theatre. Notably, those that accompanied the opening of *Jerry Springer: The Opera* in 2003 for its 'blaspheming' of Jesus, those that forced the early closure of *Behzti* (Dishonour) in 2004 at the Birmingham Repertory Theatre, principally because of its inclusion of a rape scene at a Sikh temple. In 2005 Faber and Faber decided to not publish Philip Ridley's play *Mercury Fur*, allegedly because of its repeated use of racist slurs like 'wog',[50] and Richard Bean himself censored his play *Up on Roof* in 2006, in rehearsal, during the first Muslim protests against the Danish cartoons depicting the Prophet Muhammad. In the socioreligious and cultural context that formed the backdrop to this play's 2009 life, this casting appears to be a courageous decision on the part of the RSC. Or perhaps a one-night showing in the studio of the Theatre Royal in Newcastle was seen to be low risk? I think perhaps more likely that for the RSC its focus was on re-creating their successes of the 1980s at the Pit and, until the 2009 production took place, the playtext's life as 'a gripping feminist fable' was the only life it had.

The play's characterisation places Krak at the nexus of a complex network of socioreligious markers of identity construction. Through a process of orientalism, he is objectified both positively and negatively as the 'exotic other'. Positively, he is a man able to control his emotions and provide good counsel, as well as being a draughtsman of exceptional skill. Yet, negatively he is not English, a tribal outsider in terms of ancestry and culture. He is a 'wog'. There is nothing from the critics in 1985 that suggests that either to use the term 'wog', or to attach it to the socioreligious group of Muslim, was noteworthy. However, in the life of the 2009 production, to call a Muslim prisoner-of-war a wog, in a post-9/11 world, was particularly shocking. David Rabey has noted that *The Castle* is significant in a post-9/11 culture because it 'predicts aspects of post-9/11 global politics and the paradoxical reflexes of the so-called "war on terror"'. He suggests the castle itself is emblematic of 'one upmanship, escalating terms [. . .] and concessionary sacrifice'.[51] Here I want to advance Rabey's suggestion, by noting that Krak takes us beyond this question of global politics, and invites us to consider the way individuals are treated because of their faith in a sociocultural context. Religion now operates not principally as a manifestation of practice, but rather a marker of cultural identity:[52] it is significant in the way our globalised social-economic culture identifies and targets groups, and individuals locate themselves.

The cultural foregrounding of the Muslim faith in my 2009 perceptions of *The Castle* throws some of the other religious 'norms' at work in the almost-present life of the playtext into sharp relief. In 1985 *The Castle* was termed blasphemous by critics at the time because of its profanation of Christianity. In particular in Act I, scene 4, where Stucley desecrates the Christian Church to create a new religion.[53] In the latter half of the play, the devout but shattered Christian King, in an attempt to reconstruct himself and the kingdom, sets out to re-create the Church that had been abandoned during the women's leadership. During the interregnum, its buildings were 'bunged up with cow and bird dung' (p. 19). For Stucley this decay in his former kingdom demonstrates he has been betrayed by God. He explains: 'I have just fought the Holy War on His behalf! Oh, Lord and Master of Cruelty, who has no shred of mercy for thy servants, I worship Thee. [. . .] I know the source of our religion! It is that He in his savagery is both excessive and remorseless and to our shrieks both deaf and blind!' (pp. 21–2). It is this despair that drives him to build his own vision of Christianity through revisionist liturgy and theology. The malleable priest, Nailer, becomes its sole member of the clergy. It is called 'The Church of Christ the Lover' and its new bible is 'The Gospel of Christ the Erect', which centres on Christ's sexual relationship with Mary Magdalene. This is dictated by Stucley, who takes on the role of the prophet and describes what he is seeing in his mind's eye while in an almost ecstatic state. This sacrilege was seen to continue when Christianity was further parodied through a perversion of its principal rite, the Eucharist. Stucley believes that Christ was forsaken on the cross because: 'in the body of Magdalene He found the single place in which the madness of his father's world might be subdued [. . .] once Christ is restored to cock, all contradictions are resolved'. Nailer, swept up, responds that: 'Therefore – the missing symbol of communion is [. . .] Milk! Body, blood and semen!' (p. 43). Here, the body and blood of Christ central to Christianity, symbolic for Protestants, actual for Catholics, are combined with breast milk and semen. The transcendence of Christianity is now a cult of embodied fertility. With this denigration of sacred Christian texts and practice, no wonder then that *The Castle* was termed blasphemous. What is surprising is that no direct protest was made against it in either production.

In both its lives, this playtext ridicules the most significant rite of a dominant religion, Holy Communion, and its principal deity, Christ. Yet, in both the 1980s and in the 2000s neither production was protested against. Why were Christians not offended? What might this point to in terms of how religion operates in culture? What it is to 'be Christian' in Britain is complex. The 2001 United Kingdom Census included, for the first time, a section on religious identity, which was placed along with ethnicity. It asked, 'What is your country of birth?', 'What is your ethnic group?' and 'What is your religion?' [54] In the census, 85 per cent of the population described themselves in religious terms: Christian, Muslim, Hindu, Sikh, Jewish, Buddhist, Spiritualist or other.[55] Seventy-two per cent identified themselves as 'Christian' and almost 50 per cent self-identified as being 'C of E'.[56] When compared to the Church of England's own statistical evidence gathered in the same year, these census data become more intriguing. The C of E data explain that while only 2 per cent of the population attend a monthly Church of England service, 39 per cent of the population attend a Christmas service and a notable 85 per cent of the population visit a church or place of worship during the course of the year.[57] These figures present a considerable distinction between describing oneself as Christian, or C of E, and regularly worshipping with a church community. There is a differentiation between religious identity as a cultural affiliation and religious identity expressed through worship practice.

There was not even a mention of blasphemy in relation to the

2009 performance. But this does not mean that in the new millennium there was not a universal lack of disinterest in Christian blasphemy. Unlike *The Castle*, *Jerry Springer: The Opera* was identified as blasphemous: perhaps its representation of Christ and his mother Mary along with God and Satan at the centre of a TV studio in a typical Springer show centred on a dysfunctional family made it easily accessible and identifiable as such. Or perhaps the popularity of Jerry Springer on television, or one of the musical's writers, comedian Stewart Lee, meant it reached a wider public than the exclusive realms of the RSC's Pit *The Castle* occupied? Beyond this suggestion that its high-profile public popularity meant that *Jerry Springer* was simply seen by more people who were familiar with it and this led to a groundswell of opinion large enough to generate a protest, we might suggest that Stucley's reworking of Christian doctrine and sacred texts was more doctrinally complex, and required a different sort of engagement with the play to find it blasphemous. *The Castle*'s religiosity does not fall into easy soundbites.

Moreover, this distinction perhaps reflects the way that religious education and knowledge transference has changed. I would argue that in a post-secularised, post-industrial culture, religious and spiritual identity is individualised and more likely to be constructed via a pick-and-mix approach, drawing on multiple traditions and practices, rather than communicated and burnished through societal and familial process and practices. Perhaps no one protested because Christianity, in a detailed sense, is no longer a key part of how we define ourselves as a society. This is a notion we will return to in the next section. Before we do so, I want to consider the playtext's second implicit attack on the Christian Church: the emergence of an older pre-Christian faith, what we might today see as pagan or Goddess worship.

This faith is central to the women's successful community prior to the return of the men. The women's faith is fertility-driven, collaborative, multi-stranded, about natural magic and in opposition to the Christian and Muslim monotheistic, Abrahamic traditions. These are embodied by the men, and demonstrated through power, warfare, engineering, maths and logic. Skinner is the embodiment of the pagan practice. As protector of the landscape and its people, she leads the protest when the hill, the women's kingdom's most sacred site, is defiled with the building of the castle stating, 'OLD HILL SAYS NO ... ROCK WEEPS AND STONE PROTESTS ...' (p. 30). However, like Stucley, she is challenged in her belief: she rails at the men's return, 'I HATE GOD AND NATURE, THEY MADE US VIOLABLE AS BITCHES!' (p. 19). Charles Lamb, in his important 1997 study of *The Castle*, identifies this culmination of practice as 'a feminist-type Earth-mother religion'.[58] I want to problematise that description here and reconsider its construction in a naturalised Christian culture through a richer understanding of non-Christian spirituality.

In 1985, when *The Castle* was being interpreted through its first life, scholarship exploring neo-pagan faiths was expanding beyond its usual disciplines of anthropology and folklore. Moreover, the use of religion to control women was a continuing key debate in feminisms through the 1980s. Simultaneously, several women-centric spiritual practices were beginning to formalise in northern Europe. This is a blossoming of female spirituality with which Skinner's character resonates. In order to consider how this Skinner might have been read culturally in the first life of the playtext I want to examine the way Charles Lamb uses the frame of female spirituality to give insight into her character, and to offer a different 2009 reading via a more sensitive understanding of neo-pagan practice in order to reconsider the character in a new way.

Skinner is a practitioner of natural magic who is having profound doubts about the efficacy of her faith: by the end of the play we see her accept the responsibility of creating a new one. An analysis of this process of doubt is used by Lamb to reach the conclusion that she has 'little faith in the efficacy of her witchcraft', which she has rejected to be overpowered by Ann's 'magical world of seduction'.[59] This analysis of Skinner's faith practice as that of a weak woman enables him to dismiss its significance, and to undermine her in comparison to her male counterpart, Stucley, whose faith has been 'reinforced' through 'suffering'.[60] This evidence is based on misunderstandings of neo-pagan practice. He argues that Skinner, as a feminist, will necessarily have already rejected 'God', because this is the deity of man, in order to worship 'Nature', which is 'the conventional feminist antithesis to the patriarchal deity'.[61] In 1985 this binary may have chimed with second-wave feminist attacks on patriarchal practices, but not on emerging female spiritualities. It is more problematic when reconsidered in 2009: pagan traditions venerate both the divine masculine and feminine. For Skinner one cannot assume that because she is a radical feminist, lesbian, pagan she will have absolutely rejected the masculine. More likely she will be read against a 2009 culture as attempting to reconcile the two. In this reading she is a more complex, subtle character.

We can understand Lamb's perspective more fully through his description of Skinner, as a 'feminist-type, Earth-mother'. This use of 'type' suggests inauthenticity, lack of clarity and integrity. In this framing her crisis of faith is superficial: she is a knowing fraud. This undermining is compounded further, when she wavers from her faith because of the 'seduction' of Ann. In this reading, Lamb suggests, women lack strength of character. This is not the case when, following her trial, Skinner is not outcast as she hoped, but rather as she fears, venerated: horrified, she calls on both masculine and feminine forms and says, 'Oh, God, Oh, Nature, I AM GOING TO BE WORSHIPPED' (p. 37). This power is confirmed when, by the end of the playtext, as the Church of Christ the Lover is reformed into the Holy Congregation of the Wise Womb Skinner becomes its leader, she becomes an individual of great power and reach.

Sensuality and sexuality, gender and ecological balance are at the heart of Goddess worship. To reduce her to a 'feminist-type, Earth-mother' is to deny her potency as a practitioner of a complex and rich faith. She fully understands the complexity and instability of what is taking place. This new wave of female-centred religiosity connects more strongly to what has been termed a DIY approach to religion that tends to draw on a multiplicity of folk and vernacular practices rather than liturgical foundations centred on sacred texts. These groupings are not doctrinal or theological, but a coalescence of sympathetic practices. Here, from a religion-spiritual perspective, at the very least, it seems that Lamb too might be 'caught in the very responses he seeks to dismantle', in terms of both naturalised Christian and patriarchal cultures. In 1985 women priests were still nine years away from their first ordination into the Church of England and Europe's first temple for Goddess worship in Glastonbury was a full seventeen years away. In 2009 Skinner is not a feminist-type, Earth-mother who is seduced by sex, but the leader of a new cult, one that has obliterated both Abrahamic faiths, and replaced them with a new church, one centred on the female.

The Last Supper: A New Testament (1988)

British theatre's premier doom-monger at his most declama-tory, but also his most witty. [. . .] The most entertaining play Barker has yet written.[62]

The Last Supper is the final play considered in this chapter: it was the Wrestling School's first production in 1988, a co-production with the Leicester Haymarket and Royal Court theatres. Its title and content are a reframing of the last meal Christ took with his disciples, a last supper, which is central to the Christian religion and is re-enacted in their principal rite of Holy Communion. It has been described as a 'religious play',[63] but unlike *The Castle* it is not concerned with reli-gion as its content, but rather uses religious and moral images, narratives and parodies as dramaturgical devices and exemplars: God is rejected in the play's prologue and replaced with 'the Public'. It deals instead with complex notions of self-denial and morality, responsi-bility and shame. As Lyn Gardner, writing for *City Limits*, explains, the play 'considers the nature of belief'.[64] This is a complex morality where the thirteen characters, Lvov and his twelve disciples, cannot find shame within themselves, but can only hope for salvation through the shame of others. The fable evolves against the backdrop of a long and arduous war in middle Europe. Trains pass through as rhythmic interventions in the play as Lvov diminishes in power and credibility, and in a last attempt at immortality before the end of the war, he asks his disciples to consume him in one last supper. The denouement is punctuated by a series of 'parables' whose lack of meaning disrupts the surety of the continuous narrative. This dramaturgical device mirrors a continuing trope in Barker's written and directed work that Gritzner identifies as 'unbalanced postures and uneven walks'.[65]

This unbalancing is evident in the play's chaotic closing scenes when Lvov implores his disciples to eat him. There are a range of responses from the disciples at what Victoria Radin describes as 'a bohemian dinner party where the guests flaunt their madnesses'.[66] Judith, like the eponymous heroine of Barker's 1990 play and like Bradshaw from *Victory*, is a widow. And, like Bradshaw, she anticipates the traces that will be left behind after the act is complete. When Lvov begs: 'I am the supper [. . .] Help me I am capable of such cowardice. I could so easily run in the dark crying love and kiss the wheels of filth wagons, hold me down, then!', in response Judith simply states, 'And the bones will be relics. And sterile men will plead upon them, make me fecund!'[67] There is a darkness to this detachment. One that is deepened later, as the scene unfolds and the disciples queue to take their turn to stab him. When Lvov cries out, 'JUD-ITH. It's not what I want! It's not what I want!' She leans in, demanding the description of death he promised and, as he dies, that chorus cry, 'We want to be ashamed/We want/We want to be ashamed/We want' (p. 52). Lvov dies, but there is no resurrection, nor is there reconciliation: Judith experiences neither satisfaction nor shame. There is no easy thematic or emotional coherence or resolution to the play. And one might imagine that this might make it resonate strongly with a postmodern, fractured culture, and make it a popular choice for current directors, yet *The Last Supper* has not been professionally restaged since its first production. This is not unique in the Barker canon, but unusual in his playtexts from the 1980s and early 1990s. What is it about this play that has made it unappealing to later producers?

This chapter has been concerned with comparing the lives of plays created through performances in the 1980s and in 2009. But with no later performances to consider we turn instead to the playtext itself for potential answers. We could point to this text, as *Sunday Telegraph* critic Francis King does when he explained: '[t]o read the text [. . .] after seeing a performance is to wonder at the skill of the director, Kenny Ireland, and his cast of 13. It cannot be said that what is incoherent on the page is made much more coherent, but what is inert is brought to exciting life.'[68] In performance, the play was positively received and even described as a comedy by critics from the *Evening Standard, Sunday Telegraph* and *Observer*. One can only assume Barker's displeasure. A stage direction in the second prologue explains: 'When the poem became easy it also became poor/When art became mechanised it also became an addiction/I lecture!/Oh, I lecture you! (*A terrible storm of laughter*)/Forgive! Forgive!' (p. 2). Barker's description of laughter as a 'terrible storm' reminds us of his rejection of this particular kind of 'baying' from the audience evident in *The Castle*. Perhaps then this could be one reason why the play has not had a second life: without a more nuanced reading of the text, one might see why, for a new reader, any alleviating or illuminating humour appears to have been eradicated from the playtext, leaving them with, paradoxically, a lecture.

This second prologue also points to another key theme in the play, the rejection of the communication of 'a message'. Here to give a lecture is a point of embarrassment, requiring forgiveness and, as Judith points out, 'information is nothing and expression is all' (p. 13). We have already noted Barker's rejection of any message in his work; rather the audience creates the meaning. He suggests that traditional theatre forms 'massage its audience towards a futile celebration of prior knowledge. I mean by this the hidden assumption of a shared morality.'[69] The play supports this rejection of a shared knowledge, a 'hidden assumption of a shared morality', burnished for Barker, one assumes, through the repetition of naturalism and social realism. But what is the futile, 'shared morality' that Barker is rejecting in *The Last Supper*? Does this 'shared morality' exist? Has it ever? One might assume that because of the theological and cultural framing of *The Last Supper*, Christianity is the shared morality that Barker is rejecting. He subverts the collective knowledge of the Christian story of the last supper into a tale of messianic failure and cannibalism. But such subversion can only operate if there is a sufficiency of prior knowledge to be challenged. As was established in the examination of *The Castle*, in post-secular Britain although the majority describe themselves as Christian, very few go to church. These people, described with little sensitivity by the Church of England as the 'unchurched', have little practical experience of religious worship, but nevertheless see Chrisitanity as a key part of their identity. These are cultural Christians. Within this majority, it is hard to recognise a clear, shared Christian morality in contemporary British culture. And consequently, morality and ethics are instead understood in polyvalent ways. Perhaps, then, the shared morality that Barker is rejecting with *The Last Supper* has evaporated over time, making the play itself irrelevant. This seems plausible. Even at the play's opening at the Royal Court, critic Alex Renton noted that a common sentiment among the post-show audience propping up the bar was that the play was 'old-fashioned' penned by 'the last survivor of the political writers from the Seventies'.[70] We might say, then, that the almost-present playtext of *The Last Supper* has not had a second life because it has been misunderstood as an artefact, or is already beyond relevance. Yet this is not a robust position that stands up to the scrutiny of curiosity or enthusiasm. Beyond these limitations, established by Barker's own indication of a common morality, his work does give us the opportunity to revisit discourses surrounding religious meta-narratives, ethics and morals that are still significant to how we think about ourselves as individuals and as a society. There is space for a second life still.

Via its multiphrenic lives, the almost-present play (re)lives through its cultural (re)interpretation. One of the great successes of theatre is its capacity to reinvent itself. It has a tradition of revivals of genres, and writers and plays – the notion of the retrospective 'season' thrives on it. This process allows for, depending on your point of view, new generations to rediscover classic plays for themselves, or for a capitalist system to mitigate risk by restaging previously successful works. In either case, there is a sense that theatre's past is alive in the present and is sufficiently malleable to be reshaped for an audience that evolves over time in response to sociocultural and economic change. This process of rediscovery is possible because each audience (and individual within that audience) is different. They bring their own set of understandings with them, which provides the framework through which the play is understood, meaning that even within a room of atomised individuals there is enough of a collective understanding of what is taking place for them to reach some sort of collective meaning for a new community of playgoers. However, not all plays are revived. They do not all find a sufficiently sympathetic culture, or market. And in a time that is increasingly postmodern, and postdramatic, it is difficult to know how audiences will continue to engage with a single playtext. Perhaps, as Barker hopes, audiences will no longer have collective experiences, but be atomised. One wonders, however, if this does happen, then what will become of the theatre? Here, then, the notion of multiphrenic haunting becomes increasingly significant.

JIM CARTWRIGHT
By David Lane

Career and context

Jim Cartwright's debut play *Road* was first produced at the Royal Court Theatre Upstairs in March 1986 under the direction of Simon Curtis, marking the discovery of an arresting and original new voice in British theatre. Arriving with some aplomb in one of the country's most significant new writing venues, it confronted London audiences with an uncompromising perspective on the lives of characters in a forgotten Lancastrian town ravaged by unemployment. Poetic, expressive and darkly funny, this previously unheard voice offered a frank alternative to the dramatic representation of northern England served largely through the small screen via popular 1980s soap operas such as *Coronation Street* and *Brookside*. In the Theatre Upstairs the audience shared the stage with seven performers playing a cast of multiple characters, all darting through an impressionistic structure of interwoven scenes, monologues and images to introduce us to one raucous night on the road. It captured critics' imaginations as 'an *Under Milk Wood* for the decade of the Great Unemployed'.[1] In a promenade environment with the auditorium seats removed, audiences were in close proximity to the action; jostled, shouted at and confided in, they bore witness to the deeper psychological underbelly of a small northern town communicated with passion, panache and a mordant wit. The revival in June in the Theatre Downstairs, only a few months later, was regarded as 'the most significant and original new play in London for a long time'.[2]

Cartwright's career was quickly propelled by this bold introduction. *Road* saw him named joint winner of the George Devine Award for Most Promising Playwright in 1986. The play was then adapted for the BBC under the direction of Alan Clarke, who had already begun investigating anti-establishment feeling against the Thatcher government through his film *Made in Britain* (1982) where a skinhead proclaiming white power comes up against the authorities. Clarke's uncomplicated approach to documenting working-class life resulted in 'groundbreaking films that revealed cumulatively the macabre choreography of 1980s Britain' and he was an ideal match for Cartwright's *Road*: it won the Golden Nymph Award for Best Film at the Monte Carlo Television and Film Festival (1987).[3] In 1988 a collaborative exploration of new ideas with *Road*'s original assistant director Julia Bardsley, involving working with older actors at the National Theatre Studio, led to the production of his second play *Bed* (1989) in early spring at the National Theatre, 'a strange, surreal fantasy poised somewhere halfway from Lewis Carroll to Samuel Beckett'.[4] His third stage play *Two* (first produced as *To*) was then written and devised in the summer in Bolton with director Andrew Hay and one of the country's most recognisable television couples: Sue Johnston and John McArdle, *Brookside*'s Sheila Grant and Billy Corkhill respectively. It went to the Edinburgh Festival the same year before returning to the Octagon and being awarded the Manchester *Evening News* Best New Play Award for 1989.

Considering he was developing a career across the years when dramatists were criticised for 'withdrawing from engagement with public issues', and theatre was regarded by the end of the decade as 'pretty anaemic' when it came to new plays, Cartwright's achievements seem all the more remarkable.[5] That he was giving a much-needed voice to the marginalised of the 1980s, at least in terms of cast and subject matter, is undeniable. The theatre landscape was increasingly characterised through the decade by lavish show-stopping musicals from global entrepreneurs such as Andrew Lloyd Webber on the one hand, celebrating the financial successes of commercialism by creating bigger and more impressive spectacles, and on the other hand by crippling funding deficits as public subsidy for smaller theatres was expected to make way for principles of private investment. The problem of representation was somewhat cyclical and connected economics, audiences and content: ticket prices rose and those who appeared in the auditorium became intrinsically linked to what appeared on stage. As John Bull states:

> If theatre were to be regarded as a product then its audiences would be its consumers, and as admission prices rapidly rose so the less successful consumers – the unemployed, the low-waged and the politically disaffected – would perforce stay away; and the increasingly better-off audiences would demand a drama that reflected and, indeed, celebrated their financial success.[6]

Inevitably a fall in funding and a pressure on companies to find increased sponsorship left them less manoeuvrable in terms of programming; now theatres were less able to take a financial risk, new work was more likely to be sidelined for fear of making a significant loss with an unknown author. This attitude was fiercely criticised by some practitioners. Speaking at a meeting on the current state of theatre under Thatcher in May 1988 at Goldsmiths College, John McGrath, founder of avowed socialist theatre company 7:84, labelled as 'outrageous' the Arts Council's 'specific anti-new play policy' but came down harder on artistic directors who had 'slipped very imperceptibly from the popular – in a political sense popular – to the populist, equating big working-class audiences watching silly shows with some sort of political statement'.[7] It was felt that there was a dearth of tough political analysis in playwriting which those isolated gestures from writers such as Cartwright could not live up to, with director Pam Brighton at the same conference stating: 'I don't want a subsidized theatre either, given its state at the moment. Who wants to subsidize all that nonsense? Theoretically you haven't got a leg to stand on trying to convince people that theatre matters, because the kind of theatre that's going on so patently doesn't matter.'[8] Perhaps in contrast to Brighton's comments, however, what is palpable in encountering Cartwright's work twenty-five years later is the longevity of all three of his first plays, either as historical record or as an enduring exploration of the search for human dignity in the face of adversity. While the writing may lack detailed political analysis in the manner of 1970s and 1980s heavyweight writers such as David Hare, Howard Brenton or David Edgar, this critical position also seems to miss the point of Cartwright's plays. The social and political contexts for the stories he creates may speak most clearly to an audience of each play's time, but they also provide the platform from which far bigger metaphorical departures can be taken regardless of the temporal setting. In his plays audiences can encounter the inevitable problem of what it means to be human in a world that seems determined to compromise our humanness. His work extends into the realms of magic realism, gifts working-class characters the space to speak at length with a hybrid vernacular of poetry and northern dialect, demands the audience's imagination make sense of fragmented structures and theatrical conceits and shows us characters who have lived, loved and lost. In casting off any imposed responsibility to offer specific political solutions, Cartwright instead appeals to our sense of humanity and creates a theatre that offers the experiential: not the analytical. In the following section, an identification of repeated features across all three plays provides a foundation for examining the development and production processes surrounding three of his best-known plays.

Commonalities in Cartwright

Cartwright was born in 1958 in Farnworth near Bolton in Lancashire, the son of a factory worker and a housewife. He first put his hand to creative writing in a school he describes as 'a kind of direct conveyor belt to the factory or, for the girls, the mills. If you were lucky you got a trade, as an engineer or an electrician.'[9] Embedded in a distinctly working-class environment, it is the voice of the repressed that explodes on stage in exhilarating fashion in *Road*. The effects of Thatcherism have left the inhabitants of this small northern town quite literally at the end of the road with little to do but drink, brawl, cavort and pine for a forgotten world. As the mischievous prowler and voyeur Scullery, who acts as narrator and guide for the audience through the promenade production, announces:

> **Scullery** Let me help you get your bearings. There's the town, there's this Road, then there's the slag heap. This is the last stop. All of life is chucked here. You've seen nowt yet.[10]

Repression in *Two* is more subtle in its application. Characters defined by their coupling – or lack of it – appear across numerous scenes set within a busy pub, with many of the dialogues and monologues communicating some form of repressive claustrophobia. An Old Man sits near-silent with his pint of mild mourning the death of his wife; a short timid man suffers the ignominy of a tall and overbearing partner; a young woman is bullied by her insecure and violent boyfriend and the 'Other Woman' from a love triangle seeks solace in alcohol when rejected by her married lover. *Two* pits characters against irreconcilable situations in difficult relationships. They battle with the past, with themselves, with their partners, with temptation – sometimes a chink of light is offered, sometimes they appear to be in an inescapable cycle of behaviour and sometimes they are condemned to a dead end. Yet even in the face of death, the inevitable is leavened by steely determination to look on the bright side. Alone but for his ability to feel his dead wife's presence coming and going by touching their old teapot, the Old Man finishes his monologue with the following remarks about his final day:

> **Old Man** I'll just tag on and slip off with her when she leaves. And somebody will come round to our house and find my empty shell. (*Chuckles, drinks, rests.*) Life's just passing in and out in't it? Very comfortable, very nice to know that. (*Finishes drink.*) Ta tar. (*Goes.*)[11]

In *Bed* the sense of repression is located not through a firm political or social context, but through a psychological one: seven characters in their elder years battle against the prison of insomnia from a shared thirty-foot bed in which they spend most of the play. As sleep continues to evade them – thanks in no small part to the wild and ranging interruptions hurled at them by a bust sitting on the shelf above known as the Sermon Head – dreams turn to nightmares, fetching a glass of water becomes an epic quest and the memories of each character are dredged up as if to haunt them, reminding them of the life and the country of their youth that they have now left behind. Just as *Road* and *Two* introduce multiple characters to form a mosaic of the dramatic world and a recognisable external reality of northern England, in *Bed* the characters plunder their memories and offer a broad palette of human experience as well as creating a commentary on England's fading national identity. The dapper Charles remembers an England now turned from 'decent breakfast' and 'waxy rose' to one that is 'modernly cooked, micro chumped'.[12] The scrawny Spinster tells the story of her life with no children, regimented under strict religious orders and constantly keeping account of herself, comparing Britain to an unmade bed as she remakes the actual bed on stage, describing:

Spinster   . . . a smell rising
From where our tradition has been forsaken
It's under our beds and off the shore
Putrefaction.
England hangs off the map
half scrounger, half whore.[13]

As she makes the bed she ties herself and the others into the sheets as tightly as possible, almost so they cannot move, as if tying down the physical will in some way stem the flow of embittered retrospection.

In addition to a sense of repression, the identity of self is a recurrent theme explored in relation to the shifting national identity of Britain in the 1980s. The crumbling community of *Road* shows in the strain upon the characters who, impotent to change anything, are reduced to drink and despair. Their repeated statements wishing for things to go back to the way they were before or somehow get better in the future echoes the concerns of a national community suffering from increased crime and violence, lack of social cohesion and the divisive ownership of wealth and power. Roy Hattersley, then Labour's Shadow Home Secretary, was quick to connect lack of social responsibility, crime and disproportionate wealth, stating 'the young thugs who rampage through our towns are encouraged by an ethos which urges the individual to get on at the expense of others and the expense of the community. Greed and individual gain are the gods which they are urged to worship.'[14] If the community is expendable, those within it are expendable and ready to be exploited; what is quickly eroded as a result is our identities in relation to where we live, our relationships with the people around us and any framework of shared values. The reality of 1980s Britain in a northern town is a twisted vision of Thatcher's model of economic entrepreneurship; Scullery's opportunistic raiding in *Road* of a 'derelict house . . . give it a ransacking, see if there's any coppers to be made' when in fact the inhabitants are still living there, is a prime example.[15]

When this mourning for a forgotten past, helplessness in the present and a dawning consciousness of a national identity long passed by collide, one becomes aware of the deeper layers in Cartwright's text. Characters suddenly speak for a bigger sense of loss than one which simply reflects the political specificity of the story world; caught in an existential limbo, the present is somewhere that surrounds them but the past is somewhere they still wish to live, and it is an irreconcilable conflict that penetrates their very being. Misty-eyed, remembering a nation of national service, Brylcreem, gainful employment, music halls and courting, the threadbare Jerry in *Road* can barely hold himself together:

> **Jerry**   I can't get away from the past. I just can't. But no matter what they say. I can't see how that time could turn into this time. So horrible for me and so complicated for me. And being poor and no good, no use. (*He looks up, tears in his eyes.*) I see 'em now me old friends, their young faces turning round and smiling. Fucking hell who's spoiling life, me, us, them or God?[16]

In *Bed* the past is the lens through which all the aged characters are viewed; in *Two* it is the memory of better times, gradually atrophying the marriage of Landlord and Landlady. Throughout the play their antagonistic relationship increasingly betrays a deeper unresolved complication. Only when the pub empties and the patrons disappear can the Landlord bring himself to discuss the death of their seven-year-old son, caused by a car accident when the Landlady was driving. She has perceived him to be blaming her; he has seen them as strangers since the incident. The past casts a shadow over both their lives, the void of silence in their marriage filled only by the temporary connections formed over the bar each night.

> **Landlord**   Couldn't say any . . . And from then on. All this time wouldn't talk about it, so you couldn't talk about it. I thought about it, but knew you thought I didn't. And in my quiet you thought I blamed, but I didn't. Such a lot of hurt inside. Solid. Hard.
>
> **Landlady**   We've held ourselves for all these years, sick of our own arms, squeezing, squeezing.
>
> *They look at each other. It seems they're going to embrace. But he turns and takes a glass, begins washing it.*
>
> **Landlord**   In the morning, you bring his picture down and you put it up there, will you?
>
> *She nods.*
>
> *They both start to clean up and put away a while, in silence.*[17]

Cartwright is always careful to offer a dynamic of restraint despite the highly emotive nature of his writing. Jerry continues to iron his clothes throughout his monologue, the routine like a steady ritual to keep him from disintegrating completely; the Landlord and Landlady continue with the cleaning and sweeping of the bar; the Spinster in *Bed* attends to her duties folding in the enormous sheets to secure her bedfellows. They have to find a way to carry on. The struggle to feel free and in control of their lives, despite a sense of repression, is what creates such strong internal conflicts for the characters, and perhaps also what communicates their sense of dignity and hope.

Despite the potentially melancholy examples above, Cartwright's characters are also capable of exuding hope, passion and excitement as they trawl their way through life, and it is this contrast of positivity in the face of hardship that gives the plays such humanity. We repeatedly meet characters who refuse to let circumstance erode their values or deter them from their objectives: whether they succeed or not is less important than their ability to imagine there can be a solution. In the final moments of *Road*, four drunken characters finish a disappointing night out eulogising to one another about the things they've never said and have always wanted to say, finding their voices after silently listening to Otis Redding's rousing 'Try a Little Tenderness':

> **Louise**   I want magic and miracles. I want a Jesus to come and change things again and show the invisible. And not let us keep forgetting, forge-netting everything, kickin' everyone. I want the surface up and off and all the gold and jewels and light out on the pavements. Anyway I never spoke such speech in my life and I'm glad I have. If I keep shouting somehow a somehow I might escape.[18]

This unexpected celebration of the human spirit is sprung from an awkward post-pub session with cautious expectations of a quick fumble, but escalates into something more primal and fundamental than sex – a feeling of needing to overcome, to win, to be better. Although when staged it becomes a triumphant ritual, this trend of expunging frustrations is met with some criticism by Vera Gottlieb who, in reviewing the characteristics of 'Thatcher's Theatre' through the 1980s, again conflates a lack of direct political intervention by playwrights with a lack of analysis in their work:

> In the British theatre of recent years, catharsis has frequently become collusion. 'Evil' or 'dark' forces are experienced as

located outside the self – and thus the individual feels unable to control those forces. Part of the appeal of 'law and order' is that a strong external force is seen as capable of controlling the evil 'out there'. So both the 'bad' *and* the capacity to control it are projected outwards, involving an abdication of responsibility.[19]

The implication is that both playwrights and the characters who populate their stories are part of an abdication 'which the theatre is demonstrating but not analysing', as if analysis is the catch-all solution to an interventionist theatre and unless characters are seen actively changing society within the story, theatre will remain powerless to shift audience's attitudes.[20] Julia Bardsley, assistant director on *Road* at the Royal Court, remembers it slightly differently, lauding the power of recognition that drama offers as a perfectly legitimate means of intervention, but through self-reflection. For her, the final scene was 'like something being released . . . one of those moments where you thought yes, this is what theatre is meant to be about; it's language, experience, the audience and performers all together going on a journey and really being touched, and people recognising behaviours and seeing equivalents in their own lives in a bid to work out who they are and where they fit in'.[21]

This sense of event and experience in Cartwright's work is corroborated by director Andrew Hay, who collaborated with the playwright and actors John McArdle and Sue Johnston in the creation of *Two* and who also staged a revival of *Bed* at the Bolton Octagon while Cartwright was Writer-in-Residence. Connecting the fragmented, non-linear dramaturgy of the script for *Bed* to the production, he recalls the process as 'creating an epic poem, an aural experience; giving the audience a treat and letting these older actors enjoy playing those characters, doing funny little dances – it's like variety, an extension of music hall, and I stopped trying to look for the meaning and tried to work the experience for the audience'.[22] Cartwright is never less than an entertaining writer creating a lively journey for his audience and his performers, and Hay also comments that one of their intentions in *Two* was to 'pop that balloon of Oxbridge intellectual theatre and give Bolton a community experience: he's a showman without pretension and he just didn't believe in any of that'. This is mentioned not to infantilise the work, but to emphasise how this approach serves to lighten the otherwise dark material his characters bring to the stage. Rather than somehow depoliticising the work or rendering it obsolete as a voice of intervention, content and style are crafted to create a varied journey, as Hay describes, 'pitching excitement next to silence, a bit like a ride, action and calm and then a spike and a rest. It shows control of his craft and a desire to really hit an audience where they'll respond.'

The commentary above encompasses an intentionally broad sweep of Cartwright's work, identifying familiar elements that resonate through each piece: repression, national and individual identity, the struggle between present and past and the need for some kind of redemptive hope or dream. The notion of event and experience is also relevant for discussing each of the plays and the creative processes that brought them to production; the experiences of the artists and programming venues involved is crucial in reaching a revised understanding of the work's genesis. The remainder of the chapter will investigate these contexts, drawing where relevant on contributions from directors, performers and designers, alterations and changes to scripted material through rehearsal, workshop or restaging and the thoughts of audiences and critics who saw the plays.

Road: venue and programming

Road arrived at the Royal Court as an unsolicited script from an unknown writer in 1985. At the time the Artistic Director of the English Stage Company – which had been in tenure of the Court since 1955 – was Max Stafford-Clark, approaching his sixth year in charge. A founder member of Joint Stock and previous Artistic Director at the Traverse Theatre, Edinburgh, like many company leaders in the 1980s Stafford-Clark was severely curtailed in his ability to programme the venue as he would wish thanks to a reduction in subsidy. Placing any play in the main house was a 'rigorous test for new writing' at the best of times, but the risk was further amplified within a precarious economic climate for the arts.[23] Interviewed in the year before Cartwright's debut Stafford-Clark lauds the Court's real value in 'its ability to reflect the complexity of the society we live in, and our determination to have a public voice', rating their 1980 production of unknown female playwright Andrea Dunbar's *The Arbor* – a play exploring teenage pregnancy and violent parenting on a council estate in Bradford, written at the age of fifteen – as 'the most remarkable and important work that this theatre has done because it gives voice to a section of society which is culturally disinherited, and written about almost exclusively by outsiders'.[24]

Both Dunbar and Cartwright were beneficiaries of the tireless unsolicited script-reading service provided by the Court to discover new talent; in the mid-1980s the theatre was dealing with around a thousand scripts a year. Christine Eccles, reviewing how unsolicited work was treated by theatres in 1987, notes this trend towards scripts by unknown writers and the decline of other forms of theatre in its favour: 'Back in the 'sixties the emphasis was on new ways of working, new spaces, and new audiences. Today the company-devised show, the lunchtime theatre, the tour of Welsh working-men's clubs is largely a thing of the past. What's new in theatre is a new play.'[25] What Eccles's comment fails to acknowledge is the fact that many new plays – including Cartwright's *Road* – were introducing forms and structures that indeed encouraged new ways of using space, attracted new audiences and were often created collaboratively: both *Bed* and *Two* were co-devised with the writer, following a rich tradition of work from nationally renowned companies that collaborated with playwrights through the 1970s such as Joint Stock and 7:84. The idea of a new play seems to be framed by Eccles as something inherently conservative and less exciting than the trends that preceded it, when work such as Dunbar's and Cartwright's was anything but conservative in form and content. Indeed, Cartwright's first play was originally programmed in a double-bill with Dunbar's new play *Shirley*, although *Road*'s director Simon Curtis states that this programming choice was largely due to the play's format for seven actors chiming with the seven parts in Dunbar's play. He also acknowledges the contextual influence of outfits like Joint Stock producing 'in-vogue plays with lots of

147

characters within a small company and a variety of parts' as a contributing factor.[26]

Road is a visit to a street in a Lancastrian town in the mid-1980s, taking the audience from dusk until dawn the next morning as they watch the lives of sixteen characters unfolding on a night out searching for sex, alcohol, dancing and distraction. Their 'guide' through the play is Scullery, an ever-present figure who asserts the road as 'my domain. I'm in and out and everywhere here, all about' and he is true to his word, introducing us to characters, guiding us in to scenes and allowing the walls and boundaries of the buildings on the road to disappear.[27] The writing insists upon the application of an audience's imagination in the theatre space if it is to achieve its aims. *Guardian* critic Michael Billington suggests 'the triumph of Cartwright's play was that it showed how, in large sectors of the once-industrial north, the prevailing mood was one of disillusionment and despair'.[28] *Road* reads as if it has been forcibly ejected from the writer in places, expressing characters and situations in an exhilarating fashion. It allows us a playful and painfully honest perspective of northern England but also captures the deepest, darkest nihilism of those who no longer have any direction in their lives. It carries the demand of a story needing to be told, of a boisterous world of joblessness, unemployment, sex, vice, beer and attempted survival in a forgotten corner of Thatcher's England.

The play stemmed from a monologue Cartwright wrote while training as an actor at the Central School of Speech and Drama; students were required to perform a monologue as part of the course, so he decided to write one himself.[29] This was the character of Skin-Lad, who also appears in the full playtext; he is a reformed skin-head who has exchanged fist-fighting, pornography and fried food for the dharma – the teachings and doctrines of the Buddha. On a night on the prowl he chases a new victim, a shadowy figure watching him fight who laughs and mocks his life, but who upon being struck 'opened his eyes to me like two diamonds in the night' and changes Skin-Lad's life. The monologue is vicious and brutal, describing the former life of a man who targeted his victims in search of the 'tingle': an indescribable and temporary out-of-body experience found in the moment of fighting when 'it's like you are there, you are fighting, but "you" are not there . . . (*Pause.*) You don't understand.'[30]

Skin-Lad's story is one of the few tales in *Road* that counter Billington's description in that there is a positive outcome for the character, and it is one of many monologues and speeches that punctuate the play. Cartwright gives his characters space to articulate their experience through a heightened language, offering an invitation for performers to contact the audience directly. Francis Piper refers to it as an 'unusual imbrication of the irreverent with the lyrical, the realistic with the fantastical'.[31] Cartwright's dialogue across all three plays is immensely expressive, resulting in a theatrical world that contains an operatic emotional score while touring through the deceptively simple lives of a working-class town. Language carries a textural quality, communicating a sense of place, world and atmosphere through sound and rhythm along with literal sense. Referring to *Road* as a 'noisy' play, Beth Meszaros notes how Cartwright's language evokes physical space, reflecting the promenade performances of the play where audience and spectator inhabit the dramatic world simultaneously, dissolving the boundaries of conventional performance:

> The quarrels of the shoddily housed pour out through paper-thin walls and mingle with the pandemonium of the streets below. Private noise continually penetrates public space, and community noise invades private space. This colonization of both kinds of space is so thoroughgoing that, to all intents and purposes, there is no clear demarcation between private space and public space. Simply everywhere one goes, there's noise. The denizens of *Road* must shout to be heard, and shout they do. They pound on walls and doors; they kick, they scream.[32]

Described by one critic as 'blatant in its language and confrontational in its attitude', the text of *Road* offers characters that transcend the boundaries of the usual audience–performer relationship and create an intense experience that demands a response.[33] Bill Buffery, co-creator of theatre company 'multi story' in north Devon, recalls sitting next to Cartwright's father in a production of *Road* at the Royal Court, when

Skin-Lad chose to address his pumped-up and aggressive speech towards where they were seated. Cartwright's father could clearly be heard replying to him in all seriousness, 'Just you try it lad.'[34]

While the level of urgency in Cartwright's first play seems identifiable on the page through its structure and language, the Royal Court felt it prudent to test-run the script first via a rehearsed reading, another area investigated by Eccles in her 1987 report which she describes as an 'in-between stage for the new writer. [. . .] Theatres will generally use them as a way of giving an uncertain script a try-out in front of an audience.'[35] Stafford-Clark was uncertain of *Road*, initially stating, 'I didn't rate the play at all in its earlier version' but then following the reading admitting 'by the time the first scene ended I realised that I was completely wrong'.[36] Curtis describes a similar journey of realisation with Cartwright's work, remembering 'it was quite clear from reading the scenes that they were brilliant and individual, but we weren't quite sure what they would add up to'. A first full run-through of the play in rehearsal in a room in Pimlico, southeast London, was the turning point. For Curtis it remains a seminal moment:

> I still say to people that it was one of the most exciting moments of my career. I remember all of us being absolutely stunned by the visceral comedy, the angle of it, the poetry and originality. It was absolutely clear that with the actors, Scullery, the excitement, humanity and power of the writing it added up to far more than the sum of its parts.

It is testament to the theatrical instincts of Cartwright that his plays, once manifested through the mouths and bodies of actors, are capable of enthralling an audience, more potent as live event rather than dramatic literature. However, it also exposes the dangers of the unsolicited script submission process for new writing theatres. That both Stafford-Clark and Curtis revised their initial opinions on the writing exposes the potential frailty of script-reading as a benchmark for assessing theatrical efficacy. Whether the script appears to follow known dramaturgical principles may be less important than what it does to an audience – Curtis himself describes his first impression of *Road* as 'a play without a narrative featuring a random collection of characters'.[37] As Roxana Silbert, an audience member at the second production of *Road* in the Theatre Downstairs and later Assistant Director at the Royal Court, comments:

> There is no consensus on how to think or feel about a new play. When you read a new script, you're potentially reading the future and you can't apply the old rules. When I saw *Road*, I don't know if it was a well-made play or not. I'm not sure I do now and I don't really care. I did know it was an extraordinary experience and one that spoke directly to me about the moment I was living. That was its magic.[38]

Preparing readers for an introduction to the phenomenon of 'in-yer-face' theatre, Aleks Sierz cites Cartwright as a precursor to the barrage of plays in the mid-to-late 1990s that experimented not only with taboo subject matter, but with confrontational structural forms and theatrical environments where 'what is being renegotiated is the relationship between audience and performers', usually in response to a risk or a provocation that writers are implementing 'because they have something urgent to say'.[39] The first promenade performance of *Road* in the Theatre Upstairs demanded audiences confront not only unfamiliar material that introduced marginalised experience through heightened realism, but also their assumed role as a spectator in a new writing theatre. Curtis felt the promenade choice 'was always risky' but recalls the first night where the 'frail Peggy Ramsay and Rupert Everett of all people mixed with the characters and [. . .] the sight of Max Stafford-Clark sitting cross-legged on the floor, entranced by the final scene' as unforgettable.[40]

Critical reception to this first production was polarised. Some bemoaned the promenade choice as a 'scrum . . . a disaster to anybody who needs to see things clearly', identifying the physical integration of actors and audience as a barrier to the play achieving any sense of structural cohesion.[41] Others, while acknowledging the play's questionable staging and risky collage structure, were more than happy to recognise 'a writer of outstanding talent'.[42] The decision to move the play to the Theatre Downstairs in June 1986 only two months later was a gesture that illustrated their faith in Cartwright's work. The critical reception to this second production and the sense of promenade event and experience was perfectly described by one reviewer, who simply began his review by stating 'You don't watch *Road*, a first play by Jim Cartwright, you live in it.'[43]

The final revival at the venue in January 1987 included an extended cast and some 'embellishments' (in Curtis's words) that went further in deliberately framing the piece as immersive and experiential for an audience. They encountered a pre-show scene outside the theatre where two young girls were writing obscene graffiti on the steps of the Royal Court outside the main entrance; one was actress Jane Horrocks, who would go on to reprise her role of Louise in the screenplay version of *Road* and for whom the lead role in Cartwright's play *The Rise and Fall of Little Voice* (1992) was specifically written.[44] Inside, the theatre bar was converted into a Lancashire pub incorporating a dartboard, stage, microphone, posters, photographs and glitter ribbons, where bolshy Brenda fails to squeeze a drink or perhaps some cash out of the irritable Barry. A disco took place in the main space during the interval and a low-budget striptease act 'The Electric Clutch' – which falls apart when one of the aged dancers injures her back – ran simultaneously in the bar. This was a play that foisted itself upon the audience before they even reached the auditorium, which had now been transformed into 'a huge playing area . . . achieved by building over most of the stalls seats and opening the stage up to its back and side walls, while building a raised scaffolded area to the side . . . a beautifully apt theatrical form for an impressionistic zigg-zagging piece'.[45]

Introducing additions to Cartwright's text chimes with Stafford-Clark's perspective at the time on the Royal Court's process-driven relationship with new writing, helping to illustrate the gradual shift in philosophy regarding new text-based work in British theatres through the 1980s: 'There was a belief that what came from the writer was the creative process, and you didn't interfere with it too much: there was a certain mystique about writing. Now, for better and for worse, we reassess and positively encourage rewriting more. I think that's general in theatre at large.'[46] The culture of script development noted by Stafford-Clark above also forms a bridge to Cartwright's second play *Bed*, which began from scratch with a collaborative workshop process at the National Theatre Studio where actors and director contributed to the construction and content of the text in a variety of ways. This also provides an investigative perspective for the next section in the chapter, including extensive contributions from the show's director Julia Bardsley on the nature of *Bed*'s development for the Cottesloe at the National Theatre.

Bed: process and collaboration

Following Bardsley's role as assistant director on *Road* she invited Cartwright to collaborate with her on a short residency at the National Theatre Studio: a workshop space where artists were free to experiment with new ideas in an explorative environment without the deadline of a production. The agreement between the two was that their primary interest was in working with older actors – not making a piece of work about old age. Bardsley notes that their initial casting process, finding actors with whom to collaborate, brought its own conditions and complications, many of which related to the eventual style of the piece and the laboratory-style approach:

> I was very careful in the casting and we saw an enormous amount of people so that there wouldn't be anything that would disrupt an ensemble feel: all the people we chose had already had or were having careers, doing adverts and television, and were really pleased to do some theatre because the older you get, the fewer opportunities there are. Most importantly at that age you have nothing to lose: there's no ego, no anxiety, all those things you might get with younger and newer performers. There wasn't any agenda: we were just trying something out.

Unlike *Road*, which arrived at the Royal Court as a complete script, the text for *Bed* grew from exploratory exercises, responses to collected

153

images and photographs, the performers' own personalities and physicality, and isolated lines of dialogue and poetry from Cartwright with which the ensemble could experiment. Bardsley's rehearsal notebook is full of evocative images, photos, sketches and structural diagrams that might organise the imaginative and physical space of the play's world, alongside fragments of Cartwright's typed text which have been cut and pasted, rearranged and edited. The final architecture and aesthetic of the play which we encounter in the published text echoes this process very closely: a central conceit of a thirty-foot bed anchors the seven elderly characters in one visible space, and the desire to sleep but the obstacles that get in the way (including the eighth character of Sermon Head) connect them with one singular common goal in the dramatic space. From these central tenets, however, there is no straightforward development of plot-based logic, and instead the play erupts into a whirlwind of incidents and memories, 'a strange, shapeless sleepwalk among the dreams of old people, among the litter of their lives and the fragments of their fantasies'.[47]

This erratic sequence of scenes and moments is held together through an associative structure of common themes and images: dreams, memories, the past, a fading England and a world getting bigger and faster and more alien as the protagonists become slower, older and more resigned to their fates. The potent visual elements, though poorly revealed as stage directions on the page, help communicate this theatrical world from the perspective of the elderly. Fetching a glass of water, for example, becomes a heroic escape plan involving knotting together the bedsheets, lowering two intrepid explorers down through the sheets and into the unknown before scaling a mountain of armchairs. These surreal pictures continue when towards the play's final moments a loose corner of the bedsheet is turned up to reveal a layer of soft black soil. Beneath it are hidden artefacts from the sleepers' lives that can only move them to tears: a small plaque on old wood, a little baby's shoe, a photograph, a handkerchief. Ultimately it is these tears that fill the glass of water that has originally been sought: a prime example of the play's associative structure where themes, words, images or tasks are woven through the duration of the piece. Audiences had to search for resonances and build up their own comprehension of the dramatic world's connective tissue while 'the heartbeat of an entire existence is caught in a series of interlinked memories'.[48]

After the verbal onslaught of *Road*, this new production allowed Cartwright's poetic imagination to operate alongside Bardsley's directorial vision, touching the audience most when they 'dispense with dialogue and character entirely, entering the disciplines of contemporary visual theatre and collective mime'.[49] The clarity of communication in these silent sequences may owe much to Bardsley's process with the performers through both the workshop and rehearsal periods, which borrowed from Michael Chekhov's methodology of training in Psychological Gesture. Performers are initially diverted from reason and analytical thinking in beginning their construction of character and instead encouraged to find instinctive gestures, accessible because, as Chekhov suggests, 'your [the actor's] sound intuition, your creative imagination and your artistic vision always give you at least some idea of what the character is, even upon the very first acquaintance with it'.[50] Psychological aspects of the character's experience are translated into physical dynamics, creating a symbiotic relationship between the text and the visual image. In addition, the creation of Cartwright's text may have offered its own physical shorthand to the performers, due to the close quarters in which the writing was developed. Questioned about the selection of characters within the play, Bardsley recalls:

> Jim wrote them for those people, what he saw. Charles – actually played by Charles Simon – was a fantastic guy, very dapper, sartorial, polite, had a little bit of the womaniser about him – I think he had quite a young wife – a flirter but a real English gent, so everything that was in that character was coming from his own personality. Vivienne Burgess, who played the Spinster, her nature wasn't quite as hard as the character's, but she had a very sculptured face, very birdlike. She was tiny and slim but bright-eyed, and Jim worked with that to find this sort of dry severity. John Boswall who played the Captain had a beard, was very physical, a King Lear type, evocative of the sea – and his big boats speech during the storm came from there.

Scattered throughout with individual monologues from these characters, ranging from the intimate to the fantastical, the text retains
Cartwright's familiar balancing act of grappling with the pain and
soulfulness of the past while delighting in the joy of remembrance.
These speeches also have a structural function, offering moments of
consolidation with a singular focus: islands of solid ground within the
floating, free rein of a dream world.

The structure of the original studio material, described by Bardsley
as 'a wonderfully rough scrap of a thing, a sketchy piece with a couple
of mattresses and a big duvet', had required revisiting when the
National Theatre's artistic director Richard Eyre offered the chance to
produce the play but on a very tight turnaround. A week of redrafting,
development and discussion between director and writer in a room in
Bolton was quickly implemented before rehearsals began. The decision to produce came when another programmed show had been
pulled from the intended schedule; the whole process of *Bed* being
developed from scratch, shared at the Studio, redrafted, designed,
rehearsed by the cast and eventually produced at the Cottesloe took
place over only three or four months. During the week in Bolton the
characters of The Couple were introduced to the play, bringing with
them their glass of water odyssey to create 'a more cohesive piece
rather than static little vignettes' and Cartwright introduced the
Sermon Head as the disruptive insomniac who could be threaded
through the material. Both choices were about lifting the material to a
production level, providing a stronger dramatic arc that could sustain
a whole evening rather than just an informal sharing in the confines of
the Studio.

This pressure to move towards production in only a short amount
of time was reflected in a quickly constructed stage design, dominated
by the huge bed and eiderdown and mountain of dressing tables and
armchairs. On reflection Bardsley wonders if the design was 'aesthetically slightly too fantasy . . . it lacked a bite or a disturbing kind of
vision', referencing the Beckettian nature of some of the material that
occupies a darker, grittier world. Isabel Arro's review of 15 March
1989 in *What's On in London* referred to the design as 'outrageously
spectacular', while Jim Hiley in the *Listener* the next day was more

critical, disparagingly referring to it as 'an obstacle course which would tax the fittest 20-year old'. Critical response also invited immediate comparisons with *Road*. Many identified the strong feature of first-person narration as a bridge between the two plays, but the dream elements divided critics. Paul Taylor in his review of 10 March 1989 in the *Independent* labelled them 'unstructured and plotless, moving randomly between heightened soliloquies and bizarre group activity [. . .] they tell us little that is new about the nature of dreaming', whereas Lyn Gardner found it 'sophisticated of structure and mature in content (its insights into the twilight world of old age are remarkable); Cartwright's ode to sleep fizzes with puns and free association and brims with the confidence of a craftsman who can work as happily with surrealism as naturalism'.[51] Those who criticise the play find its failings in the lack of a coherent, consolidated message or a clean narrative pathway, betraying a desire for playwriting that kowtows to realism. As Bardsley acknowledges, that was never the intention:

I was always interested in the devised thing, more interested in collage, and Jim was interested in exploring something a bit more overtly poetic and less about structure and narrative in that conventional way. I don't think we ever set out to make a play, we set out to a make a theatre performance that didn't offer a narrative thrust in the way a play does; we wanted something experiential. People were expecting the next *Road*, but Jim wanted to explore something else.

The connections between creative process and the dramaturgy of both script and production in the case of *Bed* are multiple. Actors performed text rooted in their own experience and physicality, the structure of the text shifted to accommodate the demands of the production context, and the accelerated programming timetable resulted in a set that potentially overawed the more extreme emotional terrain of the text. The determination from the outset to create something unique and particular to that specific group of actors also gave the process a consistent artistic through-line, a set of values that reflected a desire to explore the theatrical experience and push the artists, rather than serve up what audiences and critics might expect. The opportunity offered by the National Theatre Studio in providing an environment where artists could take risks through collaboration is commented upon by the critics as well, with Gardner's review above commending the production as a 'glittering tribute' to its obvious benefits. This collaborative style was so successful that Cartwright revisited it only a few months later at the Octagon with Andrew Hay, a new artistic director determined to attract audiences with 'a real hub in the centre of Bolton where people could enjoy local homegrown drama and entertainment'. Cartwright's abilities in collaboration were married with an innovative director, two of the most popular performers in 1980s British soap opera and the culture of the great British pub, leading to the creation of his most-performed play to date: *Two*.

Two: popular culture and performance

From the outset the development of *Two* (1989) was influenced by a desire to tap into popular culture. Hay had adopted the Octagon two years previously and spent two years weaning audiences off a diet of Shakespeare programmed by 'middle class, middle of the road actor-managers' and on to a menu of comedy, drama, poetry nights, folk music, amateur plays and youth theatre, opening up the studio space for local groups and broadening the audience, creating a sense of ownership for a venue with which many people had lost touch. Part of Hay's mission was to create a local voice at the heart of the theatre, and canny programming and casting choices helped avoid a resistance to new, challenging or classic drama. Audiences were offered a range of theatrical forms but often programmed with some recognisable local focus. As Hay recalls during runs of Cartwright's work – including a revival of *Road* – the impact on audiences of a northern Writer-in-Residence and a local focus was clear:

> You'd go down to the box office at 5 p.m. after finishing rehearsals and you'd see these guys queuing, hard hats under

their arms, working boots on from a day in the building yard or wherever – brickies – asking for tickets because they wanted to make sure they'd get in, and not just for popular shows: they'd come in for *Waiting for Godot* because we'd got local comic folk artists to be in it, and that's what got them in.

Theatre has always had to compete with popular forms of entertainment and the rise of numerous soap operas in the 1980s made the decade no exception. It saw the launch of *EastEnders* on the BBC in February 1985 in a desperate attempt by the channel's controller Michael Grade to win back evening audience share from ITV, who were already running *Coronation Street*, *Emmerdale* and *Crossroads* to great acclaim; he also claimed it was the channel's way of dealing with serious contemporary topics and serving the licence payers' interests rather than simply a tactical move for satisfying a mass audience.[52] In many ways the rush to develop a bigger market share of the popular audience was part of a new Thatcherist philosophy. As Lez Cooke suggests, 'television companies came under increasing pressure during the 1980s as the monetarist policies of the Tories were applied rigorously to all aspects of British culture and society', thus threatening to damage the BBC's independent responsibilities as a public service broadcaster.[53]

While this may suggest that a rush for ratings came first, countering the programmers' argument that soap opera offered some sort of social or political service by engaging with contemporary issues affecting everyday people, the government were not without their critics on the air. In October 1982 Alan Bleasdale's seminal five-part drama series *Boys from the Blackstuff* was broadcast. It followed the journey of a group of Liverpudlians tasked with a job laying tarmac in Middlesbrough, and the author was explicit about the sociopolitical focus of the programme, outlining the importance of a voice countering the opinion that 'despite the million and a half out of work and mass redundancies at every opportunity, that the majority of the unemployed are malingerers and rogues'.[54] *Brookside*, which was set and filmed around thirty-five miles from the Bolton Octagon, was also influential in countering the cultural perception of soap opera as a predominantly female genre of television drama. New weekly drama serials began to engage with contemporary issues 'in a more direct way that went beyond the plight of individual characters and dealt with the public sphere as well as the personal [. . .] new programmes sought to engage an audience which included those not normally attracted to soaps'.[55] Comparing the gaudy escapist fairy stories of *Dallas* to the gritty realism of *Brookside*, Vera Gottlieb quotes its creator Phil Redmond corroborating these aims of audience inclusion, with 'long-term unemployment, women's position in society, the black economy, the micro-electronic technological revolution' all issues he intended the series to explore, thus stimulating social debate among the viewers.[56]

By way of contrast to his first two plays, Cartwright's *Two* veered away from any obvious sense of sociopolitical agenda. The writing lacked the verbal ferocity and exuberance of form shown in *Road* and *Bed*, and perhaps as a result it is the one that conforms most closely to a sense of linear, psychological realism, presenting in many of the scenes a recognisable soap-operatic normality focused on warring couples experiencing affairs, betrayals and loss as they retreat to the pub at the end of the day. The stylistic soap-opera link may be tangential as far as the creative team were concerned – Hay describes the four-week writing and rehearsal process beginning with him, Jim, the actors and 'just a handful of characters, and we didn't really know where we'd go from there' – but the presence of *Brookside* stalwarts John McArdle and Sue Johnston in the cast was a deliberate and conscious marketing choice, offering a pre-existing relationship for an audience that instantly added another layer to their emotional journey through the play. These were figures recognised as 'Billy and Sheila' from *Brookside*, and Hay recalls as 'extraordinary' the number of audience members who felt able to chat and call out to them by name during performances at the Octagon. He adds:

We sold the actors all over the posters. Just their faces [. . .] I hated those posters, and so did Jim, but we knew they would attract an audience. That was what mattered to them, and we knew they would come for Sue and John and the play would follow behind. And we sold it as a magical mystery evening of a tour through a pub in the north of England. The matinees were fantastic – they'd been to Morrisons, and would arrive with supermarket bags, sit down in the seat, with shopping all around them, watch the matinee and then go home. It was fascinating to watch people coming in with absolute ownership and no fear.

The sense of familiarity – for the Bolton audiences at least – was accentuated by the setting of a busy northern pub, and if there is a political edge to the plot it is the struggle of the Landlord and Landlady who work tirelessly to serve the community and make economic ends meet in the pub in which they've grown up, met, got married and stayed put: the play builds a sense they are increasingly trapped by circumstances. Local audiences in Bolton were also part of a community that had been born and bred and now worked in the surrounding area, and the pub as an institution was widely acknowledged as a working-class social location, just as it is for the characters in the play.

> **Landlord** This is our life, these bar sides, to them wall sides and that's it. People and pints and measures and rolling out the bloody barrel. Working and social life all mixtured, a cocktail you can't get away from. Until night when we fall knackered to bed.[57]

The efforts articulated by the Landlord are also cleverly supported by the physical energy of the performance and the transformations from character to character. Although the performers McArdle and Johnston played a multitude of roles in the piece, it is the Landlady and Landlord who sit at the centre of the play and to whom we return as an audience. Their world extends only as far as the pub walls and the fabric of their lives is dictated by the customers they serve; all of whom are also defined in the play by their past or present relationships with partners.

Just as Sermon Head and The Couple were introduced to the plot of *Bed* to offer some sense of narrative cohesion, in the later stages of rehearsal for *Two* there was a similar problem regarding the end of the play. The idea of a dead child as the seat of the couple's antagonism was mooted, and Hay's suggestion to Cartwright was 'to reveal it in such a way that it gives us something else, that it fits into those other people's stories and so on, connecting the play together: so it actually reflects the pathos of all the other characters'. The final moments of the story when the Landlord and Landlady confront their son's death together thus echoes the dynamics of the other couples, binding together both the story world and the theatrical conceit of all the roles played by the one couple.

The containment of a whole world on stage within this central couple, telling their story with minimal props around a bare table-top bar and transforming back and forth from customer to bartenders creates a telling metaphor. It first communicates Cartwright's familiar theme of repression, externalising the psychological worlds of the Landlord and Landlady by showing how deeply they are formed or trapped by their environment. Second, the pressure and emotional strain on their lives is made tangible not only through reported experience – what the text tells us – but through the physicality of the performance, accentuating once again Cartwright's insistence on creating a unique live connection with his audience. The performance was also a timely challenge for the actors having recently left *Brookside* after seven years in the same roles. Hay insists that there was 'something of a release' in the performances as McArdle and Johnston reconnected with the presence of a live audience rather than a camera lens, adding an extra dimension to the production. The staging was kept deliberately pared-back, with all the props and other customers mimed and the atmosphere of the pub created by the audience's imaginations:

I wanted to keep the action flowing for as long as possible: hated long scene changes, hated blackouts, and I always try and find some way not to leave the audience, you can't leave that contract. With something like this they had to build a relationship with the audience, they had to connect, and I knew it was right to allow the audience into it imaginatively. So if John went off one way, Sue would be coming up the other side, and there'd be a costume change of putting on a hat or something, and that would be it. There was one moment where John walked up the runway, rolled up a sleeve, turned round and changed shape and that was amazing: people were so excited about what was coming next.

The context provided by Hay suggests there were multiple narratives unfolding for an audience during the original production of *Two*; the narrative of transformation as the 'characters' of Sheila and Billy from *Brookside* re-created themselves for an audience and they in turn adjusted their relationships to the characters/performers; the narrative of the Landlord and Landlady's story and their journey towards a sense of reconciliation and emotional transition; the individual narratives of each of the customers encountered within the pub's walls, and the theatrical narrative of the production itself as the actors continually transformed themselves and the space through the simplest of means.

This final play of the decade for Cartwright seems to signal a greater structural control over his writing, perhaps at the expense of a more anarchic and expressive voice but not at the expense of story. With this in mind, however, of all three plays *Two* may be the most conservative in terms of structure and form but despite the stronger grounding in psychological realism it is still elevated through distinct and poetic characters, the turns of phrase and linguistic choices displayed in the monologues of the Landlord and Landlady and the lonely and lost individuals seeking solace at the bar, and of course the performance choice of two actors playing all characters, which is still found as an instruction in the published text. Although the success of the play itself may have sat within a particular context in the 1980s – written for a Bolton audience in a local theatre, performed by television celebrities of the time known to that audience and written by a northern playwright – the enduring power of the play's appeal is evidenced in *Two* still being performed regularly across the world in 2011. In offering both actors and audiences an imaginative theatrical challenge, collaborating in bringing to life a funny and moving portrait of individuals facing some of life's most common human dilemmas, it is perhaps a fitting legacy for Cartwright's writing that this play should have stood the test of time.

Conclusion

An attempt to neatly compartmentalise by genre or organise an artistic narrative through these three plays is initially problematic. Cartwright's work is clearly innovative, experimental and challenging. He offers fragmented storytelling through a heightened colloquial tone in *Road*; creates a theatrical dreamscape using densely poetic language and imagery in *Bed* and in *Two* demands two actors play an emotionally fatigued Landlord and Landlady of a northern pub on a hectic night, mime all the props and in addition play all the different punters. Common characteristics are of course identifiable across all three plays, but what has primarily emerged is a writer who is always thinking theatrically, searching and probing the medium of live performance to find a unique connection with an audience.

This connection is manifested through characters that retrospectively pick their way through a life already lived, assessing the damage done and attempting to find a way to articulate it to the listening world. Each play contains direct address, twisting the conventional performance frame of realism into a form that demands physical, intellectual or imaginative engagement; all three present detailed characters written with pathos and understanding and full of passion, laughter and grim determination. To read these plays together is to wander through a vast arena of universal human problems, capturing glimpses of lives being driven to the furthest reaches of experience. Stories of love, marriage, family, friendships, old age, youthful optimism, crumbling identity, poverty and social isolation all feature. At the heart of Cartwright's work is a politics that demands the right for all people to be flawed as an expression of being human. The plays are an exploration of the right to live boldly, failing gloriously while celebrating our ceaseless determination to keep surviving.

In just over three years Cartwright left an indelible mark on new theatre writing, creating work that delighted in live performance and entertainment but always challenged its actors and audiences. All three plays explore an England dissatisfied with the present and betrothed to the past, with *Road* and *Two* especially constructing the author's identity as a spokesperson for the marginalised, socially excluded and unemployed of northern England. Framed as a 'potent phrasemaker' with 'the poetic thrust of a north country O'Casey', Cartwright attracted notoriety for his linguistically adventurous work, full of recognisable and accessible character narratives measuring the social and political temperature of the time not just in the north, but across the country as a whole.[58] Perhaps Cartwright's longevity as a playwright through the following decades is attributable in part to the insistent presence of his voice in all the varied theatrical forms he explored through his early writing. Expressionism, surrealism, heightened comedy, psychological drama and naturalism all feature, but the trademarks described above are persistent: a combination of fearless experiment, respect for the audience's desire for theatrical entertainment and a unique perspective on the commonalities of our journeys through life.

SARAH DANIELS
By Jane Milling

> I'm afraid I'm old fashioned enough to think, 'I don't care how beautiful, ritzy, glitzy, dazzly or weird anything looks, I want to be intellectually and emotionally involved in it. I want to engage with it on a gut level.'[1]

Sarah Daniels has become one of the few 'feminist canonicals' as Elaine Aston dubs them, a group of significant female playwrights whose work is aimed at enhancing women's social and political rights and representation, and who have played a significant role in remaking the tradition of British playwriting.[2] At one time these terms might have been considered antithetical, and indeed it was only during the early 1980s that the feminist works of women playwrights gained a place on mainstream stages at the Royal Court, the National Theatre and the RSC. Despite the mainstream production of some of Daniels's plays, well received by audiences, she has had a complicated relationship with newspaper theatre reviewers, those cultural mediators greatly responsible for the way performances are 'remembered'. Mary Remnant notes that many reviewers 'abandoned their tacitly agreed aesthetic criteria and gave vent to purely gut reactions'.[3] The reviews remind us how limited the cadre of theatre reviewers was, and how far a review's attribution of significance or mode of interpretation depends upon the cultural location and perspective of the individual reviewer.[4] However limited their value as reliable documentation, the reviews clearly demonstrate that Daniels achieved her desire to challenge audiences intellectually and emotionally.

There is not room here to consider all of Daniels's work during the 1980s in detail, so this chapter will take a fresh look at the production of three of her works on mainstream stages, beginning with her most notorious, *Masterpieces* (Royal Exchange Manchester, 1983), *The Devil's Gateway* (Royal Court Upstairs, 1983) and *Neaptide* (Cottesloe, 1986). Daniels's reflection on her work in the epigraph to this section captures the elements that underpin the force of her plays and their cultural location. In rejecting the 'styling' of a play in favour of its intellectual content and emotional punch Daniels appears to be reaffirming her commitment to realism and the tradition of the debate play, yet her writing differs from that traditionally understood, classic realism, and this difference forms part of her feminist armoury. In aspiring to appeal to the intellect of an audience Daniels's work centres on 'issues', an increasingly unfashionable approach to politics. At the same time, in order to engage audiences with her material, her chosen genre is most often comedy, a genre difficult to consider 'proper' political writing and often dismissed as innately conservative.

The question of realism

In the 1980s, feminist critics and writers debated whether 'classic realism', that nineteenth-century theatrical innovation which was said to produce an illusion of the unchangeable nature of the 'real world' outside the theatre, could be a useful form for feminist theatre. After all, classic realism as a style or genre emerged as a radical response to the society dramas and melodramas that focused on elite characters and reinforced the cultural and political status quo of their day.[5] By the 1980s, could feminist playwriting in the classic realist mode be politically subversive and challenge the ideas of patriarchy? Jill Dolan thought that it was impossible to represent lesbian identity because the ideology of realism was 'so determined to validate dominant culture that the lesbian position can only be moralized against or marginalized'.[6] Many feminist playwrights had a background in alternative theatre employing agitprop or street performance, cabaret, or other popular forms, and they integrated these forms into realist structures to disrupt expectations and develop their critique, in a mode Susan Carlson called the 'extrareal', or Jeanie Forte called the 'pseudo-real'.[7] Janelle Reinelt considered that the use of forms like cabaret were part of the Brechtian tradition, and might have possibilities for theatre making that contained a 'socialist-feminist analysis'.[8] Elin Diamond argued that through *performance* feminist theatre might challenge the way we think about the question of what is 'real' itself. Using a kind of performance that draws excessive attention to its 'realness', performance might spill over from mimetic representation which coerces recognition from its spectators that events on stage are 'like' life, into an excessive form that looked more like 'mimicry', and thus the feminist performer could lead an audience to question the very processes of representing the world that the theatre is undertaking – what Diamond calls the 'true-real'.[9]

Resistance to the idea of realism has particular implications for theatrical *form*. As we have seen, much of the idea of play making in the 1980s was still engaged in a battle over the value of the 'well-made' realist play:[10] a set of conventional structures which centred on plot construction, particularly cause and effect, mimetic characterisation and the use of everyday language, that audiences were trained to recognise as producing the effects of realism. Moreover, working-class gritty social realism had become, by the 1970s, the house style of the Royal Court Theatre, in its desire to develop new writing for new times.[11] Trying to subvert or challenge realism effects inevitably led to the employment of different structures, and feminist playwrights were among a set of writers with a background in alternative and political theatre who took up the challenge of form. Yet as Loren Kruger reminds us, structural disruption need not necessarily produce social or perceptual disruption: 'Techniques such as gestic acting, direct address, songs or abrupt scene changes do not *in themselves* guarantee critical effect; on the contrary, they have become so much part of the repertoire of advertising, let alone theatre, that they no longer offer a critique of convention.'[12] Kruger argued that Brecht insisted that formal experiments had to be linked to Marxist analysis and the specific historical moment of the play's production in order to have disruptive impact. It might even be, as Jeanie Forte suggested, that 'because of its structural recognizability, or "readability", realism might be able to politicize spectators alienated by the more experimental conventions of nonrealistic work'.[13]

There are many elements of Sarah Daniels's writing that appear to conform to realist expectations producing realism effects – her plays are often set in recognisable rooms, they have characters in recognisable relationships to one another, etc. However, directors who have developed her scripts to the stage note the surprising challenges she presents in creating the *mise en scène*. Daniels's work was described as 'totally anarchic' by Lou Wakefield, an actress, writer and the director of Daniels's play *Ma's Flesh is Grass* at the Sheffield Crucible (November 1981). Carole Hayman, who directed *Ripen Our Darkness* at the Royal Court, noted:

> All the men, and I include a lot of the ones who have worked with Caryl Churchill's work . . . said 'well, I don't know, well it is quite funny I suppose . . . but it is a terribly peculiar structure, isn't it? I mean, what is supposed to be important in it? I mean, who is the main character? It is just a series of scenes, isn't it? I mean where is the interval?'[14]

A particular example might be found in the penultimate scene of *Ripen Our Darkness*, where Mary, the play's oppressed housewife, has just killed herself – in the classic self-immolation an audience might expect from realist or indeed melodramatic drama (oppression is the cause that leads to the effect, suicide). But rather than end the play on Mary's tragic, individual fate, the scene offers a vision of heaven with female God as a sort of hospital matron, as director Carole Hayman describes: 'The whole thing was a dance drama. These women danced around and they did silly things, and it was very funny. But it was a totally surreal moment in what was generally a naturalistic play.'[15] Mary makes a final attempt to unsettle her oblivious husband by haunting him, but David ignores her spectral voiceover. The play leaves the men in the kitchen while Mary's character moves on to a more satisfying alternative existence elsewhere, and her exasperation with them closes the play: 'Mother Almighty, what, tell me, is the point?' (p. 71). The mixing of performance styles and registers produced a *mise en scène* that challenged expectations, and sometimes left critics nonplussed. The use of different structures was not confined to feminist theatre and it was usually intended by playwrights to carry a political force. As Susan Carlson notes, often critics 'state that it is the narration, the characterization, or the language which is at fault when it appears, actually, to be the politics' with which they disagree.[16] By rejecting classical realism's focus on Mary's death as individual failing, the play's generic playfulness mocks religion, one of the social structures that sustain the oppressive environment that drives her to suicide.

A laughing matter: issues, politics and comedy

Daniels tells an anecdote against herself that on hearing that Mark Ravenhill's play *Shopping and Fucking* was long, she joked at the box office that she would just see the shopping. The earnest response came that the shopping and fucking were all mixed up together. Daniels uses this anecdote to argue that it is not possible to separate the apparently 'ordinary' and the political in her work: 'If you write about life, doesn't that always include politics? [. . .] I know it's simplistic, but aren't they all mixed up together?'[17] The political elements of Daniels's work have not always been acknowledged; indeed she notes that often her work is described as 'issue-based', a phrase used pejoratively as if she should apologise for such an undertaking.[18] Where political writing might summon the idea of broad investigations of ideology, hegemony, structures and even theory, issue-based writing by contrast seems to imply a limited focus, a didactic or educative tone, and to suggest that success might be evaluated by a pre-imagined effect or outcome for audience members. Although agitprop had been a popular form on the alternative theatre circuit during the 1970s, increasingly by the 1980s 'issue-based' drama was most often associated with Theatre-in-Education companies, and thus frequently patronised as a lesser aesthetic form. Yet, Daniels's plays tend to meditate on an issue partly through naturalistic dialogue, where different positions and attitudes to any issue can be staged, rather than in the agitprop form of one-dimensional slogans. Daniels challenges the narrowness of any issue by piling up a whole series of related topics around the central core, although she turns this accretion of issues against herself: 'the criticism that I try and pack too much into a play is valid and this doesn't come from trying to evolve a new structure, but from lack of confidence in my ability to hold an audience's attention'.[19] Her desire to sustain and entertain an audience has produced new structure as a by-product. However, it is significant here that she articulates her praxis not as driven by formalism or stylistic experimentation, but that, in her characteristically self-deprecating way, she is concerned with affect for her audience, to be 'intellectually and emotionally involved'.

Since the 1980s, Daniels notes that one of the anxieties that commissioning editors and literary managers have about issue-based theatre is that it might appear worthy, 'which appears to be synonymous with political, politically correct, and loony'.[20] There are several agendas caught up in this concern. First, that the tone of the presentation might be earnest or too self-secure in its perspective, rather than open to debate. Second, that there might be no humour or desire to entertain an audience within the material, and this gestures towards the unspoken economic agenda underpinning the anxiety about 'worthy' work, that it might not be 'worth' very much in the marketplace. One of the reasons why Daniels's work may have found a place on mainstream stages and in the marketplace is through the variety of comedic forms she employs. 'Ridicule can often be a more devastating weapon than argument',[21] she suggests, and the organisation of the butts and objects of her satiric humour are always in line with her perspective on the issue she is raising. Her most usual form of comedic commentary comes though a gentler satiric form of mimicry and exaggeration, yet even here her use of laughter is most often as a political tool.

This use of comedy, while it serves the plays well with audiences, has sometimes meant her work has been taken less seriously by critics. Carole Hayman reflects on the reception of Daniels's work: 'Sarah's plays are very funny, consequently they can't really be very serious, they can't really be about world issues, they can't really be important in any way. They are certainly not epics because we all know epics aren't funny.'[22] Realist comedy – reflected in the social comedy of middle-class manners or farces of Alan Ayckbourn – has been dismissed as inherently conservative and sexist in its acceptance of the status quo, and there is a danger that because of its humour Daniels's work is tarred with this brush. As Daniels says herself, 'making jokes is very risky'.[23] The representation of women laughing on stage is also politically pointed, and often arises from the incongruity of situations, as in *Masterpieces* when the psychiatrist's inappropriate questioning prompts Rowena's bitter laughter (p. 207). The long history of what might be called the incongruity theory of comedy has frequently considered that women are more constrained in their laughter and use of humour in the public realm. Regenia Gagnier has suggested that in fact women employ the humour of incongruity to draw attention to, and offer critical challenge to, the status quo.[24] In Daniels's plays there are many jokes, and much comic banter and characterisation that can be sensed in the text; however, the fullest understanding of her comic work comes in performance. Looking back at comedy in performance, Lucy Delap warns, can be difficult, even if theatre texts are still living in the repertoire in an active tradition of performance, as many a toe-curlingly unfunny version of Hamlet's encounter with the gravedigger or Launcelot Gobbo's turn reminds us:

Humorous acts and texts, funny or unfunny to later inter-
preters, differ from other historical sources. Jokes have a
performative dimension and rely on gestures, pantomime,
timbre, and rhythm. [. . .] Humour is often timely and not
easily carried outside its historical context. What was intended
as satirical may now be read as neutral, as social realism, or as
grotesque.[25]

To get to the bottom of who laughs when, and why, is to get to the
point of Daniels's politics. It is clear that Daniels's issue-based plays
are political works in the fullest sense, engaging with critiques of
ideology, often specifically questions of power and masculinity. Her
plays take up political perspectives through a stretching and disrupting
of realist conventions, and through the employment of comedy, in
order to offer audiences both intellectual challenge and emotional
involvement.

Masterpieces (1983)

Masterpieces was a commission from the Royal Court, staged in
co-production with the Royal Exchange Manchester on 31 May 1983,
before transferring to the Royal Court Theatre Upstairs on 7 October,
where it followed *The Devil's Gateway*. It was a surprise success for the
theatre, in spite of reviews, and it moved to the larger Royal Court
Theatre Downstairs on 5 January 1984, assisting the Court's precarious financial situation: 'the projected deficit of £10,000 dropped in
January 1984 to less than £7,500 when *Masterpieces* produced £4,500
more than estimated'.[26] The reviews for the play were almost universally damning, with critical response split along gendered lines. Yet
the play found a keen audience, not least because of the timeliness of
the issues it raised, and its mix of intellectual and emotional passion.
Jules Wright, its director, reflected, 'it is a life-changing play and has
impacted as potently on those people who have performed it as it has
on the audiences who have witnessed it'.[27] The play has been produced
in Germany, Japan, New Zealand, Australia and the US.

The play is structurally demanding, and as Susan Carlson points out, 'Daniels does everything she can to prevent the reading/viewing of the play as a traditional narrative about Rowena. Time is jumbled [. . . m]ore noticeably, the unsettling concatenation [of voices] that occurs in the first scenes continues through the entire drama.'[28] In her review of the performance, Michelene Wandor found that the apparently causal narrative was not fleshed out with adequate realist detail, yet while there is no plot-led illustration of cause and effect, the play does build an *argumentative* implication of cause and effect summoned by Rowena's final speech:

> **Rowena** I don't want anything to do with men who have knives or whips or men who look at photos of women tied and bound, or men who say relax and enjoy it. Or men who tell misogynist jokes.[29]

A key element in the rejection of a realist plot is Daniels's refusal to let the play be a courtroom drama, and indeed to radically undercut the expected generic pleasures of the courtroom melodrama. The courtroom is suggested at the end of scene one by a soundtrack, and Rowena steps up to her position as the accused, while watched by Yvonne who then draws attention from Rowena with a direct monologue to the audience about her own working-class youth. When we eventually turn to the courtroom in scene two, the tone is almost parodic, playing up the incompetence of the rambling policeman, and characterised by Rowena's only response to the erroneous account of her pushing a man under the tube: 'I believe it is impossible to proceed in a westerly direction along Seven Sisters Road, but the rest is true' (p. 178). In the final scene of the play we return to the courtroom, this time as witnesses, having seen the encounter at the tube station silently enacted. The 'trial' is designed to frustrate the audience; it is procedurally rambling, and offers no cross-examination or demonstration of rhetorical skill in closing debate. There is no reference to justice or the law, no representation of a moral high ground. In essence the scene 'fails' because it refuses to conform to representing the narrative pleasures of a solo protagonist battling the system.

Instead it suggests the system itself is flawed. This returns us to the argumentative logic of the play, which references the 'real world' upheaval of the 1980s where there were calls for an investigation of inconsistencies in sentencing according to gender, most particularly in sexual assault cases. The play was written as a furore around prosecutions for rape had yet again arisen. In January 1982, Ipswich Crown Court Judge Bertrand Richards fined a businessman £2,000 instead of issuing a custodial sentence, for raping a teenage hitchhiker. The judge ruled that the hitchhiker was 'guilty of a great deal of contributory negligence' in asking for a lift. Public outcry led to Judge Richards being barred from trying sexual offence cases, but facing no other censure. High Court Judge Sir Melford Stevenson supported Richards's decision: 'It is the height of impudence for any girl to hitchhike at night. [. . .] She is in the true sense, asking for it.'[30] It was to this systemic injustice and gendered bigotry that Daniels's comically inept courtroom directed attention.

As always with Daniels, the play is not about a single protagonist's experience; rather it weaves a number of roles and perspectives together, not to converge in a central plot narrative, but to create the landscape of perspectives and influences that circulate around the 'issue' under discussion. In the staging at the Royal Court the role of Yvonne was doubled with Hilary, giving the actress Patti Love as much stage time, and most of the direct encounter with the audience, as Kathryn Pogson as Rowena, whose role remained within the stage frame. The play follows Hilary's experience from scene four, where Rowena as social worker asks Hilary about her earnings as a sex worker, to Hilary's comic *tour-de-force* monologue in scene seven on the inadequacies of contraception and the realities of sexual activity of young women. After the audience has had time to hear from Hilary and to laugh with her, the play stages her attempts to rebuff the advances of Ron at work before, overruled by her employer, she is manoeuvred into accepting a lift home. The audience learns about Hilary's forced sexual encounter with Ron in a conversation with Rowena, played as a soundtrack over the silent figure of Rowena in the dock. Elaine Aston considers that the use of soundtrack, rather than physical enactment of the sexual assault, ensures 'the spectator is

not seduced into the narrative of victimization, but is required to critically reflect on it'.[31] Indeed, the play carefully separates out accounts
of assault, rape or sex work from mimetic representation in order to
evacuate it of the titillating, voyeuristic function of pornography itself.
The use of soundtrack to this end occurs in scene eight, where the
disembodied voices of sex workers are played over Rowena's reading of
pornographic magazines on stage. These women's voices are not
presented as victims suffering individual tragedy or *hamartia*, but
rather are situated in relation to socioeconomic forces. Multiple
female voices recount their entry into the sex industry: 'it gave me
money and status', 'your value is your body', 'I went into the business
for money', 'I had a two-year-old daughter to support', 'if I go for a
proper job, what would I say in the interview?' (pp. 203–4). Likewise,
Hilary's account of her attempt to move from sex work to office work
marks her socioeconomic place:

> **Hilary** . . . you ain't ever going to know what it's like to be
> thrown on the shit heap. You got enough qualifications, security
> or money to have some sodding choice. Well mine is the D bloody
> HSS crap. Or on me back. What a bloody joke and I thought
> working was s'posed to give you some self-respect. (p. 226)

The lack of economic power for workers within the industry is highlighted by the contrast with the porn baron, whose entrepreneurial
boast of pure Thatcherite ambition opens the play: 'at university, my
one aim in life was to go into business and get rich quick' (p. 163).
The economic logic of the sex industry is continually returned to in
his speech: 'Profit margins are high. Our trade makes more money
than the film and record business put together. It will be the growth
industry of the eighties' (p. 163). The porn baron's speech represents
entrepreneurism at its most explicitly amoral. Indeed, the play sets out
to undercut the porn baron's claim 'ours is a perfectly normal profession run by ordinary nice people' (p. 163). This exposure of the
economic imperative of pornography is a vital component of the play
and retains its polemic force for productions today, where pornography has continued to be a growth industry and champions itself as

legitimate on the grounds of its economic success. The industry continues to divert attention from its human costs and social effects, attempting to normalise its operations as a natural expression of human sexuality. It is perhaps timely to note that at the time of writing this book Richard Desmond, who made his money through pornographic magazines like *Asian Babes* and *Penthouse*, which his company bought in 1983 as the play was staged, and pornographic television channels, has added Channel 5 (2010) to his ownership of the Express Newspapers group (2000).

For all the seriousness of the issues at the centre of the play, it is also very funny. The incongruity of witty or barbed remarks made at inappropriate moments in the dramatic narrative punctures any slide towards a comfortable realism. Recent work on neurophysiology has suggested that human laughter arises in two distinct ways, Duchenne and non-Duchenne laughter. Duchenne laughter is prompted by 'a sudden unexpected change in events that is perceived to be at once not serious and in a social context – that is, nonserious social incongruity'.[32] This kind of laughter occurs from all number of stimuli when we are 'tickled' physically or mentally by incongruity. By contrast, non-Duchenne laughter is strategic, conversational and transactional, and arises from different neural pathways. The question of where the laughs come in Daniels's *Masterpieces* is a crucial one for understanding how the puncturing force of her political critique works on stage. In reading the play alone there are many points where the jokes that characters make are funny for the reader: in reading the first scene of *Masterpieces*, after the range of dubious rape jokes, I found Yvonne's counter-joke, 'How many men does it take to tile a bathroom? Three, but you have to slice them thinly' (p. 169), prompted me to laughter. However, Chris Dymkowski reports a very different dynamic in the audience of the production at the Royal Court. During the male jokes about rape, at which all the characters laugh except Yvonne,

> the normally aware audience joined heartily in the on-stage laughter, no doubt feeling that their response was sanctioned by the playwright's sex. However, when the hitherto-silent

Yvonne finally responded with an anti-male joke [. . .] the audience fell deathly silent, their discomfort palpable. Here, Daniels' humour engaged the audience in a dialectical way, raising questions about such widely divergent responses to jokes that differ only in the objects of their malice. [33]

The effect is achieved in performance because of the non-Duchenne strategic laughter of the audience, sharing the actors' onstage performance of laughter as a form of social contract between audience and stage, early in the performance event. This laughter stutters at Yvonne's joke largely because of the performance register of the actress who delivered the line, and because it causes the audience to reflect back on their assent to the content of earlier jokes implied by their strategic, conversational laughter.

Masterpieces is, as Jules Wright noted, 'a politically confrontational work'.[34] Audience response has frequently been split along gendered lines. Robin Thurber reviewed the play in Leeds: 'I came out feeling not only threatened but muddled. The play made me angry and filled me with hate for men. But then I am one.' Jill Burrows reviewed the play in production in Ipswich and reported a woman came out saying, 'It made me think. It made me feel ill, but it made me think.'[35] The play's long journey to the stage 'involved many re-writes which continued well beyond its initial performances', as Daniels refined the effect she hoped to have. 'There are many things in the play which are not necessarily explicit or expressed directly in the dialogue.'[36] Its structure, pace, characterisation and performance mode are designed to pile example upon example of the systemic disempowering of women and the warped logic of their sexual objectification, making explicit what each structure has made 'normal'. In scene two, the teacher Yvonne meets the mother of a boy who has raped a girl, yet the scene indicates that all of the institutional structures cohere to transfer blame to the women in the situation. The headmaster 'says the same as the lawyer. She'd only been raped but was unharmed' (p. 180) and Yvonne has had to take exceptional steps to bring about prosecution. The mother of the rapist finds herself blamed by the medical profession:

Irene All those psychiatrists spent more time with me than they did with him. Where did I go wrong? [. . .] A normal healthy boy rapes a girl. Was I too prudish? Too open? To domineering? Too weak? Too much of a nag? Did I discourage him too violently from playing with his genitals as a baby? Did I sit him too viciously on the potty? Did I smother him? Did I neglect him? (p. 181)

Jules Wright suggested that the *gestic* heart of the play in performance is the scene set in the tube station where the two male figures are not threatened, but the female figure is. 'The moral questions which arise from this scene are at the centre of the play and always divide the audience.'[37] The scene's force is enhanced by its dramaturgical location – the play has built three scenes of mounting aggression and furious rows between the sexes over the use of pornography that depicts sexual violence against women. Suddenly Jennifer, Yvonne and Rowena are shown relaxing, enjoying a picnic in the sunshine, '*The pace is slow*' (p. 222), the mood relaxed, there is talk of holidays, the space and time of the moment are constructed as reverie, beyond everyday life. Immediately after this is the scene in the tube station where Rowena encounters an unknown man, late at night: '*He approaches her again very fast. Very close to her face. She shoves him violently. He falls on the track. There is the sound of a train*' (p. 224). For critics wanting the play to provide a formal debate, and argue the direct linkage as cause and effect between misogynist jokes, pornography usage, rape and violence against women, the realist logic of the play was 'flawed'.[38] But as Chris Dymkowski and Elaine Aston point out, they see the play as examining the 'prevailing social attitude'[39] as a 'materialist montage'.[40] More specifically, Daniels's critique draws explicit attention to the institutional mechanisms and the economic forces which characters in the play, and the audience, might take for granted; their operations are made strange through the play's relentless questioning.

Immediately after the play's first production there was a furore over the fact that the snuff movie to which the final scene alludes, and which has made Rowena so angry and afraid, was exposed as 'fake'.

Whether or not snuff movies as a form of fiction existed at that time is irrelevant to the significance of the play. As the policewoman in the final scene articulates, 'I've seen photos, hundreds of photos of little girls, young women, middle-aged women, old women . . . with torn genitals, ripped vaginas, mutilated beyond recognition. I try not to think about it' (p. 230). The reality of such violence against women is inescapable. As this book is being written, the news and the internet report the multiple instances of such violence, and contribute to the voyeuristic spectacle of such violence even in their apparently neutral role. The pornography industry has diffused its influence more widely through cultural artefacts, norms and commodities as 'raunch culture' than could have been imagined in 1983. In the 1980s, home video equipment broadened the market for video pornography, the teenage market for film and music was defined largely in terms of young males, and MTV (founded 1981) marketed music videos with sexualised female images aimed at this demographic. This was only compounded by the arrival of hip-hop and rap on MTV in the very late 1980s. Alterations in the way that the City of London operated and the new breed of male 'yuppie' financial services workers, hothoused in a hyper-masculine, macho culture, produced an economic demand for sexualised entertainment in London in particular. The proliferation of lap-dancing clubs was made possible by their reclassification from 'sexual entertainment' to just 'entertainment' by the Local Government (Miscellaneous Previsions) Act 1982. Today, raunch culture has so normalised an aggressive, performed, hypersexual representation of women on billboards, television, music videos, phones, the internet, in shop windows, in Playboy Bunny symbols on children's pencil cases, Tesco's toy Peekaboo pole-dancing kit and in 'slut wear' for four-year-old-girls, that Daniels's play seems positively mild in its commentary.[41]

The Devil's Gateway (1983)

'And do you not know that you are (each) an Eve? [. . .] *You* are the devil's gateway.'[42] As with many of Daniels's early plays the title of this work comes from a religious context by which she draws attention to one of the structures that has constructed a secondary social role for women through patriarchy. The play began as a result of a workshop run by Annie Castledine and Caryl Churchill, for the 'Women Live' project in May 1982, a month-long series of events organised by the collective Women in Entertainment, which was attempting to raise the profile of women in all areas of theatre and performance. In this workshop Daniels began to explore ideas around Greenham Common, at the suggestion of Annie Casteldine, but as the play developed Daniels became more interested in writing 'about a woman living in Bethnal Green'.[43] The resultant work doesn't show the Greenham protest, but uses it as a metaphor for a utopia, removed from the time and place of everyday life represented in the play, and as an 'actually existing' form of female community. The play opened in the Royal Court Upstairs on 24 August 1983, directed by Annie Castledine.

The significance of the Greenham Common Peace Camp is difficult to grasp today. As we saw in the opening chapter, in an escalation of the Cold War, American 'first strike' Cruise missiles were destined to arrive at RAF Greenham Common. Originally a small-scale protest by a group of families, not sponsored by more organised campaigning groups such as CND, it quickly became a women-only protest. It was not explicitly feminist in its aim; indeed the principle of the protest articulated a demand for a peaceful future for children and families, and creatively represented the protest as of a piece with the permitted feminine realms of the domestic and family life.[44] However, the practical expression of these principles produced a twenty-year-long public protest that saw the women imprisoned, harassed by police and army, engaged in legal battles for their right to protest and to protest on common land, draw attention to the lack of parliamentary debate on the deployment of nuclear weapons and prompted that debate, and raised the issue of nuclear deterrence itself and national independence within the 'special relationship' with the US. *The Devil's Gateway* was written during 1982, and it ends with the leading characters leaving for a key protest at Greenham: on 12 December 1982, thirty thousand women arrived at Greenham to 'Embrace the Base', forming a human chain encircling the six miles of perimeter fence. The media coverage of the protest produced fairly measured commentary by national broadcasters, while print press tended to split along party political lines. Yet despite misrepresentation in the tabloid press, the protest raised the visibility of the debate. And even the *Daily Mail* reported that in November 1983 as the missiles arrived, an NOP poll found that 94 per cent of those surveyed wanted dual control of the missiles (i.e. shared UK government control, rather than just US control) and 47 per cent were opposed to their deployment.[45] The women's protest at the arrival of Cruise missiles is the central issue that underlies Daniels's play, but her treatment of it is personalised through curious and sceptical characters, and diffracted through the lens of class and comedy.

The play is set in a working-class milieu, and centres on Betty's desire to step beyond her domestic world, where she supports mother Ivy, upwardly mobile daughter Carol, husband Jim and friend Enid: 'I'm bored with my life, everything. [. . .] Sometimes I don't feel I've done nothing with my life.'[46] Betty's growing interest in the Greenham protest, 'Makes you think, doesn't it?' (p. 111), runs parallel to a lesbian couple, middle-class social worker Fiona and working-class cook Linda, who are more directly activist in their politics, but also debate whether to become involved in the Greenham protest. Susan Carlson suggests that women's comedy often contains juxtaposed structures, as in this play where 'although thematic commonalities exist, especially a concern for global peace, the stories basically exist side by side. [. . .E]ach discrete scene in these women's plays may not move the play forward in a conventional way but will, instead, explore a moment, create a mood, speculate on a topic.'[47] Characters do move across the plot lines – Linda is Enid's daughter and reluctantly returns to her family home, and Fiona visits Betty as a social worker. The play's tight structure offers few opportunities for doubling, and writing for a small cast was encouraged by the economic realities of both the Royal Court and Royal Exchange theatres in 1983. However, the two instances of doubled roles are thoughtfully done – Lizzie Queen doubled Fiona with Betty's aspirational daughter Carol, who has moved out and up to Islington, helping the audience locate a shared sense of middle-class attitudes across the roles. Roger Frost was the only man in the cast and played Jim, the domestic abuser Mr Gardner, Mr Smith from the DHSS, and the policeman who stops Fiona and Linda in the street. On his current acting CV he lists his role as 'Patriarchy'! The setting of the play in a working-class world might seem to fit with the gritty social realism preferred by the Royal Court in the 1980s, yet Daniels's structure, comedy and characterisation offer more than classic realism.

The ostensibly familiar domestic setting of the play is undercut at every turn. Some of the stage action might seem quintessentially realist: ironing, that clichéd theatrical trope of domesticity since *Look Back in Anger*,[48] here too demarks the function of women, but is also shown as a shared act. Ivy takes over Betty's ironing in scene three and 'uses the iron with a vengeance' on Jim's shirt as she argues with him (p. 99); Fiona irons a dress to wear in court and her partner Linda finishes the task for her. Yet accounts of other events within the home, intergenerational and domestic violence, drug taking, prostitution, rape, although not staged in order to avoid producing a voyeuristic melodrama, contest any idealised domesticity.[49] Daniels draws attention to the structural economic and political realities that produce this domestic world – Jim describes the emasculation and shame of the loss of skilled employment and what he perceives as his feminised work in the black economy (p. 100), as real-world unemployment outside the theatre topped 3.1 million. Figures of the state intrude upon the private realm of the home in the form of Fiona the social worker, and Mr Smith, from the Department of Health and Social Security, and disrupt the physical (Jim must return all the kitchen appliances he bought for Betty, '*an electric toaster, liquidiser, microwave oven etc.*' (p. 120), to repay his social security benefits) and emotional environment (Enid and Betty's relationship is fractured by suspicion). The final two scenes of the play lead the women of both family sets out of the domestic environment and into the public arena of street protest – Fiona and Linda through spray-painting sex shops, and Betty, Carol, Ivy and Enid in protesting at Greenham Common. This is a realism that is not concerned with the interior psychology of individual characters, but with their social dynamics and their interaction with the political discourses, public action and socioeconomic structures of the wider world. The final scene of the play, where Betty must negotiate with Jim for the money to take the train to Newbury to join the Greenham protest, indicates the way that money and thus power flows within this 'classed' environment. It also reflects the pragmatic difficulties of cross-class consensus at the Greenham protest itself, echoed in Enid's suspicion of the Greenham project as about 'some posh woman [. . . making] sure her cut glass and Capo da Monte flowerpots are still intact' (p. 97).

Representing working-class life within a comic frame contains many pitfalls for a politically alert writer, particularly when the audience demographic of the theatre is predominantly middle class. *The Devil's Gateway* opens in Betty's living room, and the stage directions indicate the audience should understand the working-class nature of the room on display: '*Although the furniture is old everything is spotlessly clean. The room is brightened by several "cheap" ornaments, i.e. a brandy glass with a china cat up the side, a bright orange luminous ashtray on a stand*' (p. 75). These cheap ornaments are designed to evince a deliberate 'kitsch', as worthless, mass-produced items that appear 'tasteless'. They represent the distinct split in class identities between the generations of the family within the play. Late in the play Carol, Betty's daughter, confesses that she and her husband Darrel used to mock these objects, reducing them to their economic exchange value:

Carol We used to have a real laugh. Darrel used to line up all your ornaments on the floor and describe them as though it was an auction – go into detail – orange plastic ashtray.

Betty It was that funny?

Carol I used to laugh, Mum, but inside I was sad, I used to think, I still do, this collection of trinkets is all my mum's got to show for her life. I swore I'd never be like you.

Betty (*quietly angry*) Carol, I never wanted posh things, I didn't want anything else. I know this place might seem like a pile of tawdry crap to you and your friends but that's their problem. I don't want to have to go tripping round antique china, or freeze to death with pine-stripped floorboards for that matter. [. . .] A lot of this stuff was bought for me by you and John when you were kids, surely that's more important than a Rembrandt painting? (p. 141)

The items that Darrel has mocked have been part of the visual cueing of the audience about the class of the room depicted, and this moment wrong-foots the audience, who are forced to realign their understanding of the material objects of the stage, moving from any distanced position of 'knowledge' (imagined as objective and abstract) of the objects as marking class and taste horizons, to 'understanding', with the concomitant removal of distance in the comedy that has allowed us to laugh at Betty, rather than with her.

While some objects on stage are operating as souvenirs,[50] referencing the internal relationships of the home insulated from external forces of society, the use and flow of objects within *The Devil's Gateway* indicates that in fact the 'home' is porous to external pressures and explicitly located within economic and social structures. In scene three, in Betty's kitchen, in apparently realist, domestic conversation with her friend Enid, Betty uses the TV remote control as a phallic joke in a discussion about condoms. But she also brandishes the remote control to indicate the sociopolitical impact of modes of production of domestic objects: 'They can make these two a penny but they can't make nothing better than johnnies' (p. 94). As Betty furtively collects information and cuttings about the Greenham Common protests, scraps are culled from the 'high end papers' that Enid must collect and bring into the home, 'What Betty was too embarrassed to' (p. 145). The cuttings, also taken from red-top newspapers, such as the *Sun*, are concealed in a cereal packet, part of the acceptable 'reading' material for working-class homes. The other acceptable reading material Betty uses as a cover is the magazine *Women's Realm*, which through its very title summons its cultural demographic; focused as it was on television soap operas, 'homemaking' and celebrity profiles, it certainly never carried politically activist material on Greenham despite its female focus.

The play offers a comedic *tour-de-force* to the three leading roles of Betty, Enid and Ivy, who are potentially positioned as the butt of the joke, laughed at by a more knowing audience for their malapropisms, attitudes or ignorance. However, in the original production the three actresses were very accomplished comediennes, with much experience of popular theatre forms, and the script itself is provocatively self-reflexive, preventing the roles from lapsing into easy stereotype. For example, Ivy was played by Rita Triesman in the original production. Triesman was a founder member of the Unity Theatre before the Second World War who had revived the music-hall tradition at Hoxton Hall, and was a comic actress accustomed to a presentational style of performance. The audience has already seen Ivy deliberately play up the comic stereotype of deaf old lady in scene six during Fiona the social worker's visit. Then in scene nine, the play offers Ivy a comic monologue of self-reflexive resistance to type:

Ivy When you see old people on the telly in those comedy programmes what are made by morons and aren't at all funny, all they ever seem to open and shut their traps about is the war. (p. 139)

Ivy articulates a broader political perspective beyond the domestic: 'We ran the country [. . .] we invested our dreams and hopes and plans in our daughters, only to see them evaporate like pee in a lift on a hot day.' Specifically the rise of individual materialist desires has dissipated female collective energy: 'having a washing-machine, a television and a car become more important. [. . .] Bloody silly values' (p. 139). Likewise Enid might be in danger of mockery – she is repeatedly denigrated by characters within the play – specifically for her malapropisms, which delight an audience: about public weighing at Weightwatchers: 'That's what gives you the insensitive though, don't it?' (p. 92); 'You've never had an organism' (p. 109); of nuclear weapons: 'They're a detergent against those who got 'em' (p. 111).[51] Yet the play also points up that Enid is knowingly playing these word games; as Betty gently rebukes her, 'you know the difference between a deterrent and a detergent' (p. 111), and Ivy later comments, 'She does it for a laugh. She just ain't grasped the fact that you're s'posed to take the Michael outta someone else not yourself' (p. 127).

The mode of acting required by the play is not high naturalism, but a more presentational and audience-aware playing familiar from a popular theatre context. Pam Ferris, who played Betty, had a background in physical and storytelling work, having been a member of Shared Experience for some years, notably on their adaptation of *Arabian Nights*. She also brought with her the 'ghosts' of other roles, as Marvin Carlson dubs it,[52] and roles such as Betty were to become part of Ferris's professional persona, offering audiences inter-theatrical reference to other performances where she was frequently cast in motherly, working-class parts.[53] For example, in Mike Leigh's *Meantime*, a gritty drama for BBC *Play for Today* (1984) examining the impact of the dole on working-class lives, she worked with those other actors who were regularly cast as violent working-class men, Phil Daniels, Gary Oldman and Tim Roth.[54] Chrissie Cotterill, who played Linda, Enid's 'radical' lesbian daughter, had a background working with John McGrath, who had seen her perform 'a gig in the East End for old age pensioners and thought she was someone who had direct contact with the audience, big, simple, direct communication, a wonderful immediacy, a very unpretentious stage presence'.[55] The play explicitly requires this mode of performance in its comedy and moments of direct audience address, in order to unsettle the representation of the female characters as simple, realist individuals. In this, it draws on traditions of popular performance modes to represent its working-class characters.

Neaptide (1986)

All of Daniels's early plays had a fairly tortuous journey to the stage and *Neaptide* is no exception. Written in 1982, when it won her the George Devine Award for the Most Promising New Playwright, it was not staged until John Burgess championed it at the National's Cottesloe Theatre, opening on 26 June 1986. Once again the critical response to *Neaptide* was split along gendered lines. This play was also one which prompted a lengthy piece of advice about the writing of political theatre from *Guardian* theatre critic Michael Billington:

I believe that the first task of a polemical dramatist is to engage with the enemy: to present the triumph of a point of view through confrontation and argument. But Sarah Daniels' *Neaptide* [. . .] champions lesbian rights and the principle of maternal child custody while rubbishing the opposition. This may be good sexual politics but it makes for a decidedly slanted, unexploratory drama [. . .I]t is precisely because I believe Ms. Daniels [. . .] has talent that I wish she would accept that a cause triumphs only when it has worthy opponents.[56]

It is difficult to reconcile the desire for a writer to be at once a polemicist and to employ the journalistic trope of technical even-handedness, nor does one find Billington taking leftist male playwrights to task for their lack of expression of the feminist or lesbian perspective. The battle for custody of children can be brutal and underhand, as the busy family courts and more recent activist groups such as Fathers 4 Justice illustrate, and Daniels's point was to illustrate the fact that women who came out as lesbians were never awarded custody of their children in divorce cases. There is also here a misrepresentation of the play's careful treatment of the father figure. In Lawrence's second encounter with his ex-wife Claire, Daniels writes the role to articulate his love for his child, and his wistful desire to return to married life with Claire: 'Can't you see I have to go through with it?'[57] In the final scene, when he encounters the barrister on his day in court, he prevaricates, 'Do you actually think it's a foregone conclusion? [. . .] she is her mother, I suppose. [. . .] I was extremely angry when I first sought your advice' (p. 325).

In *Neaptide*, as with most of Daniels's work, lesbianism is 'presented as an implicit norm against which other relationships should be, and are, judged',[58] but also, unusually, as the central issue. Daniels establishes lesbian identity as a given within the predominantly realist plot by identifying a range of lesbians of differing ages, who gradually move from their positions of isolation into a kind of solidarity: Beatrice, Claire's headmistress, speaks up for Claire at her custody hearing, having been outed by two lesbian pupils at her school, who were themselves to be expelled before Claire intervened.

The only lesbian figure who begs to be excused is PE teacher Linda. Once again, rather than construe the battle of the play as centred on an individual protagonist, whose difficulties might therefore be identified as personal failings, by following multiple lesbian characters, it is clear that it is the institutional structures – the educational establishment and the law – that are retrograde and which need to be critiqued. By pairing Claire as a lesbian single parent with Jean as a straight single parent, and staging the chaotic but happy home they have established together, the play draws attention to the inequity of Claire's impending custody battle. Custody battles of this sort were prevalent in the late 1970s and other activist writers were tackling the subject, for example Michelene Wandor, who developed *Care and Control* with Gay Sweatshop in 1977.

One of the delights of the play's staging at the National Theatre was the five children onstage, depicting family life in all its complex glory. Claire's sister Val has two boys, who appear blissfully unaware of their mother's depression. The play opens with Val presented in a psychiatric ward, whose unreliable mutterings summon the historical and mythic frame of the witch trials. Daniels used a reading of the story of Persephone as a parallel to the intense and spotless mother-daughter relationship between Claire and her daughter Poppy. Daniels later confessed that she might have made Claire too good: 'I was speaking for a lot of women and I didn't want to blow it.'[59] However, there is a second mother–daughter relationship between Claire and Joyce that undercuts the image of family perfection. Joyce's performance in scene two is one of complete stage domination. She drags the reluctant near-silent Val in her wake, and systematically berates Claire for her lesbianism, moans about her domestic lot, and questions the decisions about work, partners and lifestyle that each of her daughters has made:

Joyce   I notice nobody bothers to ask how I am. I suppose I'm not worth bothering with.

Claire (*curtly*)   I just did, only you ignored it.

Joyce   Sometimes, frankly, it's just as well not to ask. Life's not a bowl of anything much. Especially with the neighbours banging away into the night – they've even got an hydraulic cat-flap, God alone knows why, on the twelfth floor. Still, moaning about it doesn't get you anywhere. Laugh and the world laughs with you, weep and you weep alone, that's my motto. (p. 244)

The breakneck canter through topics that Joyce sustains, leaping from unintended smuttiness through an assessment of the current Pope to the best ways to get toothpaste out of the tube, functions as a delightful corrective to the mythic Demeter. The myth contains no class, whereas the actual family is split by class, as parents Joyce and Sid, housewife and unemployed docker, through Joyce's fantasies ('I just wished that you'd all turn out like those Brontë sisters', p. 245), have produced middle-class women with tastes and desires to match. The actual reading of the myth through the play is structured so that it is comically undercut by the immediate appearance of Joyce, repeat-edly demonstrating the divergence between mythic and actual mother–daughter relations. The transition Joyce makes towards acceptance of Claire's sexuality, finally facilitating Claire's fantasy escape to America with Poppy, is a mythic one too, lying very close to the satisfactions and pay-offs of melodramatic reconciliation. Trevor R. Griffiths considers Claire's escape 'a legitimate fairy-tale ending and, in the context of production, it is a desirable one, but it also suggests that there is no point in fighting here and it displaces the struggle into a utopian realm, just as all the scenes of female solidarity appear to be set in a prelapsarian world'.[60]

The production at the National has been critiqued for not adver-tising the lesbian content in its pre-publicity. But there could be little doubt about the content of the play, were any audience member to read the reviews. While some critics have taken Daniels to task for offering Claire too simplistic a solution to her situation, what the play actually stages is Claire's expression of the difficulties with moving to the United States. Indeed, in reality, if anything the situation in some states was far more malign towards lesbian mothers than in the UK at the time of the play. That Claire is a teacher, and that lesbianism is raised within the school context is highly significant in the mid-1980s. The just-abolished GLC had issued a report, *Changing the*

World (1985), a London charter for gay and lesbian rights, and Margaret Roff, Lord Mayor of Manchester, was the first openly lesbian elected mayor in the UK, but gay and lesbian rights were not secure. In some ways *Neaptide* is a utopian play, since the positive solutions it finds in the school setting – the two schoolgirls are sustained by the role model of their headmistress, Beatrice, who herself comes out – is one that was soon to be legally questionable. What Daniels does most effectively is to gently satirise discriminatory attitudes through her mockery of the teachers. In two enormously comic scenes the dysfunction of the staffroom and staff relationships is linked to prejudice against lesbianism. The stage directions convey the lightness of performance that these group scenes in the staffroom give to the play:

> *Scene Four: Staffroom. Before school.* **Marion** *and* **Annette** *are marking exercise books.* **Cyril** *is reading the sports page in* The Times. **Linda** *is sorting out arm bands.* **Roger** *appears to be trying to mate two paper clips. There is a knock at the door.*

From this tableau the dynamic and the characteristics of each role are sketched in for the audience. The second staffroom scene parades the prejudices of the staff towards lesbians:

Annette   It's the parents I feel sorry for.

Roger   Can't be very fruitful knowing there are bent genes in the family tree.

Cyril   Luckily they can't reproduce themselves.

Marion   Public tolerance wouldn't trust them with the next generation.

Roger   Some of them do have children, though.

Annette   Don't be ridiculous, how can they? (p. 265)

By the final staffroom scene, when Claire comes out, the staff members have become more sophisticated in their responses. Cyril makes a rousing speech about the dangers of closed-mindedness and goes to the pub. Linda acknowledges her own sexuality, but refuses to make it public, and Roger appears uncharacteristically sympathetic until he propositions Claire, for the sake of her court case. The language of the staffroom is reformed, in a second utopian turn. It can be difficult to remember how vitriolic anti-gay and -lesbian discrimination was through all elements of the media, and many areas of culture during the 1980s. The play was performed *prior* to the amended Local Government Act 1988, which introduced Clause 28 into law, specifically prohibiting a local authority from permitting schools to 'promote the teaching in any maintained school of the acceptability of homosexuality as a pretended family relationship' – a clause not repealed in England until 2003. The attitudes towards lesbianism that Joyce and the teachers display might strike us today as stereotypically bigoted, and their transformation as inevitable. However, at the moment of original performance, the discriminatory attitudes were part of mainstream discourse and the transformation of attitudes struck reviewers as utopian.

Still laughing

In the teeth of Billington's assertion that polemic drama should 'present the triumph of a point of view through confrontation and argument', Daniels chooses rather to unsettle and confront through comedy and the counterpoint of perspectives. Indeed, the production of *Neaptide* was in and of itself a confrontation: it was, in 1986, the first play by a British woman to be staged at the National.[61] Against the odds Daniels has become canonical. Her writing has relentlessly examined, through comedy, the economic and institutional forces at work in preserving women's inequality in the home, the workplace, the criminal justice system and the psychiatric institution. Her work is frequently described as passionate or angry, and she readily claims, 'I like challenges ... I write issue plays.'[62] Her most frequently performed play is a community-based play she wrote for the Albany Empire Theatre about the local history of working-class women in Deptford, *The Gut Girls* (staged 2 November 1988).[63] Part of the reason for the play's enduring popularity with amateur performers is the wide range of rich lively roles for women – a trademark element of Daniels's writing – the banter the women share, and the comedy that is not at the women's expense. Yet, as Susan Haedicke points out, the play is also profoundly pessimistic, as the gut women's gentrification into domestic servants removes them from a workplace of relative autonomy back to the doubly repressive setting of the domestic and middle-class mores.[64] Daniels's writing from the 1980s does not offer utopian solutions, despite reviewers' assertions. Its operation through laughter and the rattling of realist structures returns audiences not to individual dilemmas, but to characters sharply aware of their relationship to the political, gendered and social structures that surround them.

TIMBERLAKE WERTENBAKER
By Sara Freeman

The moment: 1988

In 1988, two plays by Timberlake Wertenbaker premiered in two of England's most important theatre venues. *Our Country's Good* opened at the Royal Court Theatre Downstairs on 10 September and just seven weeks later, on 28 October, *The Love of the Nightingale* became the last show performed by the Royal Shakespeare Company at the original Other Place in Stratford. Wertenbaker won the Olivier Award for Play of the Year and the Evening Standard's Most Promising Playwright Award for *Our Country's Good*. After *Nightingale*'s move to London in 1989, it received the Eileen Anderson Central TV Drama Award. In short, 1988 culminated as an *annus mirabilis* for Wertenbaker, a development especially unexpected since as the year started she had not even begun work on *Our Country's Good*. This chapter provides a new look at Wertenbaker's three most recognised plays of the 1980s, approaching the plays as they were situated in their moment of first production and engaging anew with why the plays produce strong theatrical impact. From this perspective, the moment of 1988 takes an even more pointed position for both Wertenbaker and British theatre. For Wertenbaker, the breakthrough of 1988 held particular poignancy because in the previous year she experienced a pause in the consistent level of production she had been enjoying in London venues, with a play a year appearing since 1980, and personally, she had entered what she described as a 'period of deep mourning' after the death of her partner, actor John Price.[1]

In Britain and for British theatre, 1988 also had a different tenor. In 1987, Margaret Thatcher won re-election for the second time and started her third term, but the effects of changes from her earlier terms had already created new conditions, and cultural institutions were adapting even as they were protesting. Historian Peter Riddell notes about the 1980s that the decade almost breaks neatly into two sections: the first half 'culminating in the defeat of the miners' strike in 1984–85', a period when financial reform was most draconian and during which the 'dragon of union power was slain'.[2] As a result, the second half of the 1980s experienced a pace of change both in the labour market and in culture in general that was 'almost inconceivable to someone who did not actually see' how it played out.[3] As Andy McSmith's pop-culture history of the 1980s suggests, especially in terms of technology and class mobility, the Britain of 1979 had more in common with the Britain of 1956 than the Britain of 1989.[4] And cultural historian Robert Hewison expertly charts in *Culture and Consensus: England, Art, and Politics Since 1940* how the 'loadsamoney' juggernaut of the enterprise culture unleashed vigorous reactions and contradictory significations.[5]

What was lost and what was gained in these changes is still being sorted out in Britain and in British theatre, but nevertheless the 'loadsamoney' ethos produced a new vigour and a new terror in British theatre by 1987 and 1988 and that energy meant opportunities even within the radically changed paradigm. Although the RSC's *Carrie* failed to repeat the success of *Les Misérables* (1985), 1988 brought some brisk new developments. Funded by Canadian entrepreneurs Ed and David Mirvish, Jonathan Miller set out to revive the Old Vic with a season of controversially staged classics that year – producing *Andromache, Candide, Too Clever by Half, The Tempest* and *Bussy*

193

D'Ambois among others.[6] In 1988 Deborah Warner's RSC production of *Titus Andronicus* moved to the Pit in the Barbican and her *King John* opened at the Other Place. In fact, after the continuous agitation of women theatre artists since the 1970s, 1988 saw Ian Herbert reflecting in the 'Prompt Corner' of *London Theatre Record* that the year was notable for the achievements of extraordinary woman theatre directors. Herbert mentioned the trajectories of not only Warner, but also Di Trevis, Jude Kelly, Sarah Pia Anderson and Ireland's Garry Hynes, founder of Druid Theatre Company, who after directing *The Man of Mode* at the RSC in 1988 stayed and directed Wertenbaker's *Nightingale*. Meanwhile, by 1988, the Royal Court, where Wertenbaker had found a home, was primed to make a new statement. After a roiling scandal over *Perdition* in 1987, the Court saved itself by having a hit with Caryl Churchill's *Serious Money*, which so perfectly chronicled what had changed in Britain by the late 1980s.[7]

Some of the cultural energy in 1988 stemmed from the investigation and commemoration of 200 years of permanent British settlement in Australia that unfolded in scholarship and commonwealth public life across the year: *Our Country's Good* took part in this and benefited from it. The 1987 publication of both Robert Hughes's *The Fatal Shore* and Thomas Keneally's *The Playmaker* connected to this anniversary, which explains why Royal Court Artistic Director Max Stafford-Clark's idea to do *The Recruiting Officer* in conjunction with an adaptation of *The Playmaker*, which he had while rehearsing the Broadway transfer of *Serious Money* in New York, went from an idea to a proposal to Wertenbaker to an in-process workshop within five months (December 1987 to April 1988). *Our Country's Good* opened after only another five months, a very fast turn-around, all things considered.[8]

Wertenbaker's miraculous 1988 therefore coincided with some important trends. Yet her work across the decade maps a curious shape: Wertenbaker's content can seem a bit ahead or a bit behind the moment, anticipating the hybrid, globalised politics of the 1990s while revisiting the gender dichotomies of the 1970s; and yet, as a whole, her mode of working largely encapsulates movements of the decade. Wertenbaker began the 1980s writing for alternative theatres and expressing a strong woman-centred angle in her work. In particular, across 1980 and 1981 she had a commission from pioneering feminist company Women's Theatre Group, and for them she scripted a Theatre-in-Education piece and her first published play *New Anatomies*. Collaboration and writer's residency with Shared Experience followed: Wertenbaker produced much-admired translations of Marivaux for Mike Alfreds to direct with his group of inventive storytellers.

The absolute marker of Wertenbaker's prospects in the 1980s came when she became a Resident Writer at the Royal Court across 1984 and 1985, a role held by Hanif Kureishi, and Sarah Daniels just prior to Wertenbaker.[9] This position matters in the symbolic economy of the British theatrical scene, but beyond the symbolic realm, it also provided Wertenbaker with an artistic home base for the decade.[10] With the premiere of *The Grace of Mary Traverse* on the Royal Court's main stage in 1985 and the production of her translation of *Mephisto* at the Royal Shakespeare Company in 1986, Wertenbaker entered major venues of production and became an artist to be watched.[11] Indeed, in eight years, Wertenbaker had recapitulated the developments of the whole British theatre economy: 1970s alternative theatre artists penetrating the mainstream venues and struggling with the modes of political theatre, new writing and ensemble-based devising in that context.[12]

How, then, did Wertenbaker 'fit' in 1985 as *The Grace of Mary Traverse* gained her even wider attention? What was the nature of her voice and what about that quality demanded that she be watched? How did *Our Country's Good* and *The Love of the Nightingale* extend or disrupt Wertenbaker's encapsulation of that moment, and the trends developing after 1985? It seems apt that Sarah Daniels was Writer-in-Residence at the Royal Court just before Wertenbaker because *The Grace of Mary Traverse* thematically resonates with Daniels's concerns about rape and power within patriarchy: it had been only two years since the controversy over *Masterpieces* when *The Grace of Mary Traverse* opened. Upon re-reading *Mary Traverse* almost thirty years after its premiere, this is one of the startling aspects of it: its fatalism about gender relationships, its brutal imaging of the terrible traps that young women with both intellect and libido face. This is a way that the play almost feels 'behind' the times reading now: there's an uncomfortable sense that this territory had already been covered, well articulated by writers like Churchill, Daniels and Pam Gems, to whose radical *Camille* Victoria Radin compared the piece in the *New Statesman*, and even by male playwrights like Howard Barker, to whom the RSC was giving a 'season' in the Pit at the same time *The Grace of Mary Traverse* opened.[13] But that vision is shaped by generalisations made in the 1990s about the 'talky' and predictable political theatre of the 1980s to set up a good contrast with the in-yer-face 'explosion' of new playwriting after 1995.[14] In a lived moment, a historical 'plan view' of what will be fresh or passé is not available: artists like Wertenbaker are in the midst of the events and, as Charles Mee puts it, 'the culture writes us first, and then we write our stories'.[15] In the 1980s, it seems, the culture had written artists who needed to write stories about rape, gender, power, witches, pornography and the link of personal liberation to social and political transformation. Wertenbaker's contributions to those stories stirred powerful and revealing reactions, as the reviews to productions of *The Love of the Nightingale* from 1988 through 1991 attest.[16]

The distinctive voice of Wertenbaker's three major plays of the 1980s – *Mary Traverse*, *Our Country's Good* and *The Love of the Nightingale* – transformed a British marriage of Brechtian approaches to history plays and a Shavian theatre of ideas through a challenging and deeply contextual take on gender, identity and justice. For Wertenbaker's work, the issue of justice cannot be over-emphasised. In an interview with John DiGaetani for the 1991 collection *The Search for a Postmodern Theatre*, Wertenbaker responds to DiGaetani's praise that, compared to plays of the 1970s, her plays are sceptical, not didactic.[17] Wertenbaker counters that she thinks she's 'gone through phases of being quite didactic', and offers a telling reading of how attitudes towards Brecht on that front shift and then shift again. Wertenbaker then asserts that didactic or not, 'the search for justice should not be forgotten'.[18] Wertenbaker's interest in justice (that may never be obtained: the emphasis in her formulation is on the search) stands particularly strong in the major plays of the 1980s, which is what makes the materialist/Brechtian/feminist way they depict silence, the double-edged sword of knowledge, and the hope of transformation so searing. Wertenbaker believes 'the search for justice should continue' (p. 268), and thereby her plays entertain an ongoing humanist debate with Western intellectual history and the genre of tragedy. Wertenbaker's theatrical continuation of that debate makes clear through her exhilarating deployment of historical metaphor and literary intertext the absolutely non-metaphoric injustices troubling the contemporary world.[19]

As a playwright coming to prominence in the 1980s, Wertenbaker made theatre pieces that linked to hot cultural conversations about class and gender, race and cultural hybridity, the representation of England's 'heritage', the after-effects of Empire and developments in 'state-of-the-nation' drama. Across her career, it matters that Wertenbaker's own identity and intellectual commitments dislocate from British tradition, so her translatorial, multilingual and international ethos positions her somewhat differently in the decades of British playwriting. A perspective that David Hare or David Edgar sought to develop in the 1990s, for instance, by undertaking projects like *Pentecost* or *Via Dolorosa*, Wertenbaker nurtured from the beginning.[20] But in the 1980s in particular, Wertenbaker's work mattered because as post-war culture continued to fragment, her plays hailed a potent idea of British theatre as a place for vivid illustration of debate, provocative argument and cultural reaffirmation.

The plays: brisk sensuality

Wertenbaker's plays possess a spareness that belies the thickly contextualised realm of signification they activate. On the page, the plays present a clean look: the words are precise and eloquent. There are big ideas, but an economy of clauses and commas. Phrases turn firmly. Sentences are sharp. Periods dominate. The historical or mythic settings of the plays, the way they rework the conventions of existing dramatic genres and their dense intertextual references contrast against this spareness to produce a pleasurable frisson that might best be described as 'brisk sensuality'.[21] This brisk sensuality defines Wertenbaker's voice and it provides fertile theatrical moments to be magnified by actors, directors and designers. The fresh readings of the plays unfolded in this section attend to production history, discussing Wertenbaker's collaborators in the first staging of the plays and the context in which the plays were staged. The elements of close reading that also inform these analyses track techniques of her dramaturgy, especially how Wertenbaker evolved a skill with large group debate scenes alongside her professed love of monologues and how her plays contrapuntally contrast debate with silence.

The Grace of Mary Traverse

The Grace of Mary Traverse concerns a privileged young woman who, in defiance of her wealthy father, leaves her eighteenth-century drawing room in hopes of gaining experience. She gambles, prostitutes herself and others, reads philosophy and foments rebellion. Her encounters with the economic, political, sexual and moral systems of her society provide her a hard-earned knowledge and a different type of grace than the gentle conversation and smooth deportment she once strove to learn. The show opened at the Royal Court Theatre on 17 October 1985, just after *Aunt Dan and Lemon* by Wallace Shawn had closed, and while Upstairs *God's Second in Command* and *Basin*, both by Jacqueline Rudet, traded places.[22] Danny Boyle directed.

At that point Boyle was a Royal Court associate artist who had recently worked with Joint Stock on Howard Barker's *Victory: Choices in Reaction*, but he would go on to be famous for films such as *Trainspotting* (1997), *28 Days Later* (2003) and *Slumdog Millionaire* (2008).[23] Having Janet McTeer play the role of Mary Traverse pivotally shaped the success of what Boyle and Wertenbaker set into motion. Alongside analysis of Wertenbaker's content and conceits, the reviews for *Mary Traverse* overflow with fascination for McTeer. In the *Financial Times*, Michael Coveney enthused at the greatest length:

Mary herself is literally straining for the off, bursting at the seams, busting out of her crinoline. Janet McTeer, making her London debut, is quite simply astonishing, the most extraordinary new actress I have seen way beyond even Juliet Stevenson. Martin Hoyle's reports on this page of her Royal Exchange, Manchester, work were no idle trailer. Close your eyes and you hear Vanessa Redgrave, singing along her vowels and animating all she says with urgency and passion. Open them and you see a tall, willowy young woman full of grace and movement, total assurance and natural timing.[24]

McTeer had made her professional debut in *Mother Courage and Her Children* in Nottingham only the year before and *Mary Traverse* sensationally brought her to the attention of the London theatre scene.[25]

The sensation emerged in part because of McTeer's skill and her voluptuous beauty (the photos included with Coveney's review, and Michael Billington's in the *Guardian*, for instance, feature McTeer with neck extended, eyes and mouth wide, cleavage bursting), but also because Wertenbaker's script gave McTeer two theatrically indelible scenes to play. These two scenes would test the mettle of any actress and they carry the punch of the play's exploration of gender. The first such scene, the third of Act Two, places Mary across the room from a Mr Hardlong. She purchases his services in order to gain initiation into desire and its practice. Mary, fully clothed, observes a naked Mr Hardlong as he persuades her to take her lesson. Then, plunging in, Mary delivers a *tour-de-force* monologue built around geographic imagery of Welsh mountains and the Bay of Biscay where she describes the knowledge of pleasure she gains.[26] The script never suggests that intercourse be mimed and it seems central to the distancing effects this scene introduces around the subject of sexual autonomy and knowledge that Mary stays fully clothed,[27] but it remains a scene of astonishing revelation: the sensuality of Mary's monologue kindles a fire that collides against the stage picture of separated bodies. This contrast is further driven home by the final turn of the scene, which comes when Mr Hardlong spends his payment from Mary buying the services of Sophie, the innocent and recently raped working-class girl Mary has taken from the streets to be her servant. The crux: Mary asked Mr Hardlong to serve her pleasure. Mr Hardlong wants Sophie to serve his. When Mary declares, 'I would do that too. Mr Hardlong. I would advocate a community of pleasure. Teach me what to do and I will,' he replies, 'It's too late, Mary: you would have to learn to ask for nothing.'

The second intense, boundary-pushing scene *Mary Traverse* provides for its lead actress comes at the top of Act Three, where Mary, her state now reversed, plies her trade as a prostitute with Sophie in Vauxhall Gardens. Mary discovers her father, who thinks she is dead, starting a transaction with Sophie. Mary, masked, takes over the job and while manually bringing her father to climax also reveals to him who she is and calls him to account for all that her Faustian experience thus far has taught her about gender, power and recognition. Her speech, as she 'unbuttons' and 'massages' him, echoes Caliban's to Prospero. Giles asks if she must talk so much and she responds, 'It's my father who taught me to talk, Sir. He didn't suspect he'd also be teaching me to think. He was not a sensitive man and didn't know how words crawl into the mind and bore holes that will never again be filled' (pp. 116–17). With the way the speech develops an image of knowledge working like venereal disease, the point crystallises. Mary, unlike Sophie, 'knows' what is at stake in these exchanges (p. 115): it is not just pleasure or money or bread, it is also agency, autonomy and freedom.

Indeed, throughout the play, the pliant and blank Sophie serves as Mary's foil, her inarticulacy in opposition to Mary's silver tongue, her submission against Mary's dominance, her apparent lack of ideas and needs causing her to be desired by all the men who populate the play, but her abject state providing a distinct demonstration of the reason Mary must 'die' to her old life (accomplished by that orgasm scene) and try to find if there's some way to be both a woman and a human being. Yet, for all the vibrancy of this contrast, silence, which is always central to Wertenbaker's figuration of agency, is not Sophie's tactic. Instead, it is Jack, Sophie's lover and a working-class organiser, who in this play provides the silence that prefigures that of Liz Morden in *Our Country's Good* and Philomele in *Love of the Nightingale*.[28]

Jack appears in the play for the first time in the scene immediately following Mary's 'seduction' of her father. *The Grace of Mary Traverse* has four acts, and the interval comes between Act Two and Act Three: it marks, roughly, the play's transition from anatomising the social construction of gender and class to the play's exploration of what happens in the pursuit of material and political liberation, given those constructions. Jack brings with him a discussion of 'bread and liberty' that helps move the action of the play toward its third act culmination in riots and fourth act climax of public execution (p. 140). Jack finds his political match in Mary. He has something to say, and she has the means to say it (p. 129). When their combined voices fail to achieve their intended end, his final silence at the scaffold defies the commodification of using his last words to endorse anything, commercial or philosophical (p. 158). His protest is total.

In the first production the actor who played Jack (David Beames) had played Mr Hardlong the act before, and the world where Mary goes with Jack also demonstrates how class and gender hierarchies ghost utopian attempts at liberation so they can easily be redirected and recuperated by dominant systems. After Mary and Jack begin to agitate publicly, Lord Gordon and Mr Manners quickly target them. Then, in Act Three, scene eight, Wertenbaker provides a scene seemingly out of time, a 'midnight conversation: the last stages of a drunken dinner' that allows almost all the characters to debate together (pp. 137–8). Do they share a common cause? Initially, Mary's skill with conversation gave Jack's thoughts wings, but in this scene the cry of 'bread and liberty' twists with the manipulation of Mr Manners to become a cry for gin and against 'popery'. The way Mary falls in love with her own rhetorical skill makes her vulnerable to Mr Manners's Mephistophelean suggestion, so that suddenly, she finds herself advocating an anti-Catholic position and the revolution she and Jack dreamed of is recuperated by those in power to help reinforce the social order they want to see preserved. As the outcome, Jack is executed to the strains of Schubert's Adagio in E flat major, the 'Notturno', a punctuating use of classical music that signifies rather differently than the use of Beethoven at the end of *Our Country's Good*.[29]

The riots that consume the end of Act Three in *The Grace of Mary Traverse* are nominally the Gordon Riots of 1780, which in history were inspired by anti-Catholic sentiment. Interestingly, Wertenbaker's depiction of Lord Gordon repurposes the historical figure who headed the Protestant Association as a character also in conflict about his gender, just as Mary is about hers. This Lord Gordon (first played by Tom Chadbon, an actor best known for his later role as Lenny Monk in the TV series *Crown Prosecutor*) spends his first appearance on stage trying to figure out how best to play the social role demanded of an aristocratic man. Act One, scene two and Act One, scene three therefore serve as specific counterpoint to each other, contrasting how Mary practises the 'invisible passage of an amiable woman' and Lord Gordon prays, 'Oh God, please make me noticed, just once' (pp. 71, 74).

Lord Gordon's quest to be noticed (it is for this reason he rapes Sophie after Mary ignores him) turns into the pursuit of political power, so that as Mary and Gordon each attempt to rewrite their social identity across the first half of the play, they both come to foment political protest in the second half. Mary and Lord Gordon both misunderstand what their 'liberation' depends upon (the suffering of others), a lesson Mrs Temptwell's character history confirms. As the play reveals Mrs Temptwell's pursuit of revenge on Mary's father for his role in enclosing public lands where her family lived in order to build his fortune, it tells of the torture and execution of her grandmother as a witch in the process of clearing those lands. Mrs Temptwell, played at the Royal Court by Pam Ferris, tries to teach Mary about the cycle of revenge, even as she tries to trap Mary in it.

Wertenbaker clearly declares that *Mary Traverse* is 'not a historical play' in her note at the beginning of the script (p. 66). Despite the use of period costumes and wigs, the design of the first production relied on suggestion and minimalism in a way that reinforces Wertenbaker's description of the 'eighteenth century as a valid metaphor' by making the scene of the play not a fully detailed reality, but a framework (John Barber describes Kandis Cook's set as 'scaffolded').[30] Especially in the second half, the play invokes imagery related to atom bombs, the holocaust and contemporary sexual politics unknown in 1780. Jay Gipson-King persuasively reads these anachronistic aspects of *Mary Traverse* as metahistorical commentary that preserves a revealing alternative history.[31] Wertenbaker describes in her introduction to *Plays One* that she conceived the play influenced by having lived in a neighbourhood close to the site of the 1981 Brixton race riots (named for the unrest which took place in and around Brixton Road).[32] In addition to the actual Gordon Riots, Wertenbaker's use of the 1780s also invokes the coming French Revolution, and the recent American Revolution. Reminiscent of those historical revolutions, what lit Lambeth aflame in 1981 was not only generalised high unemployment and racial tension, but the pointed implementation of an aggressive law-enforcement policy called Operation Swamp 81 that allowed police to search subjects based on suspicion of wrongdoing. In April 1981, across only five days, plainclothes police searched over 900 people in Brixton on these grounds.[33] Yet, if the Brixton riots sent Wertenbaker looking for a metaphor by which to discuss the role of popular uprising in the pursuit of liberty and economic equality, it is worth noting that the crushing of the riots in *Mary Traverse* presents a bleak view of collective action that also seems to encapsulate the failure of the miners' strikes of 1984–85.

The collapse of the National Union of Mineworkers strike in March 1985, six months before the show opened, provides a chronologically more immediate connection to the sense of waste and defeat at the end of Act 3 than Brixton does. However, in a topical convergence of life and art, nineteen days before *Mary Traverse* opened, a new 'uprising' occurred in Brixton, in response to an invasive police search for a black man that resulted in the accidental shooting of his mother, which trigged looting, fires and the death of cameraman David Hodge in the mêlée.[34] *Mary Traverse* feels deeply of its time, capturing this jagged, tinderbox feeling about public order. Still, the Royal Court's *Mary Traverse* didn't stage race as part of its given dynamics. In the first productions of *Our Country's Good* and *Love of the Nightingale*, black performers were cast in such a way as to convey significance even in the absence of explicit dialogue about race, but no black actors were used in *Mary Traverse's* first production. While the

Brixton riots inspired *Mary Traverse*, overall the play evinces a more thematic concern with gender and labour than with race relations. This may simply be an initial result of adopting the eighteenth century as the locus for the metaphor, and when *Our Country's Good* returned Wertenbaker to the same century, her feminist-humanist debate with the continuing heritage of that time period and its philosophy sharpens about race considerably. Powerfully, as Brechtian history plays engaged in a neo-Shavian debate about equality and liberty, both *The Grace of Mary Traverse* and *Our Country's Good* stage the late eighteenth century as a moment that provocatively elucidates the tensions of liberal democracy and late postmodern capitalism.[35]

Our Country's Good

As *Our Country's Good* took shape, an Australian theatre company made a mid-year tour of London, bringing a play about the colonial displacement of indigenous peoples in Australia to England. The Australian Elizabethan Theatre Trust sponsored the Marli Biyol Company's performance of Jack Davis's *No Sugar* in a 'walkabout' production at the Riverside Studios in June 1988.[36] The first part of a trilogy written in 1985, *No Sugar* presents full force a post-colonial view of England's role in Australia. Some critics have wished *Our Country's Good* engaged more wholeheartedly with this view, rather than just suggest it through its use of a lone aborigine as chorus, who foretells the coming destruction once he figures out that the First Fleet's arrival is not a dream.[37] *Our Country's Good* dramatises how a production of George Farquhar's *The Recruiting Officer* came to be staged in Australia in 1789 by convicts and Marines who populated England's first penal colony there. *Our Country's Good* probes the divide between authority and transgression, with a strong focus on the convict women Liz Morden, Mary Brenham and Duckling Smith, but equal investment in the officers Second Lieutenant Ralph Clark (director of the play), Captain Arthur Phillip, Major Robbie Ross and Midshipman Harry Brewer. The play works in post-Brechtian epic mode, laying fragments of the colony's activities side by side in scenes that assemble as a complex composite picture.

Within this structure, the play insists on a conversation about gender and race across historical and colonial contexts, but it cannot be the work a writer with indigenous heritage would write. Despite its status as a history play 'like' *The Grace of Mary Traverse*, *Our Country's Good* doesn't include unsettling anachronistic references that shatter the illusion of the historical quite so immediately. But *Our Country's Good* set out to be a play about 'now' as much as the 'then' of its setting. The script's preface about Wertenbaker's visits to prison theatre projects and reproduction of letters from convicts to her about their transformational experiences acting in those programmes confirm this concern with the present country and its good. The dream vision of the play, I think, is that England should work for a painful, useful self-consciousness and change its structures, not that English people can relocate to colonial territories to get the freedom they can't get at home, as post-colonial critique of the play suggests. Indeed, in the moment of the premiere, the play was so successful in advocating the potential for the inclusion of otherness to transform a nation for the better that it fed a general affirmation of the arts as a means for making that change. After a decade of Thatcher's leadership and seismic changes to the way Britain conceived of itself, this idea about art, nation and identity hit home, while offering not just the desire for, but also the means of, self-examination and reinvention.

Such an excellent body of commentary already exists on *Our Country's Good* that it seems unnecessary to belabour the text's structural or thematic dynamics, or to provide a comprehensive reading of its characters.[38] Additionally, the workshop and rehearsal period for the show receives nuanced documentation in *Letters to George* and the case study on the play in *Taking Stock* by Max Stafford-Clark and Philip Roberts. *Our Country's Good* became a famous piece by being toured extensively, being produced worldwide, translated into many languages and made into a set text for British school exams. Now it needs to be rediscovered in the historical specificity of its premiere. Reading the play now and thinking about the decade it so effectively capped calls forth an excavation of the way the play's dramaturgy and production choices coincide with the tandem production of *The Recruiting Officer*, the thrilling theatrical opportunities *Our Country's Good* offered artists and audiences, and the play's ideologically complex combination of critique and affirmation.

At the time it opened, *Our Country's Good* was entirely enmeshed with the production of *The Recruiting Officer* that opened before it, used the same actors, and which ran concurrently with the show even after it transferred to the West End and during a tour to Sydney in 1989. In other words, at no point in 1988 or 1989 was *Our Country's Good* performed without *The Recruiting Officer* running in rep. This pair of productions created a significant comment on colonial history, and at the same time the project also commemorated and 'took on' Bill Gaskill's staging of *The Recruiting Officer* twenty-five years before. When Stafford-Clark's production of *The Recruiting Officer* opened in June 1988, the reviews record that the play began in a bolder way than might be expected for eighteenth-century comedy. Jim Broadbent, playing Kite (and soon to play Harry Brewer playing Kite), began while house lights were still up, delivering his recruiting speech to the audience and tossing roses to them: the play's martial and marital images landing in the audience's lap.[39] This wasn't a gorgeous picture frame version of *The Recruiting Officer*, with Broadbent's stringy, plastered-down hair and harangue of the audience, and with Peter Hartwell's 'featureless tuppence-coloured' set providing only a parish pump and 'paintings of old Shrewsbury on a cyc'.[40] Gaskill's production had won attention for being inspired by Brecht's staging, but in 1988 it was as if Farquhar were being staged as a Caryl Churchill play, the more grumpy reviews suggested. Jim Hiley enjoyed how the approach replaced 'sputtering wit and over-rehearsed conceits' with a cast able to convey 'feelings, crisply voiced' and 'subtle, absorbing' characterisations, while complaining good-naturedly about the patchwork of accents presented.[41] The cast was doubled in roles in a way that the *Daily Mail* hated and *Time Out* mocked, including having Linda Bassett, who played Melinda (and soon Liz Morden playing Melinda) cross-dressed to be Thomas Appletree.[42] Still, the overall intellectual reaction to *The Recruiting Officer* found the show to be vivifying: the 'sharpness and force' of the piece won praise and the 'troubling and intriguing' aspects of Farquhar's social critique hit home.[43]

If these critics had known what was to come in *Our Country's Good*, what might they have understood about the choices in *The Recruiting Officer*? *Our Country's Good* also has an aggressive opening, accomplished not with direct address, but by showing a contorted human body being punished. The show opens with Robert Sideway being whipped: if this is staged vividly at all, it requires a bloody-backed actor in torment for at least seven counts of the lash.[44] When he is untied, he is left in a crumpled mound on the ground, a stark embodiment of the other convicts' fragmented descriptions of life in the hold of the transport ship. Meanwhile, characters in *Our Country's Good* speak in Devonshire, Irish, Scots, Madagascan and lower- and upper-class London dialects, plus a decision is required about how the aborigine will sound. Since the actors were incubating one show as the other opened, it is no wonder that the dialects in *Recruiting Officer* ranged a bit freely. By the time both shows were up, for instance, Mark Lambert, because he played both Robbie Ross and Ketch Freeman, had to be able to move between Scots and Irish during *Our Country's Good* alone, and then turn around and play Judge Balance, the role Laurence Olivier had seemingly perfected for Gaskill in 1963! Meanwhile, the doubling of roles in *Our Country's Good* suggests ways of reading the doubling in the Farquhar as a matter of meaning-making as well as economy. In Wertenbaker's play, the doubling foregrounds the status hierarchies in the officers' ranks and among the prisoners, it highlights patterns or disjunctions in alliances and conflicts, and embodies the play's central idea that humans become the social roles they are allowed or forced to play. These same ideas applied to *The Recruiting Officer* must have helped the production's sense of edge.

Looking at the two productions, with their shared cast, Michael Billington felt they made a compelling case about 'what could be achieved if the Royal Court could afford a permanent ensemble'.[45] This sense of the plays together calling out to what might still yet be achieved by British theatre at the same time as they nod to the best of the British theatre tradition, classical and contemporary, pervades the reviews for *Our Country's Good*. Notably, the critical praise of both Farquhar and Wertenbaker's plays lauded the way the lively productions *augmented* the social critique to be found in both texts: part of the joyous reception for both plays came from the way they challenged easy ideas about honour, truth and justice. 'It is worth seeing both plays: the effect is exhilarating, like being party to a private correspondence,' wrote Kate Kellaway in the *Observer*. 'This is not as self-indulgent as it sounds, for *Our Country's Good* is about theatre's power to spill over into life and overtake circumstance.'[46] It was ideologically important that there was dialogue within the plays and dialogue between the plays. For *Our Country's Good*, the staging of debates in order to open up social issues forms the key structural strategy that secures this inter-play.

Debate scenes, in fact, form the backbone of the play, around which explode the other highly theatrical scenes of whipping, visitations by the dead, late-night confessions, seductions, couplings, fist-fights between women convicts and preparations for executions. In *Our Country's Good* the most memorable intimate scenes come when Ketch Freeman measures Liz Morden for hanging, when Duckling mourns over Harry Brewer's recently dead body, and when Ralph and a cross-dressed Mary Brenham practising her role in the play take off their uniforms for each other. What actor or director could resist these scenes? Yet their impact derives in part from momentum earned by the beautifully structured, extremely funny and intelligent debate scenes where the play's plot weaves and surges. Debate begins on a small scale in Act One, during scene three, which is titled 'Punishment'. In addition to launching the debate about rehabilitation and condemnation, the scene provides a near perfect example of Brechtian *gestus*, as the officers debate how to best to maintain order for the 'good of the colony' while they shoot birds for sport. The recreational shooting juxtaposed against the idea of hanging convicts for stealing provisions demonstrates the officer's prerogative and critiques their blindness eloquently. Three scenes later this small debate results in a large-scale debate among the assembled officers of the colony. Scene six is where 'The Authorities Discuss the Merits of the Theatre'. All ten of the actors used in the show are on stage at the same time in this scene and its overlapping, jovial, multi-focal beginning gives way to a sharply focused showdown between Major Ross and Ralph. On the way there, Wertenbaker scripts an elegant intervention for every officer character that puts another viewpoint into play, motivates actions and reactions, and builds suspense about what will happen with the play-within-the-play. Wertenbaker's skill with multi-focused, large group scenes allows for the subtle development of ideas and the exhilarating construction of dramatic tension.

Matching the scene of authorities debating is a scene that shows what happens when the convicts debate. Scene eleven, 'The First Rehearsal', also requires all ten actors, though it is not initially clear that it is a debate scene. But the scene allows the convicts to trade ideas instead of blows, an important step. Like Act One, Act Two also stages a small debate between two people (scene two, 'His Excellency Exhorts Ralph'), a scene of debate among the convicts (scene seven, 'The Meaning of Plays'), and a debate among the authorities (scene ten, 'The Question of Liz'). Act Two, scene ten provides a crucial turning point in the play: it is the place where debate, silence and monologue collide. Liz Morden's silence in this scene – she refuses to speak about the attempted escape she is accused of conspiring in – provokes the debate among the officers about whether to cancel the play. Her choice to speak at the end of the scene demonstrates the necessary effects of the debate. Liz is persuaded by Phillip's argument that 'you cannot get to the truth through silence', and she chooses to speak (p. 268).

It is not that Liz is incapable of speech, as revealed by the show-stopping top of Act Two monologue Wertenbaker created for her in canting talk of the period. Like Mary's speech with Mr Hardlong, and Niobe's meditation on her conquered homeland during Tereus's rape of Philomele in *Love of the Nightingale*, Liz's underworld aria demonstrates Wertenbaker's affection for the monologue as a set piece. 'I like monologues,' Wertenbaker told Ned Chaillet. 'I think they are an unused and rather beautiful form of communication.'[47] Liz's monologue and her famous eloquent final line in 'The Question of Liz' both turn on the issue of speaking when it matters (p. 271). Indeed, both instances in the play where convicts speak back to power, as it were, occur in the midst of debate scenes. Liz's statement, after a long silence, that she 'didn't steal the food' breaks the silence that overtakes the convicts five scenes before, when the brave way the convicts began to speak their lines from the play, rehearsing a scene to deflect Ross's abuse of Sideway, Dabby and Mary, triggers an even more brutal punishment for Arscott (pp. 271, 251–3).

Importantly, the actress who played Liz Morden in the premiere of *Our Country's Good* contributed to the final decision about how the trajectory of 'The Question of Liz' resolved. Linda Bassett, an incredibly versatile actress who had appeared in Wertenbaker's *Abel's Sister* in 1984 and acted in numerous Royal Court and Joint Stock productions, including *Serious Money* just before *Our Country's Good*, is now also well known for many television and film roles, including parts in *East is East* (1999), *The Hours* (2002), *Calendar Girls* (2003) and *The Reader* (2008). Bassett becomes the centre of gravity when she is on stage: her serious face and her light energy yet resolute choices ground the roles she plays. Wertenbaker describes how during the rehearsal process Bassett and Broadbent had improvised a scene 'about whether Lizzie would decide to talk or not'. Then, one night, Bassett made a midnight call to Wertenbaker. 'I was about to talk,' she said, and Wertenbaker took counsel from that instinct.[48] Bassett's stature as an artist and authoritative contribution to the process are reflective of the overall make-up of the cast, which contained not only Bassett and Broadbent, but also Stafford-Clark and Wertenbaker repeat collaborators like Lesley Sharp, Ron Cook, Nick Dunning and David Haig, who won an Olivier for his portrayal of Ralph Clark.

Among this cast stood Alphonsia Emmanuel, another rising star like Janet McTeer. Emmanuel is a Dominican-born actress of colour. In 1984 she had been in the RSC's production of Pam Gems's *Camille* and in 1985 she appeared with Kenneth Branagh and Josette Simon in an RSC *Love's Labour's Lost*. Casting Emmanuel as Duckling Smith, the 'she-lag' kept by midshipman Harry Brewer, capitalised on an emerging acting talent and foregrounded questions of race, without direct dialogue necessitating it. Emmanuel's presence thereby worked alongside and beyond the presence of the aborigine character and the Madagascan character 'Black' Caesar, both played by African-born actor Jude Akuwudike (who had just graduated from RADA in 1987 and who like Emmanuel has gone on to an active career on London stages as well as in film and television). Emmanuel and Akuwudike's double-casting as officers within *Our Country's Good* provides further resonance. Emmanuel playing George Johnston voiced the insight that most of the convict women had only committed small crimes, while Akuwudike, as Watkin Tench, expressed the most vitriol about the 'savage' inhabitants of New South Wales. Meanwhile, Emmanuel was playing Lucy, the lady's maid in *The Recruiting Officer*, her race giving special punch to Duckling's line 'I'm not playing Liz Morden's maid' (p. 227), and Akuwudike was playing Scruple and Justice Balance's servant. Thus, this colour-conscious casting which successfully foregrounded certain issues was also a double-edged sword that still delivered actors of colour to servant roles in classic pieces.

Tracing the actors in *Our Country's Good* also points up what happened to the play as the show was toured, revived and transferred to the West End. Broadbent, Bassett, Emmanuel, Haig and Sharp, who played Mary Brenham, left the show before its revival at the Royal Court in August and September 1989. This turnover is natural given the rhythms of an acting career. But as these actors were replaced, the cast, especially in the case of the women, got younger and then prettier. Clive Russell replaced Jim Broadbent. Suzanne Packer replaced Alphonsia Emmanuel, maintaining the presence of an actress of colour in Duckling's role. Julian Wadham stepped into Haig's boots to play Ralph. Initially Kathryn Hunter replaced Bassett as Liz Morden, a move that capitalised on Hunter's unique sense of contained violence. But by the time the show had transferred to the Garrick, Caitlin Clarke replaced Hunter. The production photos featuring Clarke as Liz Morden and Amanda Redman as Mary Brenham, for instance, convey a more conventionally sexy take on these two characters than in photos featuring Sharp and Bassett, whose brisk sensuality emerged from bold and direct action, rather than from cleavage.[49] As with its engagement with issues of race, colonialism and class, *Our Country's Good* activated a discussion of gender that was ideologically complex: even as the play critiqued dominant systems, it still moved in those systems' significations of power.

Our Country's Good affirms ideas about love and liberty even while struggling with how economic and discursive systems seem to necessitate injustice. This paradoxical combination forms the play's strength and its ongoing appeal. An unresolved, yet satisfying, movement between interrogation and affirmation in a piece of theatre serves feminist, humanist and post-colonial goals while speaking directly to postmodern audiences. In the scene titled 'John Wisehammer and Mary Brenham Exchange Words', Wertenbaker never lays out a word without giving it a complex match: there's friend and country followed by abjection and injustice; boldness and shame meet each other; lonely and loveless contend with luck and latitudinarian. Pairing these words together, the play finds language, as it has found stories, which can hold hope and condemnation at the same time.

Love of the Nightingale

Because Wertenbaker's plays unfold with a sensuality in language – it is never clearer than in the major plays of the 1980s how much she, like Wisehammer, loves words – they also insist on the sensuality of the body. Pointedly, all three of the plays discussed here pause to ponder the anatomy and linguistics of the cunt to potent effect. *Our Country's Good* famously opens with a monologue invoking the experience of the convict ship hold where Wisehammer inquires 'at night what is there to do but seek English cunt, warm, moist, soft, oh the comfort, the crannies of the crooks of England' linking cunt to countryside and homeland (p. 185). In *The Grace of Mary Traverse*, Mary insists that, just like men, part of what she pays Sophie for is pleasure. While Sophie goes under her skirt and brings her to her second orgasm on stage, Mary's monologue challenges men not to feel disgust and denies that her vividly described recesses represent a void (p. 106). In *Love of the Nightingale*, Philomele suffers violation that invades both her language and her female anatomy. After Tereus rapes Philomele, Niobe washes her face and genitals and the dialogue between them conjures Philomele's wild words against Tereus that will result in her losing her tongue.[50] The play works from the Ovidian version of the Greek mythic tale about the Athenian princesses Philomele and Procne. Procne, the elder, is married to Theban king Tereus and she asks him to bring her sister to visit her in Thebes. He transports her to Thebes, but never delivers her to Procne, cutting out her tongue to keep her silent after the rape. Later, when Procne and Philomele reunite, they revenge themselves by killing Procne and Tereus's son, Itys. Then, to end the cycle of revenge, all three are turned into birds.

Prior to that scene of washing, in counterpoint to Philomele's screams and eventual, enforced silence, Niobe delivers a gorgeous, aching monologue where she remembers the lemon trees of her childhood home, an island conquered by the Athenians. Jenni George, the actress playing Niobe, stole the show, according to Catherine Wearing's review in *What's On in London*, with that monologue of 'excruciating exactness, tact, and brilliance'.[51] That George is a 'mountainous black woman' adds another layer to this description of colonisation and drives home the male chorus's contention that the play is not a 'myth for our times' about men and women, but rather that 'if you think of anything, think of countries, silence' (p. 315).[52] George's blackness also casts in relief the increasingly anachronistic promptings of the female chorus in the play's penultimate scene, including 'why do white people cut off the words of blacks?' (p. 349). George's presence in the cast, along with that of Claudette Williams playing Iris, Tony Armatrading as the Captain and Patrick Miller in the male chorus again presents a colour-conscious signification that expresses the ideological complexity of the play's project.

Still, when *Love of the Nightingale* opened in Stratford, in many reviews its content took second place to its status as the last play in the Other Place before it closed. Many opening-night critics paused to consider the legacy of the Other Place, to remember Buzz Goodbody, and to ponder the RSC's limping new plays policy. When Jane Edwardes wrote in her review in *Time Out* that the play was a 'fitting' finale to the Other Place, she was invoking the space's associations with experimental theatre, with women's work, with agitational content.[53] *Love of the Nightingale* did exemplify those concerns, so it celebrated the goals of the Other Place. However, logistics also couched those characteristics within the RSC's remit as a huge institution dedicated to classical work. As with *Our Country's Good* and *The Recruiting Officer*, it is important to note how *Love of the Nightingale* was enmeshed in the RSC's production schedule. When the play opened in Stratford, it was up against *The Plantagenets*, the nine-hour cycle by Adrian Noble conflating the *Henry VI* plays with *Richard III* playing on the RSC mainstage. This made quite a contrast with *Nightingale's* ninety-minute, intermission-less running time. Concurrently, Cicely Berry was rehearsing a *King Lear* project slated to open in 1989 that used a significant number of *Nightingale's* actors – out of the sixteen in Wertenbaker's show, eight were simultaneously investigating and developing *King Lear*. Thus, Richard Haddon Haines channelled King Pandion while also playing King Lear; Joan Blackham as June and Jill Spurrier as Helen in the female chorus also took on Goneril and Regan; Peter Lennon played Tereus while rehearsing for Albany; and David Acton, Patrick Miller, Edward Rawle Hicks and Stephen Gordon were in the male chorus while preparing to play Cornwall, the Fool, Oswald/France and Old Man/Doctor respectively.[54] A subterranean intertextual conversation with *King Lear* cradled *Love of the Nightingale's* production.[55]

Indeed, between *Nightingale's* Other Place production in Stratford and its opening in London in 1989, nine months later, three of the actors involved with *King Lear* had left the cast and the event had been 'rethought and restaged'.[56] In Stratford, the production used classically inspired costumes and, apparently, a lot of dry ice to create effects.[57] Hynes's original staging, with choreography by Ian Spink, included 'music, masks and mimed movement' and was found to be both 'engrossing' and 'imaginative' but also 'halting and rather precious'.[58] By the time the show was remounted in London, no choreographer is credited although there is a credit for fights, and Iona McLeish had replaced Ashley Martin-Davis for 'décor'.[59] Under McLeish, what had been a classically clothed classical adaptation became a show in modern dress set on an ancient-looking set that recast classical adaptation as a type of cultural archaeology not unlike the actual archaeology surprising theatre historians in 1989 with the discovery of the remains of the Rose and the foundations of the

Globe. Wrote Charles Spencer, 'Iona McLeish's set features the ancient stones and damaged mosaics of an archaeological site, pierced by a modern steel girder. Miss McLeish might merely be suggesting that the play's themes are timeless, but I suspect that she is also making her own silent protest about the probable fate of the Rose Theatre.'[60]

Though Rhoda Koenig eviscerated the London production in *Punch*, calling it an example of a clichéd and outdated genre that should be named 'A Lot of Mythical People Running Around Screaming', the rest of the reviews of this remounted production reflect a level of contested intellectual and emotional engagement that directly channels the tension between the ancient and the contemporary, the spare and the poetical, the violent and the philosophical that define the play's text, and its 'rethought' visual and conceptual presentation.[61] Like *Miss Saigon* and Declan Donnellan's production of *Fuente Ovejuna*, which both also opened in 1989, *Love of the Nightingale* asked for a new consideration of political and sexual oppression in vividly theatrical terms.[62]

The intense theatricality of *Love of the Nightingale* proceeds not only from its meta-theatrical sequences, but also from its bold juxtapositions and its Ovidian imagery. The play-within-a-play in *Love of the Nightingale* works in a different manner to the one in *Our Country's Good* because it is performed rather than rehearsed during the course of the exterior play.[63] During the Hippolytus play, the emphasis rests on the group discussion and the revelations about individuals for the audience watching the show, while Wertenbaker's reworking of the Hippolytus/Phaedra myth develops as a foreshadowing of what will happen between Tereus and Philomele.[64] Despite the meta-commentary it offers, the Hippolytus play is not the most meta-theatrical element of *Nightingale*'s action. Philomele's re-enactment of her rape and disfigurement by Tereus with life-size dolls during the Bacchanal walks an even more dangerous line in the play, showing a moment where theatre is the means of telling the truth about actual events, a way of witnessing for justice. The play's final transformation, when Philomele, Procne and Tereus turn into birds, also offers the opportunity, depending on staging, to become a final meta-theatrical wonder, one that could be accomplished through movement alone, but which seems to have been accompanied by actual bird costumes in the Stratford premiere.[65]

The bird transformation functions as one of the script's most stark juxtapositions as the play smashes from a scene of confrontation into choral narration into a seemingly impossible transformation. Elsewhere in the script, similar brusque movements between choral narration or debate and scenes of intimacy or personal confrontation form the play's rhythm and produce laminations of moments, as when the play moves directly from Tereus kissing the now-tongueless Philomele at the end of scene sixteen to scene seventeen's meditation on mourning and desire where Procne tries to get Tereus to kiss her (pp. 338–41). The imagery of the play, meanwhile, evokes strong sensory experiences, centring on animals (tigers, serpents, dogs) and natural phenomena like water, phosphorescence and earthquakes. The birds that materialise at the end of the play fulfil an image from scene four, where Echo speaks of the 'beating of wings', after the chorus warns Procne not to ask Philomele to come to Thrace (p. 300). The sound of the birds' wings that Echo evokes haunt the play until the birds appear and play out the final scene, where Itys poses unanswerable questions to them. Questions have been thematised throughout the play as well, as when Philomele's conversation with Tereus fails because he does not allow her to ask questions, or when questions are described as being 'like earthquakes'. 'I wouldn't want to live in a world that's always shifting,' says the Male Chorus, forming an image that captures the chthonian force and political implications of questions. When Philomele-the-nightingale finds it impossible to completely define right and wrong in the final scene, Itys still presses on: 'Didn't you want me to ask questions?' he says (p. 354). Wertenbaker's plays press on: you cannot get to the truth through silence, and you cannot find justice without questions.

An assessment: interrogative affirmation

Once *Love of the Nightingale* opened in London, Paul Arnott wrote that Wertenbaker joined 'the band of playwrights' who have had two productions playing in London at the same time. This convergence of her work helped spur critical interest in her, but the first range of scholarly assessments of her work struggled with how to position theatre that probed such crucial questions but which didn't seek to shatter traditional modes of representation and often affirmed more about European culture, literature and history than expected. Wertenbaker's intelligent and dignified work carried deeply provocative insight, but it didn't emerge from a radical aesthetic or politics. By 1999, Keith Peacock wrote in *Thatcher's Theatre* that,

> in critical terms, Wertenbaker proved to be the most significant new dramatist of the 1980s. Her work, with its liberal humanistic viewpoint, suited the tenor of the times. Although it could not be considered oppositional, it raised moral concerns regarding education, justice and the treatment of women in patriarchal society, in a manner that provoked sympathy but did not fundamentally threaten or provoke its audience.[66]

Apparently, being the most significant new dramatist of the 1980s is not as simple a piece of praise as it might seem! Like Ann Wilson's reading of 'theatre, colony, and nation' in *Our Country's Good* which cannot quite resolve whether Wertenbaker improved the regressive politics in Keneally's source-text or reinscribed worse narratives, Peacock's conclusion contains a compliment but continues with apprehension. His commentary nags with a worry about the popular and the cutting edge, as opposed to the institutional and already culturally legible. And in the theoretical discourse of the 1980s and 1990s humanism could be a dirty word, prior to its reclamation after rereadings of Edward Said's oeuvre in the wake of his 2003 preface to a republication of Eric Auerbach's *Mimesis* emphasising his unwillingness to relinquish the humanist tradition.[67]

Wertenbaker contended in her interview with DiGaetani that 'you have to accept that as a playwright, you have a certain moment, and then you go out of fashion, and then you come back into fashion' (p. 268). The key dynamic of Wertenbaker's work rests in its interweaving of interrogation and affirmation, a combination that leads to an emphasis on debate and questioning, and encodes the belief that great value lies in the search for justice. The interrogative aspect of her work, and the focus it brings to moral issues, is the strength of Wertenbaker's work. Geraldine Cousin developed a sophisticated reading of *Love of the Nightingale* as an 'interrogative play' in *Women in Dramatic Place and Time*, for instance, and Ann Wilson lauded this questioning drive in Wertenbaker's work from *Our Country's Good* to *Dianeira* almost fifteen years later.[68] The affirmative aspect of Wertenbaker's work, however, paradoxically, can unsettle analysts of her work. Here the impact of DiGaetani's title finds its mark. His volume is called *A Search for a Postmodern Theatre*, and his interview with Wertenbaker seems ghosted by a larger overall question about her work in the 1980s and beyond: is Wertenbaker a postmodern writer? Can she be, if her plays stay within a verbal signifying tradition and there is a humanism at the core of her philosophy, even if feminist and post-colonial insights recognisably influence it? The interrogative fits a postmodern paradigm and aesthetic. But affirming the worth of culture and its institutions and affirming community as a human bailiwick is more difficult to characterise as a function for postmodern theatre.

Yet, across the 1980s, reviewers writing for newspapers develop a vocabulary about postmodern aesthetics that reveals the potential for affirmation to fit into an understanding of postmodernism in British theatre in the 1980s. In 1985, for instance, Milton Shulman wrote about *Mary Traverse* as a type of 'fable', a word that could sound dismissive (and Nicholas de Jongh uses it this way in his commentary on *Love of the Nightingale* in 1989). But fable also conjures associations with Brecht's theorisation of *die fable* structuring a play and invites comparisons with his evolution of 'parable' plays. When *Our Country's Good* opened, Michael Billington praised it for both this 'parabolic' aspect and for its 'bracing optimism': 'It makes for a wonderful evening's theatre,' he wrote, 'a Brechtian parable with an optimistic conclusion.'[69] This chimes with reconsiderations of Brechtian dramaturgy in the light of postmodernity, like Elizabeth Wright's 1989 volume *Postmodern Brecht: A Re-Presentation*.[70] As *Love of the Nightingale* opened, the word pastiche, so central to a description of postmodern aesthetic strategies, got applied to Wertenbaker's work, with both positive and negative overtones.[71] Billington, for one, embraced this about *Nightingale*'s structure: 'what is intriguing about the play is that it belongs to the newly-popular genre of narrative drama: heavily influenced by Peter Brook [. . .]. Intellectually I was reminded of Pinter: stylistically, of *The Conference of the Birds* in that I felt I was being confronted by an ancient myth and then allowed to unravel its meaning.'[72] Wertenbaker's reworking and reconfiguration of forms is here being recognised for the way it can de-centre and disturb audiences while providing discovery and optimism.

As Wertenbaker's oeuvre has increased after the 1980s and theo-retical vocabularies have continued to shift, it is possible to see in her work a type of Saidian humanism that depends on being able to move between an inside view of culture to an outside view of culture.[73] The cross-cultural and translational aspects of Wertenbaker's work, discussed in the most recent phases of scholarship about her, manifest in the plays of the 1980s no less than the plays of the 1990s and beyond. *The Grace of Mary Traverse*, *Our Country's Good* and *Love of the Nightingale* are dynamic cultural objects that embody and bridge the theatre trends of the 1980s through interrogative affirmation. Approached as historical artefacts of Britain in the 1980s, they reveal a great deal about the culture from inside. As they are still staged today, they provide ongoing movements that allow views from outside in and inside out. Between these poles, the debates and questions continue.

CHAPTER 4
DOCUMENTS

Howard Barker

Written interview, Howard Barker with Jane Milling, September 2011.

The 1980s saw a shift in the setting of your work – the environments you summoned for audiences – the final scene of Claw *seems pivotal, as you reflect in* Arguments for a Theatre, *both in terms of 'political meaning' but also in terms of transcending a realist* mise en scène. *I'm thinking also of some of the landscapes of your paintings. How do the places of your plays emerge? Are they primarily theatrical for you? Could you talk a little about the translation between the imaginative spaces and landscapes of the text for you as writer, and the realised actuality for you as a director?*

For one thing, I shrink from the domestic in my theatre, in any form. Consequently, there aren't many rooms, nor many families. Interiors, where I identify them, might be castles, naves, exploded sites of all descriptions, hospital wards, decayed nursing homes. These sites aren't arbitrary. The rotting library in *Found in the Ground* speaks for itself. *Blok/Eko* has mortally ill patients lying in the snow. These sites immediately communicate to the public it is privileged to be outside the familiar and decadent moral space of nearly all theatre. In my most recent work, the first image is of a child flinging itself into a bottomless well. These sound difficult to stage. In fact, they are not, they simply demand the imaginative equivalence in the director that I provide in the text. Now, from the staging point of view, my whole life in theatre has been conditioned by austerity, but I have made a style from that, and some of these productions, with few resources, have been characterised by a sense of concentrated beauty – partly through carefully chosen props, much in the costume, above all, perhaps, in the speech and bodily fluency of my actors (one could mention *Gertrude – The Cry* and *The Fence in its Thousandth Year . . .*) I 'set' my plays in particular places, but without a 'set'. I have a deep loathing for grand settings, especially if they purport to be like paintings. It's worthless seduction.

During the 1980s, were there other theatre makers whose work you saw and admired? I wonder if you felt there were kindred spirits within north European performance traditions?

There were a few. Silviu Purcarete, who did not direct my work, and Klaus Hoffmeyer, who did.[1]

Your work is extremely visceral in the images it employs in its language and in its demands on the performer. You have talked in Arguments for a Theatre, Death, the One and the Art of Theatre, *as well as* A Style and Its Origins, *about the importance of the performer as idea and as embodiment, to the realisation of your work. But I wondered to what extent particular bodies exert a pressure on your writing, as you write? Could one write for any-'body'?*

I don't write for, or direct for, the 'naturalistic body', and it is a reason why I am a demanding director. Of course, I don't write for the naturalistic voice either. Physically, I seek significant moments in which the body's gestures lend support to the character's emotional condition. Most of these gestures arise from the cultural history of this society, it stands to reason. And I try to avoid clichés. Nevertheless, there is a repertoire to call upon, and to take just one example, how an actor might pose himself whilst another issues a torrent of abuse becomes a subject of study for me. I expect actors to possess the same mysterious creative fluency with their limbs as a many-stringed puppet has in the hands of a master. Having said this, it's obvious I cannot write for 'anybody' but look always for that unity of voice and gesture that defines great acting for me. I have been privileged to work with half a dozen such people.

Looking back at writing in the 1980s, you have talked drily about the control of the 'dramaturgy' and 'the theatre'. It seemed that regional theatres, often dismissed as 'provincial' and financially cautious, were more open to challenging work, as you suggest in A Style. *I wonder whether you have found that regional theatres have escaped the 'dramaturgy' to an extent?*

I am not sure that there is a discernible distinction to be made between regional and metropolitan theatres, except perhaps in the former's relative immunity from the critical police (few of whom can travel far, it seems), and – possibly – the less fashion-conscious character of the audiences. But the political nature of dramaturgy doesn't leave many corners unturned. This is a universal system, and where unsupervised acts occur, they are perhaps best unadvertised.

You talk in A Style *about the string quartet as a formal inspiration in* Wounds to the Face, *and by contrast I think of the austerity of* Slowly. *Could you talk a little about how structure operates in your writing?*

I think I am not disingenuous in stating I have no active, intellectual sense of structure, but I nevertheless structure plays well, and sometimes immaculately. This is innate, and it can't be taught, it is an instinct, just as draughtsmanship in painting comes purely from the eye's restless working on the surface, and its satisfactions are immediate, just as when it is offended by misplaced things, the offence is immediate also. I have said how much I grieve over the shape of theatre, and how I long to alter narrative forms, and so on. I am also a passionate believer in style. A lot of this has come down to the fact that I crowd the work, unintentionally mostly, certain as I am that theatre's weakness is that it is simply not ambitious enough, it is too modest, it is, like an unhappy infant, too concerned to please, gratify and reward. That is certainly not tragedy's business.

There is a great deal of wit in your work, and often the language of the powerful provokes audience laughter. What role does laughter play in the evolution of your tragedy?

It's self-evident that laughter is complicated, and its origins various. In saying 'the language of the powerful' you identify something curious and morally stimulating. Like the mad (who I do not write about), the powerful have supreme entitlement. In a society as constrained by moral earnestness, conscience and hypocrisy, as this one is, illicit thinking creates a shock that the audience resolves by laughing. The fact is, however, the character *means* it, and that is a transformative moment for the audience, because it finds itself in the company of people who do not think as they do – or – here is the supreme *anxiety* I seek – admit to speech what they cannot dare to do.

Thinking about the range of new productions and revivals of your work over the last ten years, are there benefits, or only frustrations, in seeing your work interpreted by different directors?

I have never wanted to protect my work from directors. On rare occasions, they have surpassed my best hopes. I did want to give my plays my own interpretation in the first instance, however. This was the greatest treasure of the Wrestling School. It cared for no man's opinion. The greatest frustration in seeing these texts given by others is this – they are civilised by individuals with their own political agenda, people who think theatre is enlightening. Tragedy is not, and never can be, enlightening. Those few who understand this sadly rush into the arms of a worse nightmare – they make everything brutal and coarse. I have seen some awful *Gertrudes*. Gertrude is a character of infinite delicacy and passion. I can't direct everything.

You wryly note your delivery 'from the dramaturgs to the accountants' with the founding of the Wrestling School. You reflect on the unsettled relationship between the artist, state and patronage in many of your works, not least your most recent Blok/Eko. *What significance has the Arts Council – with all its vagaries – had for your theatre?*

Someone must pay for art, if society wants art. For myself, I don't care who that is. The Soviet-style agenda of the Arts Council is nauseating, but the politics is inevitable, the aesthetics also, in populist democracies like this which hold imagination itself in profound distrust, if not dread. In recent years, a single benefactor has provided the wherewithal. This has expired. We need not rehearse questions about the obligations of national theatres to present the best writing in English . . . in any case, what I said above applies . . . they would not know *how* to approach directing tragedy of this degree of intensity.

You are working on two linked plays on plethora and dearth. I wonder if you are finding experimenting with the idea of a dearth of words is producing a different writing process?

I opted for a single word. This had the effect of making the word – in many different mouths – lose its identity, and whilst it is a word with conventional associations, these begin to degenerate. I was doing with the solitary word what I do with all my tragedies, to de-civilise the word, and the feelings attached to it, because if I am certain of one thing, it is that the law of decay is the first law of existence (and moral existence) just as coercion is the second. The actions surrounding this word become appalling comments on it . . . in the deafening racket of the moral discourse of our day, you smell these words decaying, if you have a decent sense of smell. But it's like escaping gas; someone always smells it first. Some never smell it at all.

Jim Cartwright

Jim Cartwright rarely gives interviews. These quotations are drawn from the few significant interviews he has given over the years.

Interviewed by Benedict Nightingale in 1988, on the US opening of Road, *Cartwright reflects on the working-class environment in which he grew up, and on the creation of* Road:[2]

And on the very edge of town, almost sliding off, there's always one street where all the losers and roughs and ne'er-do-wells seem to end up. It might be in Liverpool or Bolton or Middlesbrough or Newcastle, but it's the last stop, the bottom. There's no further to fall. [. . .]

In the middle or upper classes, you're taught to think of different possibilities. If you want to be a brain surgeon, well, it's feasible. But the highest aim of most people I knew was to become a plumber or an electrician or an engineer in a factory. In a working-class environment creativity is not really expected or encouraged. I always thought it was clever people, upper-class people who wrote. [. . .]

Even within the working class there seem to be new divisions, whether you've got a job or haven't got a job, and what sort of job you have. We've lost the unity we had in the '30s and the feeling we had even in the '70s – that things could get better. Now it seems like there's dark at the end of the tunnel. It's sink or swim, and to hell with your neighbour, and grab all the material possessions you can. [. . .]

And it's the age of the square. The guy at school we used to laugh at for being a wimp is running the country. The stiffs and straights are taking revenge on the hips, the mystics, the fun-lovers and the sexy people. They're trying to put everybody in suits and ties and order everything. It can't go on, because I don't think people are really happy when they're strapped in, even if the straps are made of furs and diamonds. The grass always forces its way through the paving stones, the sun always comes through the fog. I'm not sure that all these thoughts are obviously in the play, but they're somewhere there rumbling about a bit.

When The Rise and Fall of Little Voice *opened in the West End in 1992, Cartwright reflected on writing and success in an interview with David Nathan:*[3]

On The Rise and Fall of Little Voice:
You can't write and think about the financial future of the play. You just make a work of art and that's the way this one came out.
On his background:
Where does this thing come from, this feeling to do art or writing? My father worked in a factory all his life; my mother read a lot – about

six thrillers a week. I went to a secondary modern, a low academic achievement school, a kind of direct conveyor belt to the factory or, for the girls, the mills. If you were lucky you got a trade, as an engineer or an electrician.

But the mid-1970s were a good time to be at school. There were a few teachers there who'd come from the 1960s and would encourage us, tell us we could do other things and there was the feeling, 'Yeah, I can go out there and change the world.' What angered me a bit – and actually I'm still angry about it – is that I look at the writing I did at school and it's not all that different from what I do now. But they recognise it if you're good at sport, you're instantly spotted if you're good at science or maths and even acting is possible. But writing is the kind of thing only clever people do. You have to go to university and know how to spell. I used to write poems; writing was something that was always just floating there. But you find you're going against the stream: you have to have a lot of strength to push through.

About his writing process:

I don't think about the process too much because I just like to let it happen. I'm not very well read, but in some ways it has been an advantage: I don't know about full stops properly, and I can't spell properly, and I don't know how something should be done. So I can just create fresh. It leaves me free and I like that.

I'm not saying formal education is a bad thing, I sometimes wish I could have done English at university. I'm just discovering writers, just started to read Dickens and he's brilliant. Where I come from you hear people say Shakespeare is boring and you think, how can you say that?

When I was a kid, my dad used to say: 'Whatever you want, you can do it. I haven't got any money, but I'll help you anyway I can.' My mum felt the same, but she was a bit anxious when I talked about becoming a writer. She wanted me to get a trade. Without a trade you'd be a labourer all your life, nipping from warehouse to factory. They used to say, 'You'll end up on the buses.' Not any more. All those jobs are like gold now.

In 2008, Cartwright published his first novel Supermarket Supermodel, *a moral romp that follows a young girl on her journey from checkout to model, the inability to preserve authentic relationships in that rootless lifestyle, with a guest appearance by Joan Collins as spiritual guide. Cartwright gave an interview to Carmel Thomason:*[4]

On writing a novel:

It's a very different process but I really enjoyed it because, it's just you and the page. There are no limits on your imagination – you don't have to worry about budgets, or producers or directors or actors – you can go wherever and do whatever you want.

I also liked being able to spend time exploring things. A film has to move very quickly in pictures and similarly with a play, you have to be aware of the audience and keep the action moving. All the mediums are interesting in their own right but with a book you can spend time exploring and re-entering things, you stay with your characters longer as well and can delve deeper into their background. [. . .]

On being identified as a northern writer:

My work is not always northern. I wrote a play called *Bed*, which is written for the more standard English voice. Also, sometimes it depends where the plays are produced as to how they are read. There was a really good production of *The Rise and Fall of Little Voice* in Glaswegian, which recently toured Scotland. [. . .]

On his writing process:

When I start something I don't so much think about what I'm going to do with it, I let it take me. This one took me to this fantastical area and it's almost fable-like in some ways. There is also a kind of hyper-reality and a comedy to it. She takes a very interesting journey, setting off in a supermarket and ending up going all around the world. She's rich and then poor – it's a bit of an epic journey. [. . .]

I try to do some everyday. I'm not like these people who you read about in the back of the *Sunday Times*, who say, I get up at 5.30 a.m., I have a glass of fresh orange juice, I jog for three miles, come back, walk the dog, write six chapters, make love to my wife, write another six chapters. I think, 'Oh my God – I'd be tearing my hair out.'

Sometimes it's like squeezing blood out of a stone with me. The thing is to just keep the tap dripping. Even if you just do a bit each day, keep the tap dripping and sometimes it'll come gushing and it's lovely. Some days it's just great and other days it's hard work, but you've got to show up every day and do a bit. Even if it's only a line, see how much comes. The hardest bit is always sitting down and starting.

How do you feel about people studying your work?

It's fabulous, especially when you come across a young person of sixteen telling you how much they like your work. I find it amazing that it's still relevant. That's really music to a writer's ears. To hear your work's relevant, it's great, we've had a fantastic time – you can't say more than that. I'm also lucky my work is still performed all over the world, consistently, which again is a bit of a surprise to me and something I didn't expect.

Sarah Daniels

Interviewed by Jane Milling, 20 October 2011.

Why do you start writing a play? What starts you on a play?

This is quite an easy answer *today*, the thing that starts me off is that I only write to commission, I've been very lucky. So the thing that starts me off is that I've signed a contract to do it. If you don't fulfil a contract, everybody talks to everybody else and goes, 'Oh that writer can't deliver.' You have to have the status of a genius to get away with not delivering.

You've said that some plays begin as one idea and change as you write, I'm thinking about The Devil's Gateway, *for example, which started with Greenham Common and transformed . . .*

The other thing is I can't remember what I said when, I'm sure when I said it I meant it, but you might find inconsistencies. I see my life divided up into the Chardonnay years, the Pinot Grigio years, when I've earned a bit more money there have been the Sancerre years – I've lost half my memory to white wine!

Now I mainly write for radio. When you write for Radio 4 you have to give a synopsis, give an outline for what you're proposing for the idea to be bought, so you can't stray too much, you can't turn it into a totally different play. For Radio 4, there's an afternoon play virtually every weekday of the year, so they can't suddenly have all the plays about the same subject, that's partly why they commission them. I did a play for Radio 4 quite a long time ago, which won an award, called *Cross my Heart and Hope to Fly*, which was a story about a woman who had survived breast cancer. But because they were doing a story in *The Archers* that year about one of the characters getting breast cancer, and the afternoon play comes straight after *The Archers*, they didn't want it that year, because they said people would be 'breast-cancered out' – they didn't say that I made that up – but that's what they meant.

Is that restricting? Does that alter the way you work?

I try to look at things positively. And that cliché, limitations can become strengths, is sometimes the best way to look at something. So, you're only allowed a certain number of actors because of financial constraints, but you try and look at that as a positive thing. For example, a play I did for Clean Break called *Head-Rot Holiday* could only have three actors in it. But I hope I turned that to an advantage in that each of those actors plays different sides of three very different people, so they all get a chance to play the person institutionalised, and a character who works in the institution, and one other one-off set piece. And that comes into one of your other questions. Yes, I would much rather have a company of actors and give them all meaty roles, than have someone walk on and have three lines.

You offer real gifts to actors, where they can have the audience in the palm of their hand. Do you know who is going to be performing your work as you are writing?

No, I never know that. I don't have actors in mind when I write. I think you only get disappointed if you were trying to write parts for Maggie Smith, so I just concentrate on story and the characters, as though they've got their own lives.

Do you write with actors?

I will tweak things in rehearsal, and if something isn't working, work on it – but I hardly ever do rewrites. I've never done any improvised work. The script is always there before you get to rehearsal. That is mainly because under that sort of pressure, there's a level of anxiety where I don't quite believe I can get the work done. Particularly in the radio studio, where you record a play in two days, if something isn't working I slightly panic if I'm expected to rejig or rewrite something within that time. When it is you and the blank screen, you can tell yourself you've got lots of time. One of the things about being a writer, you never know, unless you come up against other writers and their working process, exactly how slow you are. I know other people who can turn things around terribly quickly, and I think, 'Oh dear, they must be so much cleverer than I am.'

I've done a bit of television, and a bit of theatre and a bit of radio. In television and film, there is such a lot of money involved and people involved, that the writer's voice – where they are in the status of the production – is lower than in the theatre or indeed radio.

You know I used to write *Grange Hill*, and one of the writers on that was talking to me about a friend of his. This guy has written absolutely loads of television, *Brookside*, you name it. He wrote one radio play. He couldn't get over it because he went into the studio for the recording, which is part of the job, they said, 'There you are, here is your chair' and this had never ever happened to him before. It was all said in a light-hearted way. Although the writer is seen as a very important cog, you are sometimes forgotten in television. So much television is series and serials, so that you have to fit in with the machine, you can't necessarily have too much of an individual voice writing *EastEnders*.

You were writing on Grange Hill *for a long time, did you find you able to initiate or control stories because of the time you were with the production?*

It's difficult to say, because teams of people – writers, directors and producers – change, and different people work in different ways. I think it's accepting different things. Some people like original oil painting, but that doesn't mean to say that numbered screen prints are any less wonderful in their own way. I don't have a snobbery about television.

The only thing I ever heard somebody say was that you should never write for a programme that you wouldn't watch, and I thought that was such a good rule of thumb. And on that basis I could probably write for everything apart from sport and cookery programmes. If you think a certain programme is rubbish you shouldn't write for it. Otherwise people have to make a living.

And you're reaching such a large audience . . .

Yes, there are all sorts of very positive things about it.

How you find the difference between writing 'original' works, and working with adaptation?

The wonderful thing about adaptation is that by its very nature you never have to start with the blank screen. I think the key is to really like, love and admire the book and take as much pride in the work as one would in an original piece of work.

Could I lead you on to the tricky subject of politics? I think your work is very political, we don't see characters just as individuals, they are always embedded in other structures, including class structures to which they

draw attention, which show you how they got to where they are. Am I
reading too much into it?

Your question is about class, but most of my early stage work, I can't
think of any that isn't, is absolutely driven by a feminist agenda. And
to my detriment, I have forced characters to dance to my tune rather
than the other way around. I've got an agenda. I actually think that is
a major flaw in the writing – I'm not apologising for my politics, I'm
apologising of the quality of the writing. (*Laughter.*) I wish it had been
better.

But your characters are never idealised representations of feminism, they
are always much more complicated than that.

(*Sardonically*) Oh, thank you! (*Laughter.*)

I'm just thinking of Clare in Neaptide, *she's not without her flaws. For*
example, in that difficult relationship with her ex-husband, you can see
his point of view, but you end up on her side even though she is flawed.

But then to bolster my own argument, people say you should have
given her a relationship within it, but what I wanted to do was
different. At that time, my understanding was that there had only
been one woman in the country who had gained custody of her child
when her husband had challenged it because of her lesbian relationship. And the only reason she got it was that he had no address, he
was homeless. What I wanted to show was that you don't even need to
be in a relationship, this can happen to you, this has happened. So I
had a list of things that I wanted to show, the extreme of it. One of
the most fantastic things is how – that was 1986 – how things have
changed. Class is there as well, but it's really feminism.

And still drives your work?

Yes it does, although I sometimes laugh to myself, in some of my work
for Radio 4 you can see you I've got softer round the edges.

It's become more complicated.

Friends of mine are always saying to me, it's been so long since you wrote *Masterpieces* you should do a companion piece, the next step on. But I couldn't, I wouldn't know where to begin.

And working with students on Masterpieces *today, they still find it relevant to what young women are experiencing.*

As much as now nobody would take children away from lesbians, because they were lesbians, which is the positive side. I think pornography – it's worse than King Canute – the proliferation of it, the normalisation of it, the expectation of how young women are supposed to behave. I feel it's a battle lost completely. I was talking to Fiona Mackay, a sociologist, from Edinburgh University,[5] about how the whole emphasis is on looking hot, but there's a great big gap between looking hot and feeling hot. The proliferation of plastic surgery of breast enhancement, sometimes you are left without feeling, but that doesn't seem any sacrifice to make because you look hot.

You have written for different audiences and worked with Clean Break, and for Chicken Shed, for New Connections and for A.C.T. in the USA, particularly for young audiences. What draws you to write for these companies?

I was approached by Clean Break to be commissioned by them. I really wanted to do it, I'm very interested in women and mental health issues. And at that time Clean Break was a theatre group where the policy was that you employed a professional writer, director and designer, but that the actors were women who had been in prison or some sort of secure facility. That has changed over the years. I was really interested in the issues facing women in special hospitals, and there had been a big enquiry into Ashworth Hospital and abuse within in the hospital. It was something I passionately believed in. There are a lot of levels of injustice there.

A very good friend of mine works for Chicken Shed Theatre

Company, and they don't have Arts Council funding. And she was trying to get an Arts Council grant and asked me would I accept a commission, which I did. Again, because I was interested in these two young women, one of whom was in the play, Amy Golden, who had severe cerebral palsy. In fact, this connected with a play I did for Radio 4, *Humanly Possible*,[6] which fitted in alongside a series *Inside the Ethics Committee* – I have to say ethics in a pronounced way because I come from Essex, so when I've said it before people go, 'Oh that would be right up your street, writing about Essex.' (*Laughter.*)

It was about special care units and the facilities, because babies can survive earlier and earlier now. I went to the unit and I saw a baby that had been born at twenty-two weeks – you see this tiny little thing and a heart beat, it is amazing. But the question is about when life is viable. And I was thinking of these two young women, although physically they are terribly disabled [. . .] one of them has just finished university. I was interested in putting somebody with a disability centre stage.

As for the Connections[7] plays – the programme used to be run by a woman called Suzy Graham-Adriani. She contacted me and said would I like to write one. And I did really want to write one, and this is a terribly childish reason, because they'd been going for a couple of years before they got round to asking me. I kept thinking, 'All these people have been commissioned and I haven't.' (*Laughs.*) I wrote for *Grange Hill* for about twenty-two years. I really liked that. Often producers would say to me – because they changed all the time – 'You've got adolescent humour so well, how do you do that?' I never like to say anything, but it was just my own humour. (*Laughter.*) The play I did for Connections that was about gladiators, that was Suzy's idea. They'd found a grave of a female gladiator just by London Bridge. That was how that came about.

Do you write differently when you're writing for young people, or do you just get on with telling the story?

I would like to say, no, but I expect there are certain things that underneath I am taking into account. But having said that it's only the same sort of things you have to take into account for Radio 4, you know, you can't go 'fuck you' a lot.

Actually, the characters in Morning Glory, *the adolescent characters, are quite gritty representations.*

But that wasn't written for a young audience, it's really about the old ladies.

There are lots of mouthy older women in your plays, and they get loads of stage time, and I wondered if you set out to give voice to older characters?

Yes in *Morning Glory*, because the central character had to be in the S.O.E.,[8] so that character had to have that age. From a conscious point of view, it just feeds in to my feminist agenda. Women have always been centre stage in my work, whatever age. I don't think I sit down and write for older women. It's more organic than that.

I have enjoyed Ivy in The Devil's Gateway *and Grace in* Byrthrite.

To tell you the truth I haven't even looked at those plays since they were done. I feel a fraud when people phone up and ask me. Yes, there's Joyce in *Neaptide* who comes up trumps in the end.

And all those women are very funny. Not only the wordplay, puns, and the jokes but almost slapstick in places. You're allowed to laugh at them as well as with them, they are powerful comic figures on stage.

Yes . . . (*Sceptical laughter.*) . . . yes. (*Pause, laughter.*)

Would you ever write tragedy?

Some things I write are quite sad. I've just done a commission for Children in Need that will go out for *Woman's Hour*. I had to choose a group that Children in Need give money to, and it was for a group within a hospice that does things for the siblings of children with life-limiting conditions or that are terminally ill. I haven't heard the production yet, but I feel that as piece of writing that captures the mixture – it is quite sad by the nature of the thing, but I hope there are some funny things in it.

I do think humour is very important. There was a woman who used to run the Oval House Theatre in the 1980s called Kate Crutchley, she was also a part of Gay Sweatshop.[9] At a talk once, she flatly said she was never going to see another play unless it had at least three laughs in it. I can very clearly remember thinking to myself, 'Fair enough.' As a person I love making people laugh. I think laughter is a pure emotion – either something makes you laugh or it doesn't. In the moment or the second that you're laughing you feel better. So there you go. (*Laughter.*) Sarah Daniels does therapy.

I don't want to sound like I'm blowing my own trumpet but, where the agenda might be forced with the politics and the beliefs in my work, the laughter is never forced, I hope, that comes quite naturally.

Do you feel that your role as a playwright has changed over the time that you've been working – has the status of the playwright changed?

I can only really talk personally about it. When I first met Rob Ritchie, the Literary Manager of the Royal Court, who had read *Ripen Our Darkness*, and given me very positive feedback and they wanted to put it on, he had a conversation with me – I was twenty-three then, because I was twenty-four when it went on – about playwriting. And he said, 'It is hard to make a living out of writing plays.'

Of course, if you write *Mamma Mia!* or a big hit, that's really good. Sebastian Born, who was a literary agent and is now working as a Literary Manager at the National, has said, 'You can't make a living being a theatre writer, but you can make a killing.'

To go back to Rob Ritchie, he said, 'You'll probably have to do other things – bits of television and things like writing plays for Radio 4.' Being twenty-three I didn't even listen to Radio 4, I thought, 'Oh, only sad bastards listen to that.' (*Laughter.*) But now, I am feeling really positive about Radio 4, I really like writing for it. You have got your own voice, within the parameters I've talked about. You do get your own voice. You often get a fantastic cast. I don't suppose that Patricia Routledge would be in a stage play of mine, with four weeks' rehearsal, but for a radio play like *Sound Barriers* ... I really like working for radio, but it pays about a tenth of what you get for TV. But as you get older you don't need so much – not that I've ever been well dressed.

Part of the problem is how much money is set aside for new writing, or how little money is set aside for new writing. And that was a big problem in the 1980s – the Royal Court could only do a few plays at year. There are lots of regional theatres but if there's a new play on in London you have to come to London to see it, there doesn't seem to be a mechanism for taking it out to regional theatres.

Timberlake Wertenbaker

The following quotations are drawn from significant interviews with Wertenbaker over the course of her career.

In 1992 Wertenbaker's satire of the art market of the 1980s, Three Birds Alighting on a Field, *won the Susan Smith Blackburn Prize for English-language women playwrights. Following this she was interviewed, with director Max Stafford-Clark, by Michael Billington:*[10]

When you write a historical play, your first concern is to ask what its contemporary resonance is. We did a great deal of research into contemporary prisons, and that was really the key to the whole thing. We went to see a performance of a Howard Barker play, *The Love of a Good Man* (1978) in Wandsworth Prison, and that was extraordinary. *Our Country's Good* (1988) was not an illusion. Talking to convicts doing the Howard Barker play, and discovering their passion for it, inspired all of us. [. . .]

I corresponded with three or four of [the prisoners], and a few years later they did *Our Country's Good*, so everything came full circle. [. . .] And from their letters, which are published here and there, it became clear that it did change them. The whole experience did convince us all that there was something in theatre that offered hope.

[. . .] I was horrified, like most of us, by the 1980s and by Thatcherism. The play was an attempt to throw that off and get back to something I imagined England still had, which was a sense of value. I loved England then – probably more than I do now – and I felt that there was a beauty in England that was being destroyed by Thatcherism.

In 1999, Wertenbaker had a radio play, Dianeira, *broadcast on BBC Radio 3. Michael Billington interviewed Wertenbaker about her interest in classical antiquity and her experience as a woman and a playwright:*[11]

When Catherine Bailey commissioned me to write a radio play and I floated the idea of a Sophoclean translation, she said, 'Don't do me a boring Greek or no one will listen.' So what I've tried to do is review an ancient myth from a totally modern standpoint. The play's really about the way anger threads its way through the generations on both a personal and political level. I've also tried to draw parallels with the Balkans today, where the cycle of revenge continues and where neighbour is still fighting neighbour.

But I suppose I'm drawn to the Greeks by love and passion. I studied for a time at the French Lycée in New York and came across this book full of marvellous pictures of boats which turned out to be *The Odyssey*. I also did Greek at university and later hitchhiked around the country. But what I love about the Greeks is that they're trying to define what a human being is about. There's a combination of tremendous despair, which runs through Sophocles, and great hope – a terrifying bleakness and, at the same time, a love for the individual. They're also suspicious of the state and have a sense that life is out of control, something I certainly understand as a writer. But all those things are back in question again after the nineteenth century, which believed it had all the grand solutions. [. . .]

On feeling without a theatrical home.

I also resigned from the Royal Court board because I was deeply unhappy. It was partly because of the increasing encroachment of private sponsorship, which I passionately believe is dangerous for new writing – partly because of seemingly trivial things like the new leather seats. Every time I took up a cause, it was lost; and I began to feel like Don Quixote, still talking about the age of chivalry. I don't want to open up a lot of old wounds, but as the only playwright on the board, after Winsome Pinnock left, I began to feel anachronistic.

[. . .] There was a particular moment when there were all these plays by men about men with really no women present. You go to the theatre partly to be mirrored in some way and you begin to feel you don't exist. I don't think women have ever been a welcome voice. You sense a relief that we can shut those women up and get back to what really matters, which is what men are saying. It's not complete paranoia. I think we're trained from birth to listen to men. The disappearance of women from the stage may also have discouraged aspiring writers. Word got around that there was little point in sending your play to the Court or the National. So women just stopped. Or went into TV and films.

Sarah Kane did generate imitators, but I think she was incorporated into the male group of the period. She was seen as one of the boys. But if you see a dominance of male dramatists going on for a long period of time, when women are equally educated, equally able to write, equally bold on stage, you have to ask yourself why. We talk about women dramatists, but it's significant that 'woman' becomes the compound whereas 'male' is the noun. It's as if that's the norm. I don't even think the prejudice is conscious. It's just that men judge the plays, put on the plays and, on the whole, run the theatres.

In 2006, Harriet Devine, daughter of George Devine who was the first director of the English Stage Company at the Royal Court, published a series of interviews with playwrights who had written for the Court. Harriet Devine asked Wertenbaker about her playwriting in the 1980s:[12]

There were a lot of questions about what it meant to be a woman in that period, what women were capable of, and also – which was what interested me – what happened to women in history, when were they in history, or what happened to them either imaginatively, as in *The Grace of Mary Traverse*, or in other circumstances. When they became public beings, what happened to them?

[. . .] I have to find a play through the process of writing it. I don't find it and then write it. And if somebody's there to help me find it, that's great, and if they're not, they're not. But if you get a director who's an editor, it's very rewarding. If you get a director who's meddling . . .

I always think of [a play] as just shifting people slightly, you know? [. . .] Making them a little bit uncomfortable. Not too uncomfortable, because then they won't follow the play, but just a bit uncomfortable so that they question – and I think a lot of plays may try to do that and fail. A lot of plays that call themselves political are not political. They just regurgitate what's happening in political events. All this thing now about the renaissance of political theatre – I'm quite sceptical.

In 2004, Wertenbaker's play Galileo's Daughter[13] *opened at the Theatre Royal, Bath. Wertenbaker talked to John O'Mahony:*[14]

I think what interested me, and what interests me in all my plays, is really the area where the public situation hits the private person, how it affects their courage and their decisions. I wanted to explore the question of unconditional love, to try to chart the anatomy of love: what it is, and what are its consequences. Galileo didn't feel his ideas and beliefs of the Church had to destroy one another. The idea that you can hold and accept different systems is something Galileo practised; that is something we should all try to do. You can hold contradictory systems in your heart.

It is very hard for a woman to be a playwright because it is so public. It's a tough world in the theatre. The responsibility of the female playwright is to be a little more doubtful and questioning. I try to be detached, but I do have a real belief in the ability of a human being to survive and do something good. I hope I'm on the side of humanity.

Jenni Murray of Woman's Hour, *BBC Radio 4, also interviewed Wertenbaker about* Galileo's Daughter, *and the reasons for her interest in the historical figure of Sister Maria Celeste:*

It was a fascinating conflict between on the one hand a daughter and a father, and on the other hand a very famous father and the authority of the time which happened to be the Church. The period is also fascinating, and a little bit misunderstood. We think of the Catholic Church at that time as narrow-minded and, in fact, it was much more sophisticated than we know. So, Dava Sobel's book reveals all these rather unknown aspects of the period and indeed Galileo's trial. I knew nothing about it except the Brecht play. It seemed a wonderful subject, I had already read the book and I leapt on it.

How do you bring a biography to life on the stage?

It's terribly difficult because it's not just a biography, it's also a work of history. And I discarded most of it. I chose a particular period of two years. History gives you the outline and the exterior of events, and then you have to try to put something inside and that has to come from the playwright. It's mostly a process of slimming, of letting go; letting go of all that is not relevant and just fixing on what I thought were the turning points of her life and of his. [. . .]

I found tremendous contemporary relevance, because what you see are people who are stuck in their moral absolutes. And here we are in a clash of moral absolutes, and of absolute systems. The dialogue of Galileo is called *The Dialogue Concerning the Two Chief World Systems*, so he was actually writing about a clash of systems. That seemed to me such a parallel and such an interesting parallel that I didn't have to even think about the relevance, it was right there.

[. . .] We have 124 letters of hers. We don't have his letters, alas. He also visited her whenever he could. In fact, he moved to a house which was very close to the convent so he could come and visit her. [. . .] There was a great love between them. The play for me is a love story.

You've been described as a feminist playwright, how would you describe yourself?

I never describe myself. I just sit there and write, and hope for the best. I'm always a little bit surprised when somebody asks me that question – I've never found a way of answering it. I think I'm a playwright. And obviously I'm attracted to women characters because I can sense their complexity. I often see slightly simplified women characters on the stage, and I think that's partly because we don't have so many women characters in the history of plays the way we have male characters. I think it's easier for me to write a male character because I have an infinite number of models.

On the relevance of contemporary theatre.

I think it's still one of the few public arenas. You have the audience there, you have the actors – it's live. And we don't have much of that with the amount of film and television we have. You are still allowed to be a little bit intelligent in the theatre, as you are on the radio. I don't know many other places where this is celebrated. And the kind of entertainment a play can offer is different, it's much more individual. Theatre does still accept and celebrate the individual, the individual in relationship with the public.

AFTERWORD

Making a name: critical reputations

Many forces are at work in the creation of a reputation for a playwright. The plays themselves and the attributed assessment of their 'quality' are only a small component in that reputation creation. After all, who judges the 'quality' of the plays, on whose terms, for which audiences? What encourages certain new plays to be retained in the repertoire and revived more regularly than others? What's in a name? Yael Zarhy-Levo has examined some mechanisms that produce 'reputation' in post-war British theatre, in particular the gatekeepers and cultural mediators who authorise work in the cultural marketplace. She begins with a challenge from sociologist Pierre Bourdieu: 'Who is the true producer of the value of the work – the painter or the dealer, the writer or the publisher, the playwright or the theatre manager?'[1] Bourdieu's question resonates throughout his analysis of cultural and artistic production, reminding us that the distinction between commercial and 'disinterested' non-commercial art is a false one, a misrecognition of the 'interests at stake'.[2] John Frow argues this misrecognition of value in art springs from the rhetoric of the modernist avant-garde of the early twentieth century. The claim that the avant-garde stands opposed to commercial entertainment endures today in the bifurcation between the high cultural status of 'new', oppositional, difficult, experimental art judged to be more aesthetically challenging, and other cultural products designated mere entertainment for mass consumption.[3] Bourdieu dubs the economic benefits that accrue to the artist within a system that misrecognises and distinguishes 'high art' from commercialised theatre, as symbolic capital:

> The only legitimate accumulation, for the author as for the
> critic, for the art dealer as for the publisher or the theatre

manager, consists in making a name for oneself, a name that is known and recognized, the capital of consecration – implying a power to consecrate objects (this is the effect of a signature or trademark) or people (by publication, exhibition etc.) and hence of giving them value, and of making profits from this operation.[4]

Modernism's posture in rejecting the commercialisation of art was only the latest flurry in a long tussle: 'making a name for oneself' has been a crucial economic and cultural mechanism for playwrights for as long as the commercial theatre has operated. The gatekeepers and cultural mediators that craft a reputation today might include the artistic director, the literary manager (increasingly since the 1980s), the playwriting mentor, the arts funder, the theatre critic, the publisher, the university academic and the school syllabus boards, as we shall see below. The four playwrights considered more fully in this volume have 'made a name' and established their reputations from the 1980s to the present day, and their work has continued to intervene in cultural debates on the stage, screen and radio.

Howard Barker

Productions of Howard Barker's work with the Wrestling School continued at around two per year through the 1990s. *The Europeans*, turned down by the RSC in the 1980s, was staged by the Wrestling School in 1993. Some of Barker's plays of the 1980s, notably those with attractively powerful roles for leading female performers including *Scenes from an Execution* and *The Castle*, were revived and toured in Europe. In 1994 *Hated Nightfall* (UK and European tour) initiated a new mode of working for Barker, as director of his own writing. Barker increasingly took responsibility for the full scenic realisation of his drama, from a combination of personal interest, frustration with the collaborations with directors and designers as he outlines in *A Style and Its Origins*,[5] and economic necessity: 'The Wrestling School is a very poor theatre.'[6] A 'style' emerged – with monochrome costumes and settings, the appearance of at least one actress naked, usually in high heels and a hat – that is not without its ideology. While Barker does write challenging, stage-dominating roles for women, he unashamedly expresses and summons male hetero-sexual desire into the theatrical experience which repeatedly returns him to a *mise en scène* that offers naked female performers as objects of desire. This is rarely commented on in analysis of his productions. Barker's control of the staging of his own work, and his publication of his theoretical reflections on his own playwriting and its role in culture, has allowed him to exert a surprising level of control over the perception of, and discourses that surround, his work. In part because of the resistance to his work on mainstream stages, he has become the forger of his own 'reputation'.

Barker has been unusual among the writers here in that he has made a modest theatrical living from the production of his stage work. He has not written for film or television since the early 1990s. He has sustained a small company to produce his work regularly, although not as often as he would wish. His riposte might well be to suggest that this has been forced upon him by the refusal of large-scale thea-tres, notably the National and the RSC, to stage his work: 'we are driven into smaller theatres by management economies, our audience remains stable and therefore we rarely gain access to those big stages where the scale of these plays can breathe, as we did for example with *Ursula* in Birmingham'.[7] Birmingham Rep, Colchester and Leicester Haymarket have been supportive regional stages, with London Riverside Studios as his most regular London venue. In many ways the structure of the small-scale company and medium-scale touring venues has suited his desire to remain outside the explicitly commer-cialised 'market' of the West End. Barker has deliberately set out to create theatre that 'fails to provide the usual elements of the contract which lie hidden in most performance (pleasure/enlightenment [. . .for] the ticket price)' and he argues 'great art has no truck with the market'.[8] Barker's playwriting has unsettled genre and convention, and in resisting commercial imperatives he has established his theatre's avant-garde credentials, confirmed by the imprimatur of national recognition through Arts Council subsidy for the Wrestling School.

Arts Council funding ceased in 2007, and the Wrestling School has continued thorough individual patronage, European funding and other sponsorship sources, managing to stage a large-scale international festival of his work '21 for 21' across eighteen countries in 2009, to celebrate twenty-one years of production.

Barker explicitly rejects the notion that his plays find parallels in the political world, and he rejects as 'the dramaturgy' the kind of social realist or socially active role for theatre, crystallised by Myerscough's *Economic Importance of the Arts in Britain* (1988). However, there remains in Barker's work a strong sense of resonance with the political injustices or conundrums of his contemporary world. In 2003, *13 Objects* (Birmingham Rep, regional tour, Riverside Studios) reflected the twenty-first century's relentless obsession with heritage, archaeology and preservation. One of the objects of desire is a spade over which prisoners vie in order to dig a grave, their own grave. The power games played by the officer who oversees the task might issue from any conflict, but it carried a particular weight in the year the Srebrenica Genocide Memorial to the mass killings of the Serbian/Bosnian war was erected. *The Fence in its Thousandth Year* (2005) summons the paranoia that drives the construction of any symbolic state border, such as the Berlin Wall, but in 2005 this was inevitably associated with the erecting of the fence along the Gaza–Egyptian border, accompanying the apparent Israeli withdrawal from Gaza. While Barker avoids resolving each play's imagery into explanatory form, the idea of resonance captures the sense of connection to real-world contexts that the power-play of his drama summons for audiences.

While not referring explicitly to the world of politics, Barker does refer directly to other theatre texts. He developed several plays in dialogue with existing canonical texts, reworking Shakespeare in *Seven Lears* (1989) and *Gertrude – The Cry* (2002), Lessing in *Minna* (1994) and Chekhov in *(Uncle) Vanya* (1996). Barker is less interested in using the structures or content of the source plays in his intertextuality than in concentrating on the cultural status and the cultural use to which these texts have been previously put: 'I wasn't examining Chekhov but the function of Chekhov, the *use* of Chekhov, how Chekhov's status is employed for certain disguised sociopolitical ends.'[9] The status and the function of the individual artist in relation to the state has been a repeated theme in Barker's recent work – in *Hurts Given and Received* (2010, Riverside) Bach the poet bears responsibility only to his own imagination. In *Blok/Eko* (2011, Northcott, Exeter) a queen exterminates the doctors of her state and exerts a brutal patronage over poets who are required to produce art as consolation. Through these characterisations of the writer's role, through his designation of himself as a theatre *poet*, and through his theorising of his work, Barker has built a reputation that chimes with the rhetoric of the modernist avant-garde. Central to this is his process in writing, which he describes more in terms of artistry than as craft, as springing fully formed from inspiration rather than as the incremental labour of drafts:

> I will look back at yesterday's page, and I may see a single word that is not the best, and I may change it, but that is unusual. Fluency is very important and I have been doing this for 40 years, so that, to some extent, I can trust the fluency itself.[10]

Jim Cartwright

Cartwright's theatre work in the 1980s was critically well received, winning a slew of awards. *Road* in particular developed a global presence; it was filmed for BBC television, by the 'alternative' film director Alan Clarke, and won awards at the Monte Carlo Television Festival in 1987. In the US, it was produced at the La MaMa Annex with Joan Cusack and Kevin Bacon in 1988, and has been translated into over twenty languages. It is regularly professionally produced and is a set text on GCE A-level school syllabi, in part because *Road* has come to represent a period of British social history which saw the marked polarisation of the classes and an exacerbation of the north–south divide. The play's regional identity has helped establish Cartwright as a 'northern' playwright, and he has remained loyal to his local region in many of his works. *Eight Miles High* (1991) is set at an idealised north west music festival in the 1960s, and introduces audiences to a range of likely and unlikely festivalgoers, re-creating the music of the era in an interactive event. The musical has been frequently revived and was extremely successful abroad, running at Iceland's Reykjavik City Theatre for a year. It was also used as the centrepiece of a Cartwright season at the Bolton Octagon in 2005. Bolton Octagon's Artistic Director, Mark Babych, evolved the Cartwright season to activate local commitment to the theatre from the surrounding community. *Eight Miles High* was given an environmental setting that took over the whole theatre in a manner reminiscent of *Road*'s original staging. In the same season, *Two* was revived with well-known ex-*Coronation Street* actors, community participation was involved in a community theatre reworking of *Road* for Britain under New Labour and North West Playwrights ran a 'Voices of the North' showcase of staged readings of new local playwrights. In both content and mode the Bolton Octagon set out to use Cartwright to connect with local, regional audience members.

The danger of this regional focus on Cartwright's work is that it can lead to easy cliché. Comic writing and performing group, the League of Gentlemen,[11] saw *Road* at the Royal Court as students, and were initially excited by seeing their regional identity portrayed:

> We went back the next day to speak to the actors. They had been playing skinheads and were all, 'Let's get pissed tonight. There's dust in my knickers and poverty wants me', and we came into the theatre and they were like, 'Can I bum a ciggy off someone?' I thought, 'God, they were putting it on.' And then you become aware of these dreadful John Godber clichés, and that has become a real bugbear.[12]

Dave Russell's study of the representation of northern identity across fictional genres reveals the repeated designation of the 'north' as the 'other' to London's economic, internationally connected, and sophisticated self-designation as the nation's cultural heart.[13] The pejorative use of symbolic shorthand for 'northern authenticity', such as brass bands, Rugby League, racing pigeons, heavy industry, poverty and flat caps, usually centred on an uneducated masculinity, were sharply mocked in the adult comic *Viz* (founded in Newcastle 1979) and are eschewed as self-representation by northern playwrights such as Cartwright, John Godber or Willy Russell. And yet working-class industrial and post-industrial masculinity is central to all their work. Not surprisingly, the meaning of the regional identity presented in Cartwright's plays such as *Road*, *Two* or *Eight Miles High* shifts subtly in relation to its audiences, operating in a quite different culture register at the Bolton Octagon for 'local' audiences than at the Royal Court for a self-defining theatrical cognoscenti.

However, by no means all of Cartwright's work is bounded by regional identity. Cartwright's most successful play has been *The Rise and Fall of Little Voice* (1992), which began life at the National, before transferring to the West End Aldwych theatre, winning the Evening Standard Award for Best Comedy of the Year and Laurence Olivier Comedy of the Year, and arriving on Broadway in 1995. The play hinges on the musical mimicry of its lead performer – Jane Horrocks originated the role of Little Voice – a character liberated from difficult family circumstances through her ability to imitate the voices of the great divas, Monroe, Garland, Bassey, Springfield. The play was filmed in 1988, with Horrocks in the title role, and with Ewan McGregor as her lighting designer sweetheart. The play was revived in the West End in 2009, with Diana Vickers, a contestant from the televised talent show *The X Factor*, in the title role.

In many ways this play offers Cartwright's most individualistic and sustained portrayal of character – its dilemmas are personal, rather than social. Pete Postlethwaite, who played Ray Say, the manipulative agent, recalled:

> We had quite a tough time putting it together. I'd wander into rehearsals and Alison [Steadman] would come over to me. 'Have you heard?' 'Heard what?' Then she'd tell me that they'd rewritten all our lines ... again. [...] Jim Cartwright was rewriting all the time while we were rehearsing so we were learning on the hoof.[14]

Postlethwaite was unused to the more open, actor-centred evolutionary approach to writing that Cartwright employed, in contrast to

Alison Steadman, who had forged her career working with Mike Leigh in improvised creation. Cartwright didn't set out to write a 'popular' play: 'You can't write and think about the financial future of the play. You just make a work of art and that's the way this one came out.'[15] However, the play does combine many elements that sit comfortably within a West End milieu – popular music from the recent past, family-centred domestic drama and realist characterisation.

In 1996 Cartwright directed the short, bleak *I Licked a Slag's Deodorant* for the Royal Court Theatre. The two-hander followed the sympathetically portrayed, but unrelentingly grim lives of 'Man' and crack-addicted 'Slag', who come to a strange family arrangement where 'Man' inhabits a dream world under 'Slag's' bed. It played in a season that began with Pinter's *Ashes to Ashes*, Ravenhill's *Shopping and Fucking* and Ayub Khan-Din's *East is East*. Cartwright has also written television films; early works included *Vroom* (Channel 4, 1990). *Strumpet* and *Vacuuming Completely Nude in Paradise* were directed by Danny Boyle for the BBC in 2001. In the fairy-tale *Strumpet* Christopher Eccleston took the lead as a poet who picks up a strange guitar-playing girl, to form a pop duo, Strumpet. In *Vacuuming Completely Nude in Paradise*, Timothy Spall played the comic anti-hero, a door-to-door vacuum salesman, with a ruthless approach to sales among the poorest inhabitants of housing estates. Both short films offer the performers a liberating acting challenge and unrivalled screen time, although Cartwright's female characters for the screen are perhaps less fully developed. In works for both stage and screen, Cartwright's heightened realism and poetic language unsettle the domestic setting, and his actor-centred mode of writing with monologue and vignette at its core have ensured a sustained presence for his work in the theatrical canon. It is this theatrical presence that has sustained Cartwright's reputation, for there is remarkably little scholarly commentary on his work.

Sarah Daniels

Sarah Daniels's playwriting in the 1990s was closely connected to her interest in the question of women and mental health, and the condition of women in the criminal justice system. In radical contrast to Barker's rejection of theatre as social commentary, Daniels has embraced this aspect of theatre's cultural role. Her trilogy of plays on women's mental health, *Beside Herself* (1990, Women's Playhouse Trust and Royal Court), *Head-Rot Holiday* (1991, Clean Break Company, on tour) and *The Madness of Esme and Shaz* (1994, Royal Court Upstairs), depict the absurdities and iniquities of the psychiatric and criminal justice systems and their treatment of women. The plays are not vehicles for simple campaign messages, but all were based on research with women users of the mental health services, and in the case of Clean Break Theatre, written with and for women who had experience of the criminal justice system.

In the new century, Daniels collaborated more often with young people's companies and on plays for young adults. In 1999 Daniels was commissioned by the National Theatre's New Connections programme to write a short play for youth theatre groups. *Taking Breath* (1999) follows the interweaving stories of ten young people who have to deal with the complexities of idealism, the inevitability of compromise and the consequences of choice. A ramshackle group attempts an impromptu ecological protest, but the limited commitment of the members is exposed in comparison with the story of a young suffragette. At the same time, the play follows two compromised characters: Alana, a young girl who sold the drugs that caused another child to overdose, is drawn to Steve, half-brother of one of the eco-protesters, but employed by the developers. Daniels's writing for young people does not avoid the paradoxes and complexities of modern life, and the force of class that remains in the world – 'if you are poor and out of work as Steve is, you have to weigh the dignity of having a job against your principles'.[16]

Daniels was commissioned by New Connections a second time in 2003, in collaboration with the San Francisco-based American Conservatory Theatre Young Company (A.C.T.), and wrote *Dust*, a study of bullying and the challenges of independence. Inspired by the discovery of female gladiatorial remains in London, *Dust* follows Flavia, a contemporary schoolgirl cold-shouldered by a group of schoolfriends, who is caught up in a bomb blast on the London underground. Transported back to Roman London, she is taught to fight by female gladiators. The play is more complicated than a simple story of the growth of self-confidence. Flavia encounters 'Woman with a Baby' whose poverty has left her in desperate circumstances: 'You look at me like I'm the shit on your shoes, but you cannot shake my dust from your feet. [. . .] You have always revelled in reviling me [. . .] you are more concerned with making sure animals don't become extinct than with trying to eradicate me.'[17] As Daniels remarked, 'We still haven't eradicated poverty, yet we think we are so civilized.'[18] Such a distinct left-wing perspective in Daniels's writing for young people locates her work within the tradition of alternative theatre and radical Theatre-in-Education work that disappeared with changes to local education authority funding in the late 1980s, as we have seen in Chapter 1.

The 2003 commission began an ongoing relationship with A.C.T. In 2007 *Broken Wings* was co-commissioned with Bath Theatre Royal's young people's company. This demanding play presents young people coming to terms with the death of a parent. Daniels has also written for Chicken Shed, an ability-inclusive youth theatre company based in Enfield, north London. *Who's Afraid of Virginia's Sister?* was commissioned in 2006, and the lead role, Debbie, was taken by Amy Golden, a performer with cerebral palsy, who used a communication board and synthesiser to deliver her lines for the performance. The play follows the interaction between a dysfunctional mother, and two stepsisters: Alex, addicted to therapy, and Debbie. The play eschews individualistic stories of pathos or plucky heroism, in favour of commentary on the systems that impact on individuals' perceptions of themselves. As Debbie remarks, the able-bodied are 'so self-obsessed that they want to change themselves as opposed to society'.[19] Daniels comments on the therapy industry through two comic working-class characters, the therapy centre cleaners. Her harshest critique is reserved for the systems that are unable to facilitate Debbie's participation in mainstream schooling, or her attendance at university despite her ability. She mocks the gulf between need and provision in the marketisation of 'care', that sees Debbie's carer re-branded as a 'personal assistant'.

The other side to Daniels's trajectory has been her writing for *Grange Hill* (1989–2008), a television series set in a comprehensive school that garnered a reputation for its gritty representation of children's lives including drugs, self-harm, rape, suicide and knife crime. Daniels also wrote for *EastEnders* for many years. Recently Daniels has written a great deal for radio, producing two or three single dramas for BBC Radio 4 Afternoon Play slots, alongside serialised adaptations of novels for Radios 4 and 3, and the BBC World Service soap, set in a school again, but this time focused on teachers, *Westway* (1997). Daniels's radio drama has dealt with topics allied to those she pursued for the stage – women's mental health, post-natal depression, breast cancer, social work and social workers, and the experience of soldiers' wives. Her writing has remained centrally concerned with women's experience and class structures, although Elaine Aston and Gerry Harris have observed that her engagement with realism has shifted from the 'broken realism' of her stage work, to a more psychological and reparative realism in her radio drama.[20]

Timberlake Wertenbaker

Wertenbaker's large-scale plays during the 1990s were concerned with the cultural value of art, and whether art might be considered as distinct from the world of commerce. The late 1980s saw an over-inflation of the fine art market, the commercialisation of the art auction and a diversification in art ownership. This followed financial deregulation and the changes to the cultural style of City trading with the arrival of American ownership of British banks. Buyers and sellers of art were presented as the new entrepreneurs and were frequently the newly brash banks, businesses and traders. Fine art was reinvigorated as an asset class and investment vehicle, particularly Impressionist and Post-Impressionist modernist works. Wertenbaker's satiric comedy on the economic bubble in the visual art market of the late 1980s, *Three Birds Alighting on a Field* (1992), begins with a white canvas – much as Yasmin Reza's *Art* (1995) does. In Reza's play the white canvas operates as a lens for a study of individual relationships threatened by differences in taste. Through her portrayal of art investors, critics, gallery owners and artists, Wertenbaker examines what taste actually is, and how it operates in relation to personal and national identity and, inevitably, class. The play asks what cultural value remains intrinsic to art, when commercial forces are determined to view art as investment opportunity?

Wertenbaker returned to this question of the value of art and to an interrogation of those financial and cultural structures of the 1980s that so subjugated art to the logic of business in her next two plays. *The Break of Day* (1995), which toured in parallel with Out of Joint's version of Chekhov's *Three Sisters*, relocates three women to Britain just before the millennium, and concentrates on their quest for children. In a subplot Wertenbaker returns to the question of art and commerce, as the jobbing actor Robert debates whether it is better to accept a role in a Chekhov play or a TV drama – presenting an apparent contrast between the cultural capital of highbrow theatre work and the economic capital of a well-paid television job.[21] Wertenbaker seeks to champion the value of high culture and the theatre itself, as a symbol of resistance to the apparent relativism inherent in the commodification of art. The play was not well received by critics, but has been reclaimed by feminist academics who have recognised that Wertenbaker's address to a millennial 'fatigue' parallels Chekhov's depiction of ennui. The play's multiple foci relocate this ennui in a world of chaotic demand for attention and reveal the complex negotiations feminism must make in the face of a social championing of motherhood during the 1990s – the rise of the 'yummy mummy' in advertising.[22]

Her leading plays of this decade were all set against versions of post-Cold War Europe struggling to deal with the implications of its post-colonial heritage. *The Break of Day* offers a reflection on the inescapable brutality of the political fall-out in post-communist Europe and the Serbian wars. At the end of Act One of *The Break of Day*, the next-door neighbour, the widower Mr Hardache, likens the contemporaneous 'ethnic cleansing' in Bosnia to his wife's experience of the Holocaust:

> **Mr Hardache** People with suitcases, walking, walking with their
> suitcases. I thought we'd never see those images again . . . I'm
> going to march with my suitcase every day for the rest of my life.
> I'm going to protest against history.[23]

Like Diane Samuels's *Kindertransport* (1993), David Greig's *Europe* (1994) or Theatre de Complicite's *The Street of Crocodiles* (1992), the suitcase – usually old, battered, leather, suggestive of the 1930s – stands as a material trope for the trauma of middle-European brutality, and the displacement of people across cultures during the Second World War and the Cold War, a trauma that runs through all of Wertenbaker's work. The Serbian/Bosnian war challenged the assertion that the 'end of history' had arrived with the triumph of capitalism and liberal democracy after the fall of the Iron Curtain and the Berlin Wall.[24] The porous nature of national borders in the new global order, where economic migrants travel readily, and asylum seekers are detained between unwelcoming utopias and dystopian homelands is the central theme of Wertenbaker's *Credible Witness* (2001).

Wertenbaker's work has often contained a meditation on the role and cultural purpose of theatrical performance itself. *After Darwin* (1998, Hampstead) examines a theatre company putting together a play about Darwin's voyages. The play pits the traditional performer Ian, who asserts that theatre is intrinsically good for audiences, against the relativist Tom, whose pragmatic approach to career success almost stops rehearsals before the play is performed, but is ultimately defeated by Ian's act of betrayal. Two forces are at work in Wertenbaker's theatrical use of theatrical metaphor: one posits the theatre as a cultural form threatened with extinction, the other posits that art will endure through continual adaptation and evolution. Articulated by the writer figure in *After Darwin*, the black American professor Lawrence offers a challenge to the commercial cynicism of the actor Tom: 'When I see a character on the stage, I think, ah, where is he going, he's emerged from the tragic, is he a hybrid, a completely new form? And I never stop being excited by the human possibilities – that struggle for exist-ence on this small space.'[25] Ultimately the play figures the theatrical possibilities of continual reinvention and translation across cultures. The translation of cultural identities is picked up in Wertenbaker's *Credible Witness* (2001, Royal Court Upstairs), which depicts a refugee drama therapy group for youngsters. The question of the effi-cacy of theatre in the New Labour context, which further emphasised the instrumentality of art as social panacea, is one from which Wertenbaker does not shrink. The potential irrelevance of theatre in a mediatised and globally interconnected world must be challenged, she asserts: 'There is a danger of English theatre being primarily about English subjects. And that raises the bigger question of whether theatre is best when it stays within its own country or when it reflects that, in the contemporary world, we have fewer borders.'[26]

In the new millennium Wertenbaker's work has focused even more on translation, adaptation and reworkings of myths and classic texts. For Wertenbaker, 'a translation not only changes something, but also moves it, displaces it', and she identifies herself as from the 'faithful wives school' of translation, attempting to work very closely from the original language.[27] Given that several of her early plays are concerned with the silencing and repression of cultural articulation that comes with brutal colonial oppression, it is not surprising, perhaps, that she should consider loyalty to an original text a crucial contribution of the translator. By contrast, she distinguishes adaptation as a process of modification, allowing the play to live in new surroundings. 'By their modification of the parent work, [adaptations] may actually help a work survive. But we also have to ask, does the adaptation then supplant the original. Does a film adaptation make the reading of the book unnecessary?'[28] As we have seen, Wertenbaker's adaptations tend to come in response to canonical texts from the classical era, or key theatre texts from a traditional European theatrical canon. As she articulates, 'My favourite way of working when not writing an "orig-inal" is by basing a work on another one.'[29] This produces a kind of theatrical writing that sits at the heart of mainstream British culture, both displaying and requiring a level of cultural competence that is distinctly highbrow, and summoning a frame of reference that draws in the widest range of European literary and performance heritage.

Other histories

The four playwrights who have formed the central study for the volume have all entered the theatrical mainstream and the theatre canon, to differing degrees – Elaine Aston argues that Sarah Daniels's work has been kept from the large-scale mainstream stages since the 1980s because of her explicitly feminist agenda.[30] Nevertheless, all four playwrights have had works revived, have had new works staged and have written for film, television or radio, have entered school syllabi as examination texts or are regularly performed by amateur groups. Yet in this volume there are other routes and careers that we might have focused on. The canonisation of a writer into the theatrical repertoire is no straightforward recognition of the 'success' of their work with audiences or maximisation of profit from minimum production outlay. Indeed, under these terms we should have spent most of our time analysing the smash hit mega-musicals of the 1980s. Christopher Balme has noted that, as theatre historians, we are too loyal to the modernist narratives of art for art's sake where, 'only those works that programmatically defy commodification find a place in the archive. [. . .Theatre history's] frames of reference are still conditioned by a definition of theatrical canonicity in which attention is focused on the aesthetic component defined by the players themselves.'[31] With this warning in mind, we might instead have focused on Alan Ayckbourn, who was the most economically successful playwright of the 1980s, outside the realm of musical theatre. He had fourteen plays staged between 1980 and 1989, including four at the National Theatre – *Sisterly Feelings* (Olivier, 1980), *Way Upstream* (Lyttelton, 1982), *A Chorus of Disapproval* (Olivier, 1985) and *A Small Family Business* (1987, Olivier) – and five in the West End – *Taking Steps* (Lyric, 1980), *Season's Greetings* (Apollo, 1982), *Intimate Exchanges* (Ambassadors, 1983), *Woman in Mind* (Vaudeville, 1986) and *Henceforward*

(Vaudeville, 1988). Alongside the West End and National Theatre locations for his new plays, revivals and multiple productions of his existing texts were in the repertoires of regional theatres of Britain and Europe throughout the 1980s. Yet Ayckbourn is very rarely considered as producing 'new writing'. Indeed, because of his success, Ian Brown and Robert Brannen separated Ayckbourn out from the categories of 'new writing' and of 'post-war drama', in their statistical articulation of the repertoire in regional theatres for the Cork Report of 1986. While Ayckbourn has been a canonical figure in the repertoire for audiences and for theatre directors, producers and practitioners since the 1970s, he is rarely studied on school syllabi or at university level. There are very few scholarly articles about his work and those books that do refer to him tend to be written by theatre practitioners.[32] This is in part because he is perceived as too populist, as predominantly writing comedy, and as confining his work to the gentle satire of middle-class mores. As John Bull suggests, Ayckbourn's study of the minutiae of middle-class England integrates experimental dialogue forms from the so-called absurdists of the 1950s. For Bull, this produces structurally complicated versions of the genre of domestic farce, regenerating the mainstream form but without offering radical political challenge.[33] A comparison between Ayckbourn's *A Woman in Mind* (Stephen Joseph Theatre, Scarborough, 1985) and Sarah Daniels's *Ripen Our Darkness* (Royal Court, 1981) perhaps illustrates why Ayckbourn's political stance has made him so popular with audiences, and so little studied by the academy. Both plays centre on a vicar's wife who is oppressed within her domestic context and has a breakdown. For Ayckbourn's Susan, the audience follows her experience of a double life – one fantasy, one disappointingly real – entirely from Susan's perspective confined within the heterosexual norms of domestic life. When fantasy daughter Lucy praises her mother's fantasy career as a brain surgeon it provides a belly-laugh moment for audiences. Ayckbourn's play ends with Susan about to be bundled into an ambulance and off to hospital. By contrast, as we have seen, Daniels's play is explicitly feminist. It sets out to reveal the social and political structures that produce individual oppression, rejects heterosexual norms as norms, and refuses to position Mary's breakdown and suicide as personal, individual failing. The contrast makes clear why Daniels has readily been championed by academic feminism, and at the same time why her play has been less commercially successful or revived on mainstream stages.

We might have followed a different trajectory in the work of Winsome Pinnock (born Islington, 1961), who began her writing life as part of the Royal Court Young Playwrights group, a privileged entry to the playwriting élite. The Royal Court writers' group offers valuable patronage and mentoring, as well as the reputation-enhancing possibility of staging her work – indeed her first play *A Hero's Welcome* (1986) was given a staged reading at the Royal Court Upstairs. However, it was through feminist networks of patronage with the Women's Playhouse Trust that the play was revised and finally produced into the repertoire. *A Hero's Welcome* was printed with Aurora Metro, an explicitly feminist press arising from new writing at the Drill Hall. Pinnock has talked about her relationship with one of the first set of gatekeepers, the director: 'As a writer you're dependent on directors championing your work and if there isn't interest in the sort of work you're doing, you fade out of the picture.'[34] Pinnock's work centres on the black British experience, particularly that of black women. She notes the difference in significance that her play *Leave Taking* (1988, Liverpool Playhouse Studio; 1990, Lyric Studio; 1996, National Theatre and tour) had at its revival at the National. It was

> quite an extraordinary thing when it had its few performances at the National Theatre last year, to see a woman like Enid centre-stage at the National with the usual National Theatre audience going to watch her. Because when you watch a performance of a play, you are forced to identify with whoever is the heroine at that point. So people were identifying with someone who was seemingly 'other' and yet the feedback I got was brilliant, 'Yes, that's me.'[35]

While Pinnock's work may have made its way to short runs at the National and into an accepted repertoire of black British writing, the question remains whether the theatrical institutions will facilitate her work's entry into the mainstream canon without marking her work as 'black'.[36] And she has not yet been absorbed on to school syllabi, although she is much studied at university level as part of an academic interest in black writing and feminist writing, both figured as oppositional political positions.

From the 1990s onwards there has been a conscious attempt by the Arts Council, theatre venues and the wider media to ensure that non-discriminatory policies are in place and that the diversity of British cultural experience is heard. Given the many black playwrights, male and female, now writing for established stages Pinnock asks whether the Alfred Fagon Award for playwrights of African and Caribbean descent still seems necessary in 2010? She concludes that awards 'offer a tremendous career boost to both winners and short-listed writers, bringing their names to the attention of literary managers and producers who might have overlooked them, effectively showering what one of the award's advisors called "gold dust" on to a writer'.[37] Within mainstream theatrical culture black playwriting still has ground to make and sustain. While within schools and universities, John Guillory has argued, the question of canonisation resides in the problem of 'syllabus and curriculum, the institutional forms by which works are preserved as *great* works'.[38] University arts and literature courses, on both sides of the Atlantic, went through several convulsions during the 1980s over two key questions. First, whether critical and philosophical theory was more significant than the study of literature itself, and second whether female-authored work or black-authored work should be adopted on to mainstream courses, or reserved as special interest subjects for particular constituencies.[39] Books such as this one contribute to the privileging of particular subjects and reputations; as Bourdieu reminds us, 'discourse about a work is not a mere accompaniment, intended to assist its perception and appreciation, but a stage in the production of the work, of its meaning and value'.[40] So, there are at least three fields that matter for the forging of individual literary reputations and a writer's acceptance into a 'canon': the theatrical repertoire of production, the university syllabus and the school curriculum. Each field is traversed by competing demands and all are involved in commodified production and in establishing economic value as much as cultural capital.

One emergent aspect of theatrical culture during the 1980s was the mainstream visibility of theatre groups engaged in what the Arts Council dubbed 'experimental' work, including devising performance, live or performance art, physical or dance theatre. Text operated within all these performance genres, but it was less likely to be identified as playwriting – since such work desired to be marked out as 'alternative' or experimental, and the well-made play seemed to some companies to be quite unable to respond to, or contain, their aesthetic explorations. Nevertheless, 'text' or performance writing was a key aspect of such performance work; as Claire MacDonald argues, it was a more writerly mode than has been acknowledged. The difficulty for such texts, as Claire MacDonald reflects through the work of Deborah Levy, is that the material traces left in the text itself are only a small part of the experience of the performance as a conceptual whole, 'an inadequate vehicle for the complexity of the work, which [. . .] can only be appreciated in the context of its production'.[41] This difficulty might in part explain why study of such genres of work was increasingly championed in the university, but only appeared on school syllabi as a process-centred exploration for making theatre, not in relation to text or new writing. The 1980s saw increasingly high-profile productions of physical theatre, dance theatre, or performance art, with the work of Theatre de Complicite at the National Theatre, the regular visits of Pina Bausch's Tanztheater Wuppertal to Sadler's Wells or the Barbican, or DV8's staging at the ICA. As Sally Banes and Philip Auslander have argued, performance art, with its interest in reusing and referencing mass popular culture, was easily assimilated into mainstream culture during the 1980s. Visits from high-profile US performance artists such as Laurie Anderson or Spalding Gray also illustrated another element of autobiographical, confessional performance art that was to become more accepted in mainstream repertoires.[42] As the cultural cachet of alternative genres grew with their assimilation into mainstream theatres, these genres exerted increased pressure on theatrical writing and the 1990s was to see a far more diverse range of structure, form and production in plays on its mainstages as a result.

The making of a reputation and the building of a theatrical career has always been a complex negotiation with a variety of networks: with theatrical gatekeepers and cultural mediators who nurture a play-text into production; with critics and academics who reinterpret the playtext, often searching for radical or oppositional interpretations; and with an education system at school level tasked with inculcating appropriate cultural capital in their pupils. In the 1980s the interrelation between the economic value of art and its cultural value seemed to have become compressed. In 1988 the Arts Minister Richard Luce directly aligned economic success with artistic success, warning the Regional Arts Associations, 'if it's any good people will be prepared to pay for it . . .The only real test of our ability to succeed is whether or not we can attract enough customers.'[43] By 1991, Fredric Jameson suggested that the dominance of multinational capital and of the dizzying relativism of postmodernist thought had all but eradicated the possibility of a resistant political art by which we might 'begin to grasp our positioning as individual and collective subjects and regain a capacity to act and struggle'.[44] Yet the 1980s did find a host of resistant voices from the stage in community and school halls, in fringe and alternative venues, in regional theatres, as well as on the major subsidised national stages: voices whose resistance was not always based on a readily interpretable left-wing agenda. The political force of this resistance from multiple voices was only partially diffused by Conservative rhetoric which set groups against each other in competition for dwindling resources. Such competitive rhetoric led political thinkers Ernesto Laclau and Chantal Mouffe to propose the need for a 'chain of equivalence' across political struggles.[45] The pluralising and authorising of multiple voices, multiple perspectives and multiple identities, both as theatrical subject matter and in terms of the authors whose work was staged, was a crucial development in the political and theatrical landscape of the 1980s.

NOTES

Introduction to the 1980s

1. www.statistics.gov.uk/downloads/theme_social/Social-Trends40/02 Chapter 2: House-holds and Families.
2. http://family.jrank.org/pages/737/Great-Britain-Nature-Family-Change-in-Great-Britain.html.
3. www.statistics.gov.uk/downloads/theme_social/Social-Trends40/02 Chapter 2: House-holds and Families
4. Office of National Statistics General Household Survey 2000, summary of changes.
5. Sue Anderson (ed.), *The CML Mortgage Market Manifesto: Taking the Past into the Future* (Council of Mortgage Lenders; February 2004).
6. www.statistics.gov.uk/articles/economic_trends/ET626_CPI.pdf.
7. www.statistics.gov.uk/downloads/theme_social/Social-Trends40/24.
8. www.mind.org.uk/help/research_and_policy/the_history_of_mental_health_and_community_care-key_dates.
9. Sheila Peace, 'The Development of Residential and Nursing Home Care in the UK', in Jeanne Katz and Sheila Peace (eds), *End of Life in Care Homes: A Palliative Care Approach* (Oxford: Oxford University Press, 2003), pp. 15–42.
10. www.statistics.gov.uk/downloads/theme_social/Social-Trends40/18.
11. www.unionhistory.info/timeline/1960_2000_5.php.
12. Steve Machin, 'Unto them that hath . . .', Centre for Economic Performance cep.lse.ac.uk/pubs/download/CP138.pdf.
13. D. Greenaway and M. Haynes, 'Funding Higher Education in the UK', *Economic Journal*, Vol. 113 (2003), pp. 150–66.
14. http://news.bbc.co.uk/1/hi/uk/4733330.stm.
15. Victor Middleton, 'Whither the Package Tour?' *Tourism Management*, Vol. 12, No. 3 (1991), pp. 185–92.
16. Richard Davies et al., 'Evolution of the UK Banking System', *Bank of England Quarterly Bulletin*, Vol. 50, No. 4 (2010), pp. 321–32.

1 Theatre in the 1980s

1. Fredric Jameson, *The Political Unconscious: Narrative as Socially Symbolic Act* (Ithaca, NY: Cornell University Press, 1981), p. ix. Paradoxically Jameson posits radical

historicity as 'the one absolute, and we may even say "transhistorical" imperative of all dialectical thought'.

2. Public Enemy, 'Fight the Power' (Tamla Records, 1989).

3. Valerie, the abused wife, in Jim Cartwright's *Road* in *Jim Cartwright: Plays 1* (London: Methuen, 1996), p. 60.

4. In this phrase I mean both the delimitation of the present from the past, and I summon the Brechtian sense of using historical material to sustain a critical reflection on the present.

5. www.vh1.com/shows/i_love_the_80s/series.jhtml (accessed 2 June 2011).

6. Andreas Huyssen, *Twilight Memories* (London: Routledge, 1995), p. 3.

7. Susan Stewart, *On Longing* (Chicago, IL: Duke University Press, 2003; eighth edition), p. 23.

8. Susan Bennett, *Performing Nostalgia: Shifting Shakespeare and the Contemporary Past* (London: Routledge, 1996).

9. Robert Hewison, *The Heritage Industry: Britain in a Climate of Decline* (London: Methuen, 1987).

10. David Edgar (ed.), *State of Play: Playwrights on Playwriting* (London: Faber and Faber, 1999), p. 15.

11. Broadly speaking, this is the position of Fredric Jameson's *Postmodernism: or, the Cultural Logic of Late Capitalism* (London: Verso, 1991).

12. Raphael Samuel, *Theatres of Memory* (London: Verso, 1994), p. 95.

13. Brian Walden interview, *Weekend World*, London Weekend Television, Sunday 16 January 1983, transcript available at www.margaretthatcher.org/document/105087, fo. 29.

14. Voluntary school provision was patchy for the lowest classes, and schooling was not free to all until the state stepped in with the 1891 Free Education Act.

15. Picking up Williams's procedure, Fredric Jameson begins the decade with the publication of *The Political Unconscious: Narrative as a Socially Symbolic Act* (1981), which examines the act of interpretation in its historical context and deduces 'there is nothing that is not social and historical – that everything is "in the last analysis" political' (p. 20). Jameson finished the decade with *Postmodernism: or, the Cultural Logic of Late Capitalism* (1991), which argues that parody (a mode which requires moral judgement) has been replaced by pastiche, and that there is a crisis in historicity, by which he means there is no relation between learned history and lived experience in everyday life.

16. Michel Foucault, *The History of Sexuality: Volume 1*, trans. Robert Hurley (New York: Pantheon Books, 1978).

17. Barbara Kirshenblatt-Gimblett becomes chair. The academic journal *The Drama Review* adds a subtitle *Journal of Performance Studies* in 1980.

18. Catherine Itzin, *British Alternative Theatre Directory* (Eastbourne: John Offord, 1980), p. 15.

19. Andrew Lavender, 'Theatre in Crisis: Conference Report, December 1988', *New Theatre Quarterly*, Vol. 5, No. 19 (1989), pp. 210–16.

20. Cited in D. Keith Peacock, *Thatcher's Theatre* (Westport, CT: Greenwood Press, 1999), p. 35.

21. Andrew Feist and Robert Hutchison (eds), *Cultural Trends in the Eighties* (London: Policy Studies Institute, 1990).

22. Feist and Hutchison, *Cultural Trends*; Baz Kershaw, 'British Theatre, 1940–2002', in Baz Kershaw (ed.), *Cambridge History of British Theatre: Volume 3* (Cambridge: Cambridge University Press, 2004), pp. 291–325.

23. Kingsley Amis wrote a pamphlet for the Conservative think tank Centre for Policy Studies, calling for the Arts Council's abolition because it subsidised the middle classes (*An Arts Policy?* 1979). Paul Johnson called the Arts Council a 'baroque institution' in the *Evening Standard*, 26 June 1979; see Jim McGuigan, *Culture and the Public Sphere* (London: Routledge, 1996), p. 64.

24. Cited in John Bull, *Stage Right: Crisis and Recovery in British Contemporary Mainstream Theatre* (Basingstoke: Macmillan, 1994), p. 16.

25. Robert Protherough and John Pick, *Managing Britannia: Culture and Management in Modern Britain* (Corbridge: Brynmill Press, 2002), pp. 101–2.

26. John Myerscough, *The Economic Importance of the Arts* (London: Policy Studies Institute, 1988).

27. See Baz Kershaw, 'Discouraging Democracy: British Theatres and Economics, 1979–1999', *Theatre Journal*, Vol. 51, No. 3 (1999), pp. 267–83, for a fuller discussion of the complexity of this contention.

28. Max Horkheimer and Theodor W. Adorno, 'The Culture Industry: Enlightenment as Mass Deception', in Horkheimer and Adorno, *Dialectic of Enlightenment* (Stanford, CA: Stanford UP, 2002).

29. Peter Smith, 'Dr Hoggart's Farewell', *Marxism Today*, March 1982, pp. 31–2.

30. Richard Hoggart, *A Measured Life* (London: Chatto & Windus, 1994), p. 232.

31. Having failed to win a seat as a Conservative, Rees-Mogg worked as a journalist, editor and political speech writer for Conservative ministers. Immediately upon leaving *The Times* in 1981, Rees-Mogg was appointed as deputy chair of the Board of Governors of the BBC – a regulatory role supposedly beyond party politics (1981–86); concurrently he was chair of the Arts Council (1982–89). He was made a life peer in 1988.

32. For fuller discussion of this see Robert Hewison, *Culture and Consensus* (London: Methuen, 1995) and Kershaw, 'Discouraging Democracy'.

33. However, Maria Delgado and Caridad Svich offer a timely reminder that British theatre in the 1980s was not as party political as in Spain, for example, where the Artistic Directorate of the National Theatre Madrid was removed when the next government were elected to office. Maria Delgado and Caridad Svich (eds), *Theatre in Crisis: Performance Manifestos for a New Century* (Manchester: Manchester University Press, 1999), p. 41.

34. Cited in Vera Gottlieb, 'Theatre Today – a New Realism', *Contemporary Theatre Review*, Vol. 13, No. 1 (2003), p. 12.

35. Nobuko Kawashima, 'Planning for Equality: Decentralisation in Cultural Policy' (Warwick: Centre for Cultural Policy Studies, 2004), p. 1.

36. Kate Dorney and Ros Merkin (eds), *The Glory of the Garden: English Regional Theatre and the Arts Council* (Newcastle: Cambridge Scholars Press, 2010), p. 8.

37. Cited in Peacock, *Thatcher's Theatre*, p. 142.

38. Colin Tweedy presented on Filling the Funding Gap, quoted in Alistair Smith, 'Theatres Should Give Up Charitable Status Says Arts & Business', *The Stage*, 9 March 2011.

39. Peacock, *Thatcher's Theatre*, p. 48.

40. Feist and Hutchison, *Cultural Trends*, p. 34.

41. Tracy C. Davis, *The Economics of the British Stage 1800–1914* (Cambridge: Cambridge University Press, 2000), p. 349.

42. Simon Shepherd, *The Cambridge Introduction to Modern British Theatre* (Cambridge: Cambridge University Press, 2009), p. 112.

43. David Edgar, 'Towards a Theatre of Dynamic Ambiguities: An Interview with David Edgar', *Theatre Quarterly*, Vol. 9, No. 33 (1979), pp. 3–23.

44. Alan Plater, playwright and screenwriter, in Mike Bradwell (ed.), *The Bush Theatre Book* (London: Methuen, 1997), p. 63.

45. Ros Merkin, 'Devolve and/or Die', in Dorney and Merkin, *The Glory of the Garden*, p. 78.

46. Ian Brown, a key member of the Drama Panel and Cork Report team, has written an insightful reflection on the report and its outcomes: Ian Brown and Rob Brannen, 'When Theatre was for All: the Cork Report, After Ten Years', *New Theatre Quarterly*, Vol. 12 (1996), pp. 367–83.

47. See Robert Hewison on the GLC budget in *Culture and Consensus*, pp. 237–41.

48. Kershaw, 'Discouraging Democracy', p. 270; Kershaw suggests that the rise of populist programming, defended as widening access, in fact is more likely to 'reduce potential for social critique'.

49. Kershaw, 'Discouraging Democracy', p. 276. In considering audiences, Kershaw notes that the newly populist theatre of the 1980s has produced an emphasis on individual consumers, dispersing power that came from membership of a collective social formation, and this has led to 'a paradoxical image of an highly hierarchical "democratized" estate' (p. 279).

50. Michael Billington, *One Night Stands* (London: Nick Hern, 1993), p. 174.

51. Ibid.

52. D. J. Taylor, 'The Sound of the Suburbs: The Idea of the Suburb in English Pop', in Roger Webster (ed.), *Expanding Suburbia* (Oxford: Berghahn Books, 2000), pp. 161–71; at p. 170.

53. Susan Croft, 'Black Women Playwrights in Britain', in Trevor R. Griffiths and Margaret Llewellyn-Jones (eds), *British and Irish Women Dramatists Since 1958* (Buckingham: Open University Press, 1993), pp. 84–98; at p. 86.

54. Kershaw helpfully notes the debate between left-wing critics such as Graham Woodruff, who finds the work complicit with capitalism's agenda, and others who applaud the participatory ethos as strengthening community; see Baz Kershaw, *The Politics of Performance* (London: Routledge, 1992).

55. David Johnston, Tangere Arts, www.tangere-arts.co.uk/tinsoldier.htm (accessed 20 March 2011).

56. Nicolas Whybrow, 'Young People's Theatre and the New Ideology of State Education', *New Theatre Quarterly*, Vol. X, No. 39 (1994), pp. 267–80.

57. Jim McGuigan, *Culture and the Public Sphere* (London: Routledge, 1996).

58. Chin-Tao Wu, *Privatising Culture: Corporate Art Intervention Since the 1980s* (London: Verso, 2002), p. 131.

59. Hewison, *Culture and Consensus*, p. 257.

60. Andrew Faulds to Paul Channon, Arts Minister, *Hansard 1803–2005*, House of Commons Debate, 22 February 1982, Vol. 18, cc. 603–45. Online at http://hansard. millbanksystems.com/commons/1982/feb/22/the-arts (accessed July 2010).

61. Brendan Evans, *The Politics of the Training Market* (London: Routledge, 1992), especially pp. 56–65.

62. Owen Kelly, *Community, Art and the State: Storming the Citadels* (London: Comedia, 1984).

63. Colin Chambers and Mike Prior, *Playwrights' Progress: Patterns of Postwar British Drama* (Oxford: Amber Lane Press, 1987), p. 21.

64. Ibid., p. 23.

65. Ibid., p. 25.

66. Elaine Aston and Geraldine Harris, *Performance Practice and Process: Contemporary Women Practitioners* (Basingstoke: Palgrave, 2007), p. 86.

67. Brown and Brannen, 'When Theatre was for All', p. 377.

68. Susan Carlson, 'Collaboration, Identity and Cultural Difference: Karim Alrawi's Theatre of Engagement', *Theatre Journal*, Vol. 45, No. 2 (1993), pp. 155–73.

69. Arts Council Annual Report, 1981–82. For 1983–84, there were twenty-five bursaries awarded, including to Howard Barker, Tunde Ikoli, Errol John, Bryony Lavery, Snoo Wilson (three went to black authors, three to women playwrights); thirty-nine Contract Writers Awards were made to theatre companies; and twelve Resident Dramatist Awards. Royalty Supplement Awards supported thirty-one plays in production. In 1985, twenty-seven bursaries, forty-four Contract Writers, eight Resident Dramatists and twenty-nine plays were supported with the Royalty Supplement Awards. In 1988–9, only seven writers' bursaries were awarded, including to David Johnston, Deborah Levy and Sheila Yeger; twenty-four Royalty Supplement Awards were given to plays; the Second Production scheme had been set up to underwrite the first revival of a play, nine were awarded; sixty-one commission or option awards were given, several were won by a single playwright within a year (April De Angelis had three commissions in 1988); eleven Resident Dramatist attachments were awarded including to Sarah Daniels (at the Combination) and Jim Cartwright (at Bolton Octagon).

70. The Welsh Arts Council in 1981–82 set aside £28,690 for playwright commissioning, according to the Arts Council Annual Report of that year.

71. Theodore Shank, 'The Playwriting Profession', in Theodore Shank (ed.), *Contemporary British Theatre* (Basingstoke: Palgrave, 1996), pp. 181–204; at p. 185.

72. The TWU joined with the Writers' Guild in 1997.

73. Victor Bonham-Carter, *Authors by Profession* (London: Society of Authors, 1984), p. 194.

74. Award schemes running during the 1980s were often subsidised by print or broadcast media included Thames Television Best Play Award; *Drama* Magazine Award; John Whiting Award; Samuel Beckett Award; *Evening Standard* Most Promising Playwright Award; *Time Out* Best Play; LWT Plays on Stage Award; George Devine Award; Kenneth Tynan Award for Outstanding Achievement; the Olivier Awards; London Fringe Award; and *Plays and Players* Most Promising Playwright Award.

75. Cited in Elaine Aston, *Feminist Views on the English Stage* (Cambridge: Cambridge University Press, 2003), p. 1.

76. Michael Billington, 'Making a Drama out of Crisis', *Guardian*, 4–5 May 1991.

77. Christopher Innes, *Modern British Drama 1890–1990* (Cambridge: Cambridge University Press, 1992), p. 448.

78. Ibid.

79. Emma Dunton, Roger Nelson and Hetty Shand, *New Writing in Theatre 2003–2008* (London: Arts Council, 2009).

80. Arts Council Green Paper on Drama 1995, discussed by Ben Payne in John Deeney (ed.), *Writing Live* (London: New Playwrights' Trust, 1998).

81. Dromgoole in Bradwell, *Bush Theatre Book*, p. 72.

82. Interview with Ben Payne, in New Playwrights' Trust Newsletter, No. 78 (March 1993), cited in Deeney, *Writing Live*, p. 20.

83. Timberlake Wertenbaker, in Edgar, *State of Play*, p. 75.

84. Carol Rosen, 'Literary Management at the RSC Warehouse, London', *Theater*, Vol. 10, No. 1 (1978), pp. 43–6; Donohue estimates he received around twelve plays a week, all of which were read and commented upon.

85. *Nickleby* won the Society of West End Theatre (later the Laurence Olivier) Play of the Year Award, 1980. It was revived at Stratford-upon-Avon in 1986. *Educating Rita* won the Society of West End Theatre Best New Comedy in 1980.

86. Although *Educating Rita* was not considered a 'state-of-the-nation' play, in the tradition of Shaw's *Pygmalion* it is a reflection on class politics, the acquisition of education and cultural value.

87. Aston and Harris, *Performance Practice and Process*, p. 85.

88. Bradwell, *Bush Theatre Book*, p. 50.

89. It was expensively refurbished in 1985 and, as with a similar round of capital building projects in regional theatres during the mid-1990s, the company found itself servicing debts for the building work from its operating grant, and was eventually forced into voluntary liquidation in 1989.

90. Bradwell, *Bush Theatre Book*, p. 7.

91. Hedley made this claim in 1983, cited in Michael Coren, *Theatre Royal: A 100 Years of Stratford East* (London: Quartet, 1984), p. 99.

92. Ann Considine and Robyn Slovo (eds), *Dead Proud: Second Wave Young Women Playwrights* (London: Women's Press, 1987) and Frances Gray (ed.), *Second Wave Plays: Women at the Albany Empire* (Sheffield: Sheffield Academic Press, 1990).

93. The Drill Hall became the first building-based performance space committed to gay and lesbian theatre. It was run by a management company, Central London Arts Limited.

94. George Rowell and Anthony Jackson, *The Repertory Movement: A History of Regional Theatre in Britain* (Cambridge: Cambridge University Press, 1984).

95. Peacock, *Thatcher's Theatre*, pp. 44–52.

96. Brown and Brannen, 'When Theatre was for All', pp. 367–83.

97. Interview with Lynn Gardner, 'The Power Behind the Scenes', *Guardian*, 4 April 2001.

98. Kate Dorney, 'Touring and Regional Repertory', in Dorney and Merkin, *The Glory of the Garden*, p. 108.

99. Edgar, *State of Play*, p. 20.

100. Claire MacDonald, 'Writing Outside the Mainstream', in Elaine Aston and Janelle Reinelt (eds), *The Cambridge Companion to Modern British Women Playwrights* (Cambridge: Cambridge University Press, 2000), pp. 235–52; at p. 237.

101. Some of the complexity of ownership over text in collaborative processes emerges from the court case that arose from the phenomenal success of *Stones in His Pockets* on Broadway, after which director Pam Brighton argued that her contribution to the development of the play in rehearsal made her joint author of the piece.

102. For a fuller discussion see Alda Terracciano, 'Mainstreaming African, Asian and Caribbean Theatre: The Experiments of the Black Theatre Forum', in Dimple Godiwala (ed.), *Alternatives within the Mainstream: British Black and Asian Theatres* (Newcastle: Cambridge Scholars Press, 2006), pp. 22–50.

103. Baz Kershaw, *Radical in Performance: Between Brecht and Baudrillard* (London: Routledge, 1999), p. 74.

104. Michael Billington, *Guardian*, 10 May 1974. This is cited in Gareth and Barbara Lloyd Evans, *Plays in Review: 1956–1980 British Drama and the Critics* (London: Methuen, 1985).

105. John Elsom, *Post-War British Theatre* (London: Routledge & Kegan Paul, 1976), p. 73.

106. Itzin, *Stages*, p. 256.

107. Michael Billington, *State of the Nation: British Theatre Since 1945* (London: Faber and Faber, 2007).

108. Dan Rebellato, 'From the State of the Nation to Globalization: Shifting Political Agendas in Contemporary British Playwriting', in Mary Luckhurst and Nadine Holdsworth (eds), *A Concise Companion to Contemporary British and Irish Drama* (Oxford: Blackwell, 2008), pp. 245–62; at p. 246.

109. Simon Shepherd, 'Theatre and Politics', in Laura Marcus and Peter Nicholls (eds), *The Cambridge History of Twentieth-Century English Literature* (Cambridge: Cambridge University Press, 2004), p. 637.

110. Janelle Reinelt and Gerald Hewitt, *The Political Theatre of David Edgar: Negotiation and Retrieval* (Cambridge: Cambridge University Press, 2011), pp. 7–27.

111. Reinelt and Hewitt, *Political Theatre*, p. 12.

112. May Joseph, 'Bodies Outside the State: Black British Women Playwrights and the Limits of Citizenship', in Jill Lane and Peggy Phelan (eds), *The Ends of Performance* (New York: New York University Press, 1998), pp. 197–215; at p. 197.

113. Newman is perhaps better known for his television writing, *Judge John Deed* and on *Law and Order*.

114. An equally likely butt of the satiric joke might have been Britain's other newspaper magnate, Robert Maxwell, who, in July 1984, had added the Mirror Group Newspapers to his publishing empire, which included the European rights to MTV.

115. Anger at *The Satanic Verses* was global: bookshops that sold it were bombed, its Japanese translator was stabbed to death in the street, other translators were attacked and Rushdie was placed under police protection.

116. See Akbar Ahmed's polemic *Postmodernism and Islam: Predicament and Promise* (London: Routledge, 1992).

117. Janelle Reinelt, *After Brecht: British Epic Theatre* (Ann Arbor: University of Michigan Press, 1994), p. 97.

118. Formally recognised as genocide by a Dutch court in The Hague in 2005, who successfully prosecuted Frans van Anraat for supplying the chemical weapons used at Halabja.

119. David Edgar in *State of Play* and Aleks Sierz in *In-Yer-Face Theatre* (London: Faber, 2001).

120. George Michael and Andrew Ridgeley, 'Wham Rap (Enjoy What You Do?)', Innervision 1982.

121. Speech to Conservative Party conference, Blackpool, 15 October 1981.

122. Jim Cartwright, *Road* (London: Methuen, 1996), p. 59.

123. www.bis.gov.uk/files/file23914.pdf.

124. The a cappella group who provided the music for the show, formed as The Flying Pickets, had a Christmas number 1 with Yazoo's 'Only You' in 1983.

125. Cited in Nadine Holdsworth, 'Good Nights Out: Activating the Audience with 7:84 (England)', *New Theatre Quarterly*, Vol. 13, No. 9 (1997), pp. 29–40; at p. 32.

126. Lizbeth Goodman, *Contemporary Feminist Theatres* (London: Routledge, 1993), p. 104. For a fuller analysis of the play see Peacock, *Thatcher's Theatre*, pp. 151–4.

127. See Aston and Reinelt, *Cambridge Companion to Modern British Women Playwrights*, p. 153.

128. See Heidi Stephenson and Natasha Langridge (eds), *Rage and Reason: Women Playwrights on Playwriting* (London: Methuen, 1997) for detailed interviews on this topic. Lynette Goddard, *Staging Black Feminisms* (Basingstoke: Palgrave, 2007), notes Winsome Pinnock and Jenny McLeod wanted their plays 'recognised for their universal worth rather than as black women's plays' (p. 31).

129. Margaret Thatcher Foundation, 27 January 1978. Interview on Granada TV http://www.margaretthatcher.org/document/103485 (accessed September 2011).

130. The Vagrancy Act of 1824 allowed police to stop and search people on 'reasonable suspicion' of their felonious intent, hence 'sus' law. These stop and searches were extremely disproportionately applied to black and Asian young men.

131. Stanton Garner, *Trevor Griffiths: Politics, Drama, History* (Ann Arbor: University of Michigan Press, 1999).

132. Keeffe is a white East End playwright, who has frequently written about black experience, for example in *Sus* (1979).

133. Cited in Bennett, *Performing Nostalgia*, p. 55.

134. Cited in Gerry Cousin, *Women in Dramatic Place and Time* (London: Routledge, 1996), p. 50.

135. For fuller discussion of these developments see Gabriele Griffin, *Contemporary Black and Asian Women Playwrights in Britain* (Cambridge: Cambridge University Press, 2003); Dominic Hingorani, *British Asian Theatre* (London: Routledge, 2010); Graham Ley and Sarah Dadswell (eds), *Critical Essays on British South Asian Theatre* (Exeter: University of Exeter Press, 2011).

136. Geoffrey Davis and Anne Fuchs (eds), *Staging New Britain: Aspects of Black and South Asian British Theatre Practice* (Brussels: Peter Lang, 2006), p. 42.

137. Goddard, *Staging Black Feminisms*, p. 31.

138. For a fuller discussion see Goodman, *Contemporary Feminist Theatres*, pp. 104–7.

139. John Muellbauer, 'The Assessment: Consumer Expenditure', *Oxford Review of Economic Policy*, Vol. 10, No. 2 (1994), pp. 1–41.

140. Ann D. Morgan, *British Imports of Consumer Goods: A Study of Import Penetration 1974–1985* (Cambridge: Cambridge University Press, 1988), p. 6.

141. George Soros, *A New Paradigm for Financial Markets: The Credit Crisis of 2008 and What It Means* (Philadelphia, PA: Perseus Books, 2008).

142. For a detailed analysis of the repercussions of *The Romans in Britain*, see Richard Boon, *Brenton the Playwright* (London: Methuen, 1991).

2 Introducing the Playwrights

1. Writewords.org.uk interview with Julie Balloo (accessed 10 June 2011).

2. Participation of eighteen- to twenty-one-year-olds in higher education ran at around 13 per cent in 1980, 15 per cent in 1988, and was at 30 per cent by 1993.

3. Robert Holman in Mike Bradwell (ed.), *The Bush Theatre Book* (London: Methuen, 1997), p. 62.

4. Timberlake Wertenbaker interview in Harriet Devine, *Looking Back* (London: Faber and Faber, 2006), p. 275.

5. Patricia Hilaire, Paulette Randall and Bernadine Evaristo had met at Rose Bruford Drama School and wanted to create their own work. Susan Croft, 'The Theatre of Black Women', in Alison Donnell (ed.), *Companion to Contemporary Black British Culture* (London: Routledge, 2002); Meenakshi Ponnuswami, 'Small Island People: Black British Women Playwrights', in Elaine Aston and Janelle Reinelt (eds), *Cambridge Companion to Modern British Women Playwrights* (Cambridge: Cambridge University Press, 2000), pp. 217–34; at p. 218.

6. www.famouspoetsandpoems.com/poets/jackie_kay/biography (accessed March 2011).

7. Jill Davis, *Lesbian Plays: Volume 1* (London: Methuen, 1987), p. 82.

8. New Playwrights' Trust became writernet in 1999, when its subsidy was cut, and morphed into the blog- and web-based network It isn't Fixed in 2008.

9. The Black Audio Film Collective, founded in Hackney, London, in 1982 by students of sociology and fine art, made experimental films and documentaries about black British life. Notably *Handsworth Songs* (1986) centred on people's perspectives on the 1985 urban unrest and the way it was portrayed by the media. See also Yvonne Brewster's introduction to *Black Plays: Volume 2* (London: Methuen, 1989) and Gabriele Griffin's *Contemporary Black and Asian Women Playwrights in Britain* (Cambridge: Cambridge University Press, 2003).

10. In 1988 the work of North West Playwrights won the *Manchester Evening News* Horniman Award for contribution to new writing. See the 'North West Playwrights Archive' held at the John Rylands Library, University of Manchester http://archives. li.man.ac.uk.

11. Barker in Charles Lamb, *The Theatre of Howard Barker* (London: Routledge, 1997), pp. 39–40.

12. Barker interviewed in Catherine Itzin, *Stages in the Revolution: Political Theatre in Britain Since 1968* (London: Routledge, 1980), p. 251.

13. 'Departures from a Position', interview broadcast 14 February 1999, Radio 3, presented by Ian McDiarmid.

14. Interview collected in Mark Brown (ed.), *Howard Barker Interviews 1980–2010: Conversations in Catastrophe* (Bristol: Intellect, 2011), p. 19.

15. Barker quoted in Theodore Shank, 'The Playwriting Profession', in Theodore Shank (ed.), *Contemporary British Theatre* (Basingstoke: Palgrave, 1996), p. 202.

16. Howard Barker, *Arguments for a Theatre* (London: John Calder, 1989), p. 56.

17. The death scene of Noel in the bath invites the audience to reflect on the well-known painting by Jacques-Louis David of 'The Death of Marat', French revolutionary polemicist.

18. Brown, *Howard Barker Interviews*, p. 35.

19. Eduardo Houth/Howard Barker, *A Style and Its Origins* (London: Oberon Books, 2007), p. 93.

20. Arts Council funding to the Wrestling School was cut in 2007.

21. Barker, *A Style*, p. 62.

22. Interview with David Nathan, 'Double Take: Playwright Jim Cartwright has finally made it to the West End', *Independent*, 19 October 1992.

23. Benedict Nightingale, *New York Times*, 24 July 1988. It is difficult to remember how conservative Central School used to be; it expelled Rupert Everett.

24. Steve Davies, 'Class Act', *Guardian*, 2 August 2008.

25. Playwright Trevor Griffiths reviewed the play: 'despite the sordid catalogue of brutal events portrayed in graphic detail, ranging from the anal impaling of a canary via the killing of a baby and occasional razor slashings to vomiting into roadworks and onto

workmen, the production achieved a kind of manic lyricism amid several moments of high comedy' (*Scotsman*, 19 January 1988).

26. Nightingale, *New York Times*, 24 July 1988.

27. Nathan, *Independent*, 19 October 1992.

28. Jeremy Kingston, *The Times*, 22 January 1987.

29. Nathan, *Independent*, 19 October 1992; Benedict Nightingale, *New York Times*, 24 July 1988.

30. Nathan, *Independent*, 19 October 1992.

31. Ibid.

32. Elaine Aston and Geraldine Harris, *Performance Practice and Process: Contemporary Women Practitioners* (Basingstoke: Palgrave, 2007), p. 81.

33. www.bbc.co.uk/writersroom/insight/writing_for_radio-4.shtml (accessed 10 April 2011).

34. Susan Brown, Patricia Clements and Isobel Grundy (eds), Sarah Daniels entry, *Orlando: Women's Writing in the British Isles from the Beginning to the Present* (Cambridge: Cambridge University Press Online, 2006). http://orlando.cambridge.org/ (accessed 9 March 2011).

35. Sarah Daniels, 'Introduction', *Plays: Volume 1* (London: Methuen, 1991), pp. x–xi.

36. Sarah Daniels, 'Foreword', in Lizbeth Goodman and Jane De Gay (eds), *The Routledge Reader in Politics and Performance* (London: Routledge, 2000), p. xxvi.

37. Lizbeth Goodman, with Jane de Gay (eds), *Feminist Stages: Interviews with Women in Contemporary British Theatre* (London: Routledge, 1996), p. 102.

38. 'Sarah Daniels', in Heidi Stephenson and Natasha Langridge (eds), *Rage and Reason: Women Playwrights on Playwriting* (London: Methuen, 1997), p. 8.

39. Timberlake Wertenbaker, 'First Thoughts on Transforming a Text', in Maya E. Roth and Sara Freeman (eds), *International Dramaturgy: Translation and Transformations in the Theatre of Timberlake Wertenbaker* (Brussels: PIE Peter Lang, 2008), pp. 35–40; at p. 39.

40. Devine, *Looking Back*, p. 273.

41. Devine, *Looking Back*, pp. 273, 274.

42. Devine, *Looking Back*, p. 274.

43. For a brief discussion of this see Sophie Bush, 'The Inevitable Need to Speak in Order to Be: On the Loss of Voice in Two Plays by Timberlake Wertenbaker', *Forum: University of Edinburgh Postgraduate Journal of Culture and the Arts*, 9 (Autumn 2009) www.forumjournal.org/site/issue/09 (accessed November 2010).

44. Elaine Aston, *Feminist Views on the English Stage* (Cambridge: Cambridge University Press, 2003), p. 222 says Wertenbaker talked of this time in interview on *Writers Revealed* on Radio 4, 20 June 1991.

45. Susan Carlson, *Women and Comedy: Rewriting the British Theatrical Tradition* (Ann Arbor: University of Michigan, 1991), p. 263.

46. Stephenson and Langridge, *Rage and Reason*, p. 143.

47. Aston, *Feminist Views*, p. 163, and an audio recording is held in the British Library

National Sound Archive. The play was a combined project with the Royal Court's Young People's Theatre Scheme.

48. Stephenson and Langridge, *Rage and Reason*, p. 137.
49. Timberlake Wertenbaker, in Devine, *Looking Back*, p. 276.
50. Stephenson and Langridge, *Rage and Reason*, p. 137.
51. Timberlake Wertenbaker, in David Edgar (ed.), *State of Play: Playwrights on Playwriting* (London: Faber and Faber, 1999), p. 76.
52. Timberlake Wertenbaker in Devine, *Looking Back*, p. 279.

3 Playwrights and Plays: Howard Barker

1. Howard Barker, Programme for *Victory: Choices in Reaction* (London/Leicester: Wrestling School/Leicester Haymarket Theatre, 1991).
2. Simon Shepherd and Peter Womack, *English Drama: A Cultural History* (Oxford: Blackwell, 1996), p. viii.
3. Kenneth Gergen, *The Saturated Self: Dilemmas of Identity in Contemporary Life* (New York: Basic Books, 1991), p. 49.
4. The challenge of estrangement might be reduced if one is writing from an intercultural position. For an examination of intercultural theory through the lens of performance histories, and an insight into historical-cultural estrangement, see the preface to Phillip Zarrilli, Bruce McConachie et al., *Theatre Histories: An Introduction* (London: Taylor & Francis, 2006).
5. Elisabeth Angel-Perez, 'Reinventing "Grand Narratives": Barker's Challenge to Postmodernism', Howard Barker's Art of Theatre Conference (10–12 July 2009, University of Aberystwyth, UK).
6. Ian Herbert, '*Crimes in Hot Counties* – a Review', *London Theatre Record*, October 1985, p. 1011.
7. Dan Rebellato, 'Sarah Kane: An Appreciation', *New Theatre Quarterly*, Vol. 15, No. 3 (1999), p. 280.
8. Milton Shulman, '*Victory: Choices in Reaction* – Review for the *London Standard*', *London Theatre Record*, October 1985, p. 1017.
9. For an excellent longitudinal study of Barker's four decades, see David Ian Rabey's two volumes: *Howard Barker, Politics and Desire: An Expository Study of His Drama and Poetry, 1969–1987* (Basingstoke: Macmillan, 1989) and *Howard Barker, Ecstasy and Death: An Expository Study of His Drama, Theory and Production Work, 1988–2008* (London: Palgrave, 2009).
10. Howard Barker, *Sheer Detachment* (London: SALT, 2009).
11. Howard Barker, 'The Wrestling School' www.thewrestlingschool.co.uk/tws.html (accessed 1 September 2011).
12. Robert Shaughnessy, 'Howard Barker, the Wrestling School, the Cult of the Author', *New Theatre Quarterly*, Vol. 5, No. 19 (1989), p. 270.

13. Howard Barker, *Arguments for a Theatre* (Manchester: Manchester University Press, 1989).
14. Howard Barker, *Death, the One and the Art of Theatre* (Abingdon: Routledge, 2005).
15. Eduardo Houth/Howard Barker, *A Style and Its Origins* (London: Oberon, 2007).
16. For a description of this 'anti-reconciliatory' form, see Rabey, *Howard Barker, Ecstasy and Death*, pp. 19–20.
17. Shaughnessy, 'Howard Barker', p. 269. This was also the moment of the publication of the first volume of Rabey's study of Barker, *Howard Barker, Politics and Desire*.
18. Rabey, *Howard Barker, Ecstasy and Death*, p. 248.
19. Ibid.
20. Eduardo Houth/Howard Barker, *A Style*, p. 9.
21. Anthony Curtis, '*Victory*', *Financial Times*, 26 March 1983, p. 217.
22. Andrew Haydon, 'Do we really watch plays for pleasure?', 22 October, *Guardian*, 2009 www.guardian.co.uk/stage/theatreblog/2009/oct/22/howard-barker-play-pleasure (accessed 1 September 2011).
23. Howard Barker, *Victory: Choices in Reaction* (London: John Calder, 1983), p. 63; all quotations from this edition will be noted in the text in parenthesis.
24. Jack Tinker, '*Victory: Choices in Reaction* – Review', 26 March, *Daily Mail*, March 1983.
25. Ros Asquith, '*Victory* – Review', *City Limits*, 28 March–5 April 1983.
26. Ned Sherrin, '*Marilyn!*', *Plays and Players*, May 1983, p. 28.
27. Charles Spencer, '*Call Me Madam*: Victoria Palace', *Plays and Players*, May 1983, p. 30.
28. Barker, *Arguments*, p. 17.
29. Ibid.
30. Ibid.
31. Joint Stock, the theatre company performing *Victory* in 1983, had already performed Caryl Churchill's Civil War play *Light Shining in Buckinghamshire* in 1976. Unlike *Victory*, it attempted an accurate representation of religious factions within the complex Civil War structure. In the early 1980s, the Civil War presented an interesting totem with key scholarly texts like Christopher Hill's *The Century of Revolution 1603–1714* published in its second edition in 1980.
32. Ros Carne, '*Victory* – Review', *Guardian*, 26 March 1983.
33. Asquith, '*Victory* – Review', 1983.
34. Nigel Lawson, House of Commons transcript (24 November 1983), Hansard, House of Commons Debates, Series 6, Volume 49 http://hansard.millbanksystems.com/commons/1983/nov/24/international-banking-crisis (accessed June 2011).
35. Benedict Nightingale, '*Victory* – Review', *New Statesman*, 26 March 1983.
36. Barker, *Arguments*, p. 38.
37. Kevin Quarmby, '*Victory: Choices in Reaction* – Review for the British Theatre Guide' (2009) www.britishtheatreguide.info/reviews/victorychoices-rev (accessed 1 September 2011).

38. Barker, *Arguments*, p. 17.

39. Howard Barker, 'Don't Exaggerate: a Political Statement in the Form of Hysteria', *Don't Exaggerate (Desire and Abuse)* (London: John Calder, 1985), p. 23.

40. John Barber, '*The Castle* – a Review for the *Daily Telegraph*', *London Theatre Record*, 9–22 October 1985, p. 1017.

41. Martin Banham (ed.), *The Cambridge Guide to Theatre* (Cambridge: Cambridge University Press, 1995), p. 78.

42. Steve Grant, '*Victory*: Royal Court', *Plays and Players*, March 1983.

43. Howard Barker, *The Castle: A Triumph* in *Barker – Plays Two* (London: Oberon, 2006), pp. 7–78; at pp. 28–9. All quotations from this play are from this edition and noted in the text in parenthesis.

44. Barber, '*The Castle* – a Review for the *Daily Telegraph*'.

45. A. Rissik, '*The Castle* – a Review for *Time Out*', *London Theatre Record*, 9–22 October 1985, p. 1016.

46. Michael Billington, '*The Castle* – a Review for the *Guardian*', *London Theatre Record*, 9–22 October 1985, p. 1016.

47. Mary Karen Dahl, 'The Body in Extremis: Exercises in Self-Creation and Citizenship', in Karoline Gritzner and David Ian Rabey (eds), *Theatre of Catastrophe: New Essays on Howard Barker* (London: Oberon Books, 2006), p. 97.

48. Jim Hiley, '*The Castle* – a Review for the *Listener*', *London Theatre Record*, 9–22 October 1985, p. 1016.

49. Barney Bardsley, '*The Castle* – a Review for *City Limits*', *London Theatre Record*, 9–22 October 1985, p. 1017.

50. Although the play has since been published by Methuen.

51. David Ian Rabey, 'Raising Hell', in Gritzner and Rabey, *Theatre of Catastrophe*, p. 19.

52. A rich academic discourse surrounding this phenomenon centres on the key text by sociologist of religion, Grace Davie, *Religion in Britain Since 1945: Believing without Belonging* (Oxford: Blackwell, 1994).

53. Charles Lamb, *The Theatre of Howard Barker* (London: Routledge, 2005), p. 123.

54. Office for National Statistics, 'Census 2001 – Ethnicity in England and Wales' (2007) www.statistics.gov.uk/census2001/profiles/commentaries/ethnicity.asp (accessed 22 August 2008).

55. This particular census return is notable for two reasons. First, it was the first census that carried questions specifically on religion. But, second, it was the year when a campaign to make 'Jedi Knight' the dominant UK religion saw marked success, with 390,000 describing themselves as such, and only 329,358 describing themselves as Sikh.

56. Office for National Statistics, 'Census 2001'.

57. The Archbishops' Council, *Church Statistics 2001* (London: Church House Publishing, 2003), pp. v–vi.

58. Lamb, *Theatre of Howard Barker*, p. 95.

59. Ibid.

60. Lamb, *Theatre of Howard Barker*, p. 96.

61. Ibid.

62. A. Renton, 'Review: *The Last Supper* at the Royal Court', *Plays and Players*, May 1989, pp. 22–3.

63. Shaughnessy, 'Howard Barker', p. 268.

64. Lyn Gardner, 'The Last Supper', *City Limits*, 17 March 1988.

65. Cited in Rabey, *Howard Barker, Ecstasy and Death*, p. 14.

66. Victoria Radin, '*The Last Supper*', *New Statesman*, 17 March 1988.

67. Howard Barker, *The Last Supper* (London: John Calder, 1988), p. 50; all references to this play come from this edition and are noted in parenthesis in the text.

68. Francis King, 'The Last Supper', *Sunday Telegraph*, 20 March 1988.

69. Barker, *Arguments*, p. 80.

70. Renton, '*The Last Supper*', p. 23.

3 Playwrights and Plays: Jim Cartwright

1. Ros Asquith, review of *Road*, *City Limits*, 19 June 1986.

2. Michael Ratcliffe, review of *Road*, *Observer*, 15 June 1986.

3. Paul Greengrass, 'My Hero Alan Clarke', *Guardian*, 1 February 2002.

4. Sheridan Morley, review of *Bed*, *Herald Tribune*, 29 March 1989.

5. Michael Billington, 'Review of the Eighties', *Guardian*, 28 December 1989.

6. John Bull, *Stage Right: Crisis and Recovery in British Contemporary Mainstream Theatre* (London: Macmillan, 1994), p. 17.

7. Andrew Lavender, 'NTQ Symposium, Theatre in Thatcher's Britain: Organizing the Opposition', *New Theatre Quarterly*, Vol. 5, No. 18 (1989), p. 118.

8. Pam Brighton in Andrew Lavender, 'NTQ Symposium'.

9. David Nathan, 'Playwright Jim Cartwright has Finally Made It to the West End', *Independent*, 19 October 1992.

10. Jim Cartwright, *Road*, in *Plays: 1* (London: Methuen, 1996), p. 16.

11. Jim Cartwright, *Two*, in *Plays: 1*, p. 141.

12. Jim Cartwright, *Bed*, in *Plays: 1*, p. 99.

13. Ibid., pp. 113–15.

14. Quoted in Peter Riddell, *The Thatcher Era and Its Legacy* (Oxford: Blackwell, 1991), p. 173.

15. Cartwright, *Road*, in *Plays: 1*, p. 27.

16. Ibid., p. 31.

17. Cartwright, *Two*, in *Plays: 1*, p. 173.

18. Cartwright, *Road*, in *Plays: 1*, p. 83.

19. Vera Gottlieb, 'Thatcher's Theatre – or, After *Equus*', *New Theatre Quarterly*, Vol. 4, No. 14 (1988), p. 100.

20. Ibid., p. 101.

21. Interview with Julia Bardsley on 10 January 2011: this and further quotations from Bardsley are attributed to this interview.

22. Interview with Andrew Hay on 7 December 2010: this and further quotations from Hay are attributed to this interview.

23. Max Stafford-Clark in Tony Dunn, '"A Programme for the Progressive Conscience": the Royal Court in the Eighties', *New Theatre Quarterly*, Vol. 1, No. 2 (1985), p. 144.

24. Ibid., p. 145.

25. Christine Eccles, 'The Unsolicited Playscript . . . and Its Almost Inevitable Return', *New Theatre Quarterly*, Vol. 3, No. 9 (1987), p. 25.

26. Telephone interview with Simon Curtis, 17 January 2011. This and further quotations from Curtis are attributed to this interview unless otherwise stated.

27. Cartwright, *Road*, in *Plays: 1*, p. 9.

28. Michael Billington, *State of the Nation: British Theatre Since 1945* (London: Faber and Faber, 2007), p. 312.

28. From interview with Simon Curtis.

29. Ibid.

30. Cartwright, *Road*, in *Plays:1*, pp. 26–7.

31. Francis Piper, 'Contemporary Writers: Jim Cartwright, Critical Perspective' www.contemporarywriters.com/authors/?p=auth252 (accessed 27 November 2011).

32. Beth Meszaros, 'Internal Sound Cues: Aural Geographies and the Politics of Noise', *Modern Drama*, Vol. 48, No. 1 (2005), pp. 118–31.

33. Nicholas de Jongh, review of *Road*, *Guardian*, 14 June 1986.

34. Conversation with Bill Buffery, 22 November 2011, Barnstaple.

35. Eccles, 'The Unsolicited Playscript', p. 27.

36. Max Stafford-Clark in Ruth Little and Emily McLaughlin (eds), *The Royal Court Theatre: Inside Out* (London: Oberon, 2007), p. 248.

37. Simon Curtis, in Little and McLaughlin, *The Royal Court Theatre: Inside Out*, p. 248.

38. Roxana Silbert in Little and McLaughlin, *The Royal Court Theatre: Inside Out*, p. 249.

39. Aleks Sierz, *In-Yer-Face Theatre: British Drama Today* (London: Faber and Faber, 2001), p. 5.

40. Simon Curtis in Little and McLaughlin, *The Royal Court Theatre: Inside Out*, p. 248.

41. Victoria Radin, review of *Road*, *Guardian*, 7 April 1986.

42. Francis King, review of *Road*, *Sunday Telegraph*, 30 March 1986.

43. David Nathan, review of *Road*, *Daily Mirror*, 20 June 1986.

44. David Nathan, 'Playwright Jim Cartwright has finally made it to the West End'.

45. De Jongh, review of *Road*.

46. Max Stafford-Clark in Dunn, '"A Programme for the Progressive Conscience"', p. 140.

47. David Nathan, review of *Bed*, *Jewish Chronicle*, 17 March 1989.

48. Michael Ratcliffe, review of *Bed*.

49. Michael Coveney, review of *Bed*, *Financial Times*, 9 March 1989.

50. Michael Chekhov, *To the Actor* (Abingdon: Routledge, 2002), p. 67.

51. Lyn Gardner, review of *Bed*, *City Limits*, 9 March 1989.

52. Edward Buscombe, *British Television: A Reader* (Oxford: Oxford University Press, 2000), pp. 146–8.

53. Lez Cooke, *British Television Drama: A History* (London: British Film Institute, 2003), p. 128.

54. Alan Bleasdale, in Cooke, *British Television Drama*, p. 130.

55. Christine Geraghty, in Cooke, *British Television Drama*, p. 154.

56. Vera Gottlieb, '*Brookside*: 'Damon's YTS Comes to an End' (Barry Woodward)' in George W. Brandt (ed.), *British Television Drama in the 1980s* (Cambridge: Cambridge University Press, 1993), p. 40.

57. Cartwright, *Two*, in *Plays: 1*, p. 129.

58. Milton Shulman, review of *Road*, *London Standard*, 17 June 1986.

3 Playwrights and Plays: Sarah Daniels

1. Heidi Stephenson and Natasha Langridge (eds), *Rage and Reason: Women Playwrights on Playwriting* (London: Methuen, 1997), p. 6.

2. Elaine Aston, *Feminist Views on the English Stage* (Cambridge: Cambridge University Press, 2003), p. 39.

3. Mary Remnant (ed.), 'Introduction', *Plays by Women, Volume 6* (London: Methuen, 1987), p. 8. Extended discussion of Daniels's reception by critics is found in Elaine Aston, 'Daniels in the Lion's Den', *Theatre Journal*, Vol. 47, No. 3 (1995), pp. 393–403.

4. Elaine Aston finds the reviews of *Masterpieces* were bifurcated along gendered lines, in 'Daniels in the Lion's Den'.

5. The force of realism's political effects have been much debated since Roland Barthes's classic article 'The Reality Effect' in *The Rustle of Language*, trans. Richard Howard (New York: Hill & Wang, 1986), pp. 141–8, and most recently in Jacques Rancière's *The Politics of Literature* (London: Polity, 2011).

6. Jill Dolan, '"Lesbian" Subjectivity in Realism: Dragging at the Margins of Structure and Ideology', in Sue-Ellen Case (ed.), *Performing Feminisms: Feminist Critical Theory and Theatre* (Baltimore, MD: Johns Hopkins University Press, 1990), pp. 40–53; at p. 44.

7. For discussions on this see Susan Carlson, *Women and Comedy* (Ann Arbor: University of Michigan Press, 1991) and Jeanie Forte, 'Realism, Narrative, and the Feminist Playwright – A Problem of Reception', in Helene Keyssar (ed.), *Feminist Theory and Theatre* (Basingstoke: Macmillan, 1996), pp. 19–34.

8. Janelle Reinelt, 'Beyond Brecht: Britain's New Feminist Drama', *Theatre Journal*, Vol. 38, No. 2 (1989), pp. 154–63; at p. 163.

9. Elin Diamond, 'Mimesis, Mimicry, and the "True-Real"', *Modern Drama*, Vol. 32, No. 1 (1989), pp. 58–72; and for a fuller discussion of how this links to Brechtian notions of gestic acting, see her *Unmaking Mimesis* (London: Routledge, 1997). This

is interpreted into a method for making theatre by Elaine Aston in *Feminist Theatre Practice: A Handbook* (London: Routledge, 1999), pp. 119–21.

10. For a fuller discussion from George Bernard Shaw – 'Against the Well Made Play' (1911) – onwards, see Ann Marie Adams, 'Look Back in Anger: The Making and Unmaking of Dramatic Form in the Reception of the British New Wave', *Journal of Midwest Modern Language Association*, Vol. 40, No. 1 (2007), pp. 75–86.

11. Sheila Stowell, 'Rehabilitating Realism', *Journal of Dramatic Theory and Criticism*, Vol. 6, No. 2 (1992), pp. 81–8.

12. Loren Kruger, 'The Dis-Play's the Thing: Gender and Public Sphere in Contemporary British Theatre', in Helene Keyssar (ed.), *Feminist Theatre and Theory* (Houndmills: Macmillan, 1996), pp. 49–78; at p. 53.

13. This is Dolan's gloss on Forte's approach in '"Lesbian" Subjectivity in Realism', pp. 44–5.

14. Cited in Susan Carlson, 'Empowerment on Stage: Sarah Daniels' Agenda for Social Change', *Viewpoints* (1989), pp. 2, 3.

15. Carlson, 'Empowerment on Stage', p. 2.

16. Carlson, 'Empowerment on Stage', p. 6.

17. Sarah Daniels, 'Foreword', in Lizbeth Goodman and Jane de Gay (eds), *The Routledge Reader in Politics and Performance* (London: Routledge, 2000), p. xxv.

18. 'Some plays are more political than others, but within a context of challenging a status quo and putting forward ideas or ideology that have a different perspective, then my work is political. I do want my plays to be challenging. [. . .] I have also been accused of being didactic. *Masterpieces* is an issue-based play and in that sense it is didactic.' Interview with Sarah Daniels, in Stephenson and Langridge, *Rage and Reason*, pp. 4, 5.

19. Stephenson and Langridge, *Rage and Reason*, p. 6.

20. Daniels, 'Foreword', p. xxvi.

21. Stephenson and Langridge, *Rage and Reason*, p. 5.

22. Carlson, 'Empowerment on the Stage', p. 4.

23. Sabine Durrant interview, 1990; cited in Chris Dymkowski, 'Breaking the Rules: the Plays of Sarah Daniels', *Contemporary Theatre Review*, Vol. 5, No. 1 (1996), p. 64.

24. Regenia Gagnier, 'Between Women: a Cross-Class Analysis of Status and Anarchic Humour', in Regina Barreca, *Last Laughs: Perspectives on Women and Comedy* (New York: Gordon & Breach, 1988), pp. 135–48.

25. Lucy Delap, 'Kitchen-Sink Laughter: Domestic Service Humour in Twentieth Century Britain', *Journal of British Studies*, Vol. 49, No. 3 (2010), pp. 623–54; at p. 628.

26. Philip Roberts, *The Royal Court and the Modern Stage* (Cambridge: Cambridge University Press, 1999), p. 183.

27. Jules Wright, in Lizbeth Goodman and Jane de Gay (eds), *Feminist Stages: Interviews with Women in Contemporary British Theatre* (London: Routledge, 1996), p. 112.

28. Carlson, *Women and Comedy*, p. 198.

29. Sarah Daniels, *Masterpieces* in *Sarah Daniels: Plays 1* (London: Methuen, 1997), p. 230; all further references from this play are noted in parenthesis in the text.

30. Gerry and Ann Millar Chambers, *Investigating Sexual Assault* (Edinburgh: HMSO, 1983), p. 6.

31. Elaine Aston, *An Introduction to Feminism and Theatre* (London: Routledge 1999), pp. 131–2.

32. Matthew Gervais and David Sloane Wilson, 'Evolution of Laughter and Humour', *Quarterly Review of Biology*, Vol. 80, No. 4 (2005), p. 399.

33. Dymkowski, 'Breaking the Rules', p. 65.

34. Wright, *Feminist Stages*, p. 112.

35. Remnant, 'Introduction', p. 8.

36. Wright, *Feminist Stages*, p. 112.

37. Ibid.

38. Nicholas de Jongh, *Guardian* review, cited in Remnant, 'Introduction', p. 5.

39. Dymkowski, 'Breaking the Rules', p. 73.

40. Aston, 'Daniels in the Lion's Den', p. 399.

41. For a discussion of raunch culture see Ariel Levy, *Female Chauvinist Pigs: Women and the Rise of Raunch Culture* (New York: Free Press, 2005); Natasha Walter, *Living Dolls: the Return of Sexism* (London: Virago, 2011).

42. Tertullian, a radical theologian writing around 200 CE, condemns women to permanent mourning for the sin of Eve in tempting Adam. 'On the Apparel of Women', Book 1, Chapter 1, Tertullian (*c.* 202 CE), in K. Kvam et al. (eds), *Eve and Adam: Jewish, Christian, Muslim Readings of Genesis and Gender* (Bloomington: Indiana University Press, 1999), p. 132.

43. Daniels, 'Introduction', *Plays: Volume 1*, p. x.

44. Indeed, the protest shared much with the long, if little-known, tradition of women's peace campaigning. See Jill Liddington's illuminating *The Road to Greenham Common: Feminism and Anti-Militarism in Britain Since 1820* (London: Virago, 1989).

45. 'News Content, Language and Visuals', in John Eldridge and Greg Philo (eds), *The Glasgow Media Group Reader: Volume 1* (London: Routledge, 1995), p. 325. Peggy Seeger's song 'Carry Greenham Home' was written for the protesters.

46. Sarah Daniels, *The Devil's Gateway*, in *Sarah Daniels: Plays 1* (London: Methuen, 1997), p. 109; all further references from this play are noted in parenthesis in the text.

47. Carlson, *Women and Comedy*, pp. 196, 197.

48. Carina Bartleet, 'Sarah Daniels: Feminist Enque[e]ry within the Mainstream', *New Theatre Quarterly*, Vol. 26, No. 2 (2010), pp. 145–60.

49. Linda is thrown downstairs by her father for being a lesbian (p. 138); Darrel throws a tin of tomatoes at Carol on honeymoon (p. 117), an indication that this is the beginning of a violent relationship; Enid hits her husband with a chip pan (p. 155); John, Betty's unseen son, is a glue-sniffer (p. 88); Enid's son Dennis is a drug dealer (p. 107); Enid was involved in East End gang culture epitomised by the Krays (p. 118); Ivy was an occasional sex worker (pp. 118, 154).

50. See Susan Stewart, *On Longing* (Durham, NC: Duke University Press, 1984) p. 136,

on the souvenir as 'a sample of the now-distanced experience, an experience which the object can only evoke and resonate to, and can never entirely recoup'.

51. Susan Porrett, who had played the mother Mary in Tunde Ikoli's *Scrape off the Black* at the Riverside (1980) and in the Royal Court's version of *The London Cuckolds* (1979).

52. Marvin Carlson, *The Haunted Stage* (Ann Arbor: University of Michigan Press, 2001).

53. 'Intertheatrical' is a term coined by Jacky Bratton to usefully articulate the fuller richness beyond intertextuality that the performance produces, 'a theatrical code shared by writers, performers and audience which consists not only of language but of genres, conventions and memory – shared by the audience – of previous plays and scenes, previous performances, the actors' previous roles and their known personae on and off stage'. 'Reading the Intertheatrical', in Maggie Gale and Viv Gardner (eds), *Women, Theatre and Performance* (Manchester: Manchester University Press, 2000), p. 15.

54. She was also cast in multiple servant or prostitute roles in an adaptation of Aphra Behn's *The Lucky Chance* at the Royal Court in 1984 and in Wertenbaker's *The Grace of Mary Traverse*, as Sara Freeman discusses later in this volume. She is now best known for her television role as Ma Larkin in an adaptation of H. E. Bates's *The Darling Buds of May* (1991–93) or a gardening detective with Felicity Kendal in *Rosemary and Thyme* (2003–06), and has been attempting to resist roles that consign her to the 'mother function' (*Daily Mail*, 22 November 2008).

55. John McGrath and Nadine Holdsworth (eds), *Naked Thoughts that Roam About* (London: Nick Hern, 2002), p. 90. Chrissie had just played Annetta Brady, a brutal young mother sent to borstal for petty theft, in a Handmade British film *Scrubbers* (1982), described as 'almost unwatchably grim'.

56. *Guardian*, 4 July 1986; *London Theatre Record*, 2–15 July 1986, p. 716.

57. Sarah Daniels, *Neaptide*, in *Sarah Daniels: Plays 1* (London: Methuen, 1997), p. 312; all further references from this play are noted in parenthesis in the text.

58. Dymkowski, 'Breaking the Rules', p. 66.

59. Goodman, *Contemporary Feminist Theatre*, p. 130.

60. Trevor R. Griffiths, 'Waving Not Drowning: the Mainstream 1979–88', in Trevor R. Griffiths and Margaret Llewellyn-Jones (eds), *British and Irish Women Dramatists Since 1958* (Buckingham: Open University Press, 1993), p. 62.

61. Lillian Hellman's 1941 play, *Watch on the Rhine* had been staged in 1980, some monologues from *One Woman Plays* (Dario Fo and Franca Rame) reached the Cottesloe in an anodyne form in 1981, and two of Debbie Horsfield's plays had been given one-night showings as part of the National Theatre Studio's new writing initiative, on the Cottesloe's reopening in 1985.

62. Interview cited in Goodman, *Contemporary Feminist Theatres*, p. 128.

63. Sarah Daniels, 'Introduction', *Sarah Daniels: Plays 2* (London: Methuen, 1994). A sign of how canonical this feminist writer has become is perhaps that extracts from *The Gut Girls* feature as texts for GCSE and A-level drama.

64. Susan Haedicke, 'Doing the Dirty Work: Gendered Versions of Working Class Women in Sarah Daniels' *The Gut Girls* and Israel Horovitz's *North Shore Fish*', *Journal of Dramatic Theory and Criticism*, Vol. 3, No. 2 (1994), pp. 77–88.

3 Playwrights and Plays: Timberlake Wertenbaker

1. Timberlake Wertenbaker, Introduction to *Plays One* (London: Faber and Faber, 1996), p. viii, and Carole Woddis, 'The Healing Art: As *Our Country's Good* Arrives in the West End', *City Limits*, 30 November–7 December 1989. Also see Philip Roberts and Max Stafford-Clark, *Taking Stock: The Theatre of Max Stafford-Clark* (London: Nick Hern Books, 2007), p. 153.

2. Peter Riddell, *The Thatcher Decade: How Britain Has Changed During the 1980s* (Oxford: Basil Blackwell, 1989), pp. 43–4.

3. Riddell, *Thatcher Decade*, p. 45.

4. Andy McSmith, *No Such Thing as Society: A History of Britain in the 1980s* (London: Constable & Robinson, 2010).

5. Robert Hewison, *Culture and Consensus: England, Art, and Politics Since 1940* (London: Methuen, 1995). See particularly pages 209–94.

6. Hewison, *Culture and Consensus*, p. 287, and William A. Henry, 'Theater: New Life at London's Old Vic', *Time Magazine*, 1 February 1988 www.time.com/time/magazine/article/0,9171,966589,00.html.

7. Roberts and Stafford-Clark, *Taking Stock*, pp. 124–6.

8. Roberts and Stafford-Clark, *Taking Stock*, pp. 147–66, especially at p. 150.

9. Writers take on the 'in residence' or Resident Dramatist designation for different durations and around different tasks at the Royal Court, like running playwriting groups or having year-long residencies (personal email, Nic Wass, Royal Court Literary Office, 13 January 2011). The unpublished manuscript of *Abel's Sister* describes that Wertenbaker met Yolande Boucier, the disabled teenager whose poetry sourced the script, during a Royal Court Young Writers programme in 1981, which suggests that she might initially have been helping run a writers' group.

10. The concrete benefits of that home base for Wertenbaker are best documented by her descriptions of how she experienced its absence, when she felt out of place among the wave of 'lads' plays' and the visceral in-yer-face style emerging from the Court in the mid-1990s and she resigned from the Court's Board of Directors as the company responded to the changing climate in arts funding by seeking more co-sponsorship with industry. See Heidi Stephenson and Natasha Langridge's interview with Wertenbaker in *Rage and Reason: Women Playwrights on Playwriting* (London: Methuen, 1997), pp. 136–45, and the conversation between Wertenbaker, Michael Billington and Max Stafford-Clark in Alexis Greene (ed.), *Women Writing Plays: Three Decades of the Susan Smith Blackburn Prize* (Austin: University of Texas Press, 2006), pp. 54–68. For discussion of Wertenbaker's distaste for the 'encroachment of private sponsorship' see her interview with Michael Billington in the *Guardian* on 25 November 1999 www.guardian.co.uk/culture/1999/nov/25/artsfeatures9.

11. See Maya Roth's comprehensive introduction to Maya Roth and Sara Freeman (eds), *International Dramaturgy: Translation and Transformation in the Theatre of Timberlake Wertenbaker* (Brussels: Peter Lang, 2008), pp. 11–33, for a chronological discussion of

Wertenbaker's career into the early twenty-first century, its development in 'waves', and the most prominent thematic links in her writing.

12. Wertenbaker's first London production was *This is No Place for Tallulah Bankhead* in 1978 at the King's Head Theatre Club, so eight years covers 1978–86. Also, *Mephisto*, an under-appreciated translation in Wertenbaker's oeuvre, needs to be understood as an ensemble-based piece that even if *no longer in process* (because the RSC was restaging the work created by Théâtre du Soleil's process), then *in structure and aesthetics* participated in the trends represented by rising 1980s companies such as Theatre de Complicite and Shared Experience. In other words *Mephisto* represented another way for the RSC to import and capitalise on those trends within its own system. For the only scholarly considerations of *Mephisto* as part of Wertenbaker's body of work, and for how the content and structure of Ariane Mnouchkine and Soleil's work connects to the structure of *Our Country's Good* (also created after an ensemble workshop process) see Christopher Swanson's 'Translations and Transmutations: Timberlake Wertenbaker's *Mephisto*', in Roth and Freeman (eds), *International Dramaturgy*, pp. 93–107.

13. Collected reviews for Barker's *Crimes in Hot Countries, The Castle,* and *Downchild* in *London Theatre Record*, Vol. 5. No. 21 (9–22 October 1985), pp. 1013–22. See *London Theatre Record*, Vol. 5, No. 22 (23 October–5 November 1985), p. 1109, for Radin's commentary on *Mary Traverse*.

14. See for instance Mel Kenyon's comments about this tactic quoted in the introduction to Part I of Rebecca D'Monte and Graham Saunders (eds), *Cool Britannia: British Political Drama in the 1990s* (London: Palgrave Macmillan, 2008), p. 20.

15. Charles Mee, 'The Culture Writes Us', in Caridad Svitch (ed.), *Divine Fire: Eight Contemporary Plays Inspired by the Greeks* (New York: Backstage Books, 2002), pp. 9–10.

16. Ably documented by Susan Carlson in 'Issues of Identity, Nationality, and Performance: The Reception of Two Plays by Timberlake Wertenbaker', *New Theatre Quarterly*, Vol. 9, No. 35 (1993), pp. 267–89. Pointedly, in her commentary for the 1997 Birmingham Theatre Conference reprinted in David Edgar (ed.), *State of Play: Playwrights on Playwriting* (London: Faber and Faber, 1999), pp. 73–6, Wertenbaker declared 'Sarah Daniels's blisteringly funny first play at the Royal Court caused as much discomfort as Sarah Kane's' (p. 75).

17. Didactic reads as a reference to 1970s 'agitprop' or 'political theatre' in this interview, the type of theatre Catherine Itzin wrote about in *Stages in the Revolution: Political Theatre in Britain Since 1968* (London: Methuen, 1980).

18. John DiGaetani, *A Search for a Postmodern Theatre: Interviews with Contemporary Playwrights* (New York: Greenwood Press, 1991), p. 268. Subsequent quotations from this interview will be cited parenthetically in the text.

19. For discussions of Wertenbaker's reworking of tragedy, see Victoria Pedrick's 'Ismene's Return from a Sentimental Journey', in Roth and Freeman (eds), *International Dramaturgy*, pp. 41–59, about Wertenbaker's translation of *Antigone*; Jennifer A.

Wagner's 'Formal Parody and the Metamorphosis of the Audience in Timberlake Wertenbaker's *The Love of the Nightingale*', *Papers on Language and Literature*, Vol. 31, No. 3 (1995), pp. 227–54; my own 'Group Tragedy and Diaspora: New and Old Histories of Exile and Family in Wertenbaker's *Hecuba* and *Credible Witness*', in Roth and Freeman (eds), *International Dramaturgy*, pp. 61–75 and 'Tragedy *After Darwin*: Timberlake Wertenbaker Remakes "Modern" Tragedy', *Comparative Drama*, Vol. 44, No. 2 (2010), pp. 201–27.

20. See David Ian Rabey, 'Defining Differences: Timberlake Wertenbaker's Drama of Language, Dispossession, and Discovery', *Modern Drama*, Vol. 33. No. 4 (1990), pp. 518–28; Carlson, 'Issues of Identity'; and Roth's introduction and my afterword to *International Dramaturgy*.

21. Michael Coveney described Max Stafford-Clark's staging of the premiere of *Our Country's Good* as 'briskly sensuous', *Financial Times* review reprinted in *London Theatre Record*, Vol. 8, No. 19 (9–22 September), p. 1264.

22. Ian Herbert (ed.), *London Theatre Index 1985*, pp. 27–9.

23. Rob Ritchie, *The Joint Stock Book* (London: Methuen, 1987), p. 83, and 'A Film Director in a Class of His Own,' *Observer* Profile, 4 January 2009 www.guardian. co.uk/film/2009/jan/04/danny-boyle-interview-slumdog-millionaire.

24. Coveney, *Financial Times*, 24 October 1985. In the *Guardian* on the same day, Michael Billington also wrote of her 'conjuring memories of a young Vanessa Redgrave'.

25. See the discussion of McTeer in Greene, *Women Writing Plays*, p. 56.

26. Timberlake Wertenbaker, *The Grace of Mary Traverse*, in *Plays One* (London: Faber and Faber, 1996), pp. 56–160; at pp. 89–91. Subsequent quotations from this play are cited parenthetically in the text.

27. Billington's review records that the scene transpired with 'delicate verbal eroticism and minimal physical contact'.

28. See Ann Wilson, 'Forgiving History and Making New Worlds: Timberlake Wertenbaker's Recent Drama', in James Acheson (ed.), *British and Irish Drama Since 1960* (London: Macmillan, 1993), pp. 146–61, at p. 156, for strong discussion of silence.

29. Ann Wilson initiates a discussion of how the use of Beethoven's 'triumphant' music troublingly 'orchestrates' the audiences reaction in '*Our Country's Good*: Theatre, Colony, and Nation in Wertenbaker's Adaptation of *The Playmaker*', *Modern Drama*, Vol. 34, No. 1 (1991), pp. 23–34. Peter Buse develops a full critique of this 'happy ending' in *Drama+Theory: Critical Approaches to Modern British Drama* (Manchester: Manchester University Press, 2001).

30. *London Theatre Record*, Vol. 5, No. 21 (9–22 October 1985), p. 1056.

31. Jay Gipson-King, 'Wertenbaker and the Metahistorical: Fracturing History in *The Grace of Mary Traverse, Love of the Nightingale* & *After Darwin*', in Roth and Freeman, *International Dramaturgy*, pp. 223–34.

32. Wertenbaker, 'Introduction', *Plays One*, pp. vii–ix. See also Greene, *Women Writing Plays*, p. 56.

33. www.met.police.uk/history/brixton_riots.htm.

34. www.information-britain.co.uk/famdates.php?id=731.

35. Esther Beth Sullivan's Althusserian concern with how Wertenbaker's plays represent 'significant action' in 'Hailing Ideology, Acting in the Horizon, and Reading Between Plays by Timberlake Wertenbaker', *Theatre Journal*, Vol. 45, No. 2 (1993), pp. 139–54, turns on the problematic of the 'postmodern malaise' about 'what's to be done when it seems nothing can be done?' within this system (pp. 140, 149).

36. See the assembled reviews for *No Sugar*, *London Theatre Record*, Vol. 8, No. 13 (17–30 June 1988), pp. 837–40.

37. See Buse for a critique of *Our Country's Good* in light of Edward Said's *Culture and Imperialism*. Sullivan also probes this problematic.

38. See the annotated bibliography included in this volume. For *Our Country's Good* in particular see Wilson 1991; David Ian Rabey, 'Defining Differences: Timberlake Wertenbaker's Drama of Language, Dispossession, and Discovery', *Modern Drama*, Vol. 33, No. 4 (1990), pp. 518–28; Val Taylor, 'Mothers of Invention: Female Characters in *Our Country's Good* and *The Playmaker*', *Critical Survey*, Vol. 3, No. 3 (1991), pp. 331–8; Esther-Beth Sullivan, 'Hailing Ideology, Acting in the Horizon, and Reading Between Plays by Timberlake Wertenbaker', *Theatre Journal*, Vol. 45, No. 2 (1993), pp. 139–54; Christine Dymkowski, '"The Play's the Thing": The Metatheatre of Timberlake Wertenbaker', in Nicole Boireau (ed.), *Drama on Drama: Dimensions of Theatricality on the Contemporary British Stage* (London: Macmillan, 1997), pp. 121–35; Stephen Weeks, 'The Question of Liz: Staging the Prisoner in *Our Country's Good*', *Modern Drama*, Vol. 43, No. 2 (2000), pp. 147–56.

39. Kate Kellaway describes catching one of the roses in her *Observer* review, reprinted in *London Theatre Record*, Vol. 8, No. 15 (15–28 June 1988), p. 991.

40. Steve Grant in *Time Out* and Charles Spencer in the *Daily Telegraph*, reprinted in *London Theatre Record*, Vol. 8, No. 15, pp. 991, 994.

41. Michael Coveney and Jim Hiley in *London Theatre Record*, Vol. 8, No. 15, at p. 995 and p. 992.

42. Kenneth Hurren wrote in the *Mail on Sunday* that the play's satire 'is mostly lost in the ramshackle dreariness of a production in which actors barely adequate in one role are invariably asked to play two', *London Theatre Record*, Vol. 8, No. 15, p. 991.

43. Francis King in the *Sunday Telegraph* and Dominic Gray in *What's On in London*, reprinted in *London Theatre Record*, Vol. 8, No. 15, p. 992.

44. Timberlake Wertenbaker, *Our Country's Good*, in *Plays One* (London: Faber and Faber, 1996), pp. 162–281, p. 185. Subsequent quotations from the play will be cited parenthetically in the text.

45. *London Theatre Record*, Vol. 8, No. 19 (9–22 September 1988), p. 1267.

46. *London Theatre Record*, Vol. 8, No. 19, p. 1265.

47. Ned Chaillet, 'Timberlake Wertenbaker', in D. L. Kirkpatrick (ed.), *Contemporary Dramatists*, 4th edn (Chicago, IL: St James Press, 1988), pp. 553–5; at p. 554.

48. Greene, *Women Writing Plays*, pp. 59–60.

49. See the collected reviews and pictures of the 1989 revival and the transfer to the

Garrick in *London Theatre Record*, Vol. 9, No. 16 (30 July–12 August 1989), pp. 1045–9, and Vol. 9, No. 24 (19 November–December 1989), pp. 1645–6.

50. Timberlake Wertenbaker, *The Love of the Nightingale*, in *Plays One* (London: Faber and Faber, 1996), pp. 283–354; pp. 333–5. Subsequent quotations from the play will be cited parenthetically in the text.

51. Reprinted in the collected reviews of the 1989 London production of *The Love of the Nightingale*, *London Theatre Record*, Vol. 9, No. 17 (22 August–4 October 1989), pp. 1070–2.

52. Paul Taylor in the *Independent* notes this detail. See the collected reviews of the play's premiere in *London Theatre Record*, Vol. 8, No. 23 (4–17 November 1988), pp. 1599–602.

53. Reprinted in *London Theatre Record*, Vol. 8, No. 23, p. 1599.

54. From the RSC's online archive http://calm.shakespeare.org.uk/dserve/dserveexe? dsqIni=Dserve.ini&dsqApp=Archive&dsqCmd=Show.tcl&dsqDb=Performance&dsqPos=6&dsqSearch=%28%28UserInteger1=%271988%27%29AND%28Venue=%27The%20Other%20Place%27%29%29.

55. In her remarks at the 2006 symposium on her work at Georgetown University that became 'First Thoughts on Transforming a Text', in Roth and Freeman (eds), *International Dramaturgy*, pp. 35–40, Wertenbaker commented that *King Lear* was one of her favourite plays.

56. De Jongh in the *Guardian*, reprinted in *London Theatre Record*, Vol. 9, No. 17, p. 1072.

57. See Coveney on the dry ice and Marmion on the costumes in reviews reprinted in *London Theatre Record*, Vol. 8, No. 23, pp. 1600–2.

58. Billington, then Taylor, Schmidt and Coveney respectively in the collected reviews in *London Theatre Record*, Vol. 8, No. 23, pp. 1600–1.

59. *London Theatre Record* has cast lists for both productions in Vol 8, No. 23, p. 1599, and Vol. 9, No. 17, p. 1070.

60. *Daily Telegraph* review reprinted in *London Theatre Record*, Vol. 9, No. 17, p. 1072.

61. Reprinted in *London Theatre Record*, Vol. 9, No. 17, p. 1070.

62. On this point, see Maya Roth's 'The Philomele Myth as Postcolonial Feminist Theatre: Timberlake Wertenbaker's *Love of the Nightingale*', in Sharon Friedman (ed.), *Feminist Theatrical Revisions of Classic Works* (New York: McFarland, 2009), pp. 42–60.

63. See Christine Dymkowski, '"The Play's the Thing"', pp. 121–35.

64. See also Joe Winston, 'Recasting the Phaedra Syndrome: Myth and Morality in Timberlake Wertenbaker's *Love of the Nightingale*', *Modern Drama*, Vol. 38, No. 4 (1995), pp. 510–19.

65. Dan Jones in the *Sunday Telegraph*, reprinted in *London Theatre Record*, Vol. 8, No. 23, p. 1601.

66. Keith Peacock, *Thatcher's Theatre: British Theatre and Drama in the Eighties* (Westport, CT: Greenwood Press, 1999), p. 199.

67. See especially Emily Apter, *The Translation Zone: A New Comparative Literature* (Princeton, NJ: Princeton University Press, 2006), pp. 65–81.

68. Geraldine Cousin, *Women in Dramatic Place and Time: Contemporary Female Characters on Stage* (London: Routledge, 1996), at pp. 115–20; Wilson, 'Forgiving History' and '*Dianeira*, Anger, and History' in Roth and Freeman (eds), *International Dramaturgy*, pp. 209–21.

69. *London Theatre Record*, Vol. 8, No. 19, p. 1267.

70. Elizabeth Wright, *Postmodern Brecht: A Re-Presentation* (London: Routledge, 1989).

71. See Carlson's reading of this word in 'Issues of Identity', at p. 269.

72. *London Theatre Record*, Vol. 8, No. 23, p. 1602.

73. After Apter's discussion of Saidian humanism, Sheila Rabillard applied the term to Wertenbaker in 'Translating the Past: Theatrical and Historical Repetition in Wertenbaker's *The Break of Day*', in Roth and Freeman (eds), *International Dramaturgy*, pp. 135–53.

4 Documents

1. Silviu Purcarete is a Romanian director, who specialises in opera and classic texts, working at the Little Theatre of Bucharest and the National Theatre in Craiova during the 1980s. In 1996 he became Director at the Centre Dramatique National de Limoges. Klaus Hoffmeyer, a Danish director specialising in Danish writing, was appointed head of Drama at the Royal Theatre in 1997.

2. Benedict Nightingale, *New York Times*, 24 July 1988.

3. David Nathan, *Independent*, 19 October 1992.

4. Carmel Thomason, *Manchester City Life*, 15 October 2008.

5. Fiona Mackay was discussing the work of Ariel Levy, *Female Chauvinist Pigs* (New York: Free Press, 2005) and Natasha Walter, *Living Dolls* (London: Virago, 2010).

6. BBC Radio Four, *Afternoon Play*, broadcast 27 July 2010.

7. Started in 1995, the National Theatre's *New Connections* (originally sponsored by Royal Dutch Shell), now known as Connections, is an annual youth theatre scheme. The National Theatre commissions ten plays from established playwrights which are performed by youth theatres across the country, and productions are selected to play at the National at the end of the festival.

8. The Special Operations Executive was a clandestine organisation, sometime known as Churchill's Secret Army, working with resistance movements during the Second World War.

9. Kate Crutchley is a performer and director, who worked with Gay Sweatshop. In 1977 she devised *Care and Control*, with Michelene Wandor and the company, about lesbian parenthood and custody. She programmed the Oval House Theatre during the 1980s and ran her own company, Character Ladies.

10. Greene, Alexis (ed.), *Women Writing Plays: Three Decades of the Susan Smith Blackburn Prize* (Austin: University of Texas Press, 2006), pp. 58–61.

11. Michael Billington, *Guardian*, 25 November 1999.

12. Harriet Devine (ed.), *Looking Back: Playwrights at the Royal Court, 1956–2006* (London: Faber and Faber, 2006), pp. 278–81.

13. *Galileo's Daughter* has since been retitled *The Line*.

14. John O'Mahony, *Guardian*, 30 June 2004.

Afterword

1. Yael Zarhy-Levo, *The Making of Theatrical Reputations: Studies from the Modern London Theatre* (Iowa City: University of Iowa Press, 2008), p. 1. Her study is focused on London, and on the Royal Court Theatre as a mechanism for establishing playwrights' cultural capital.

2. Pierre Bourdieu and Randal Johnson (eds), *The Field of Cultural Production*, (London: Polity Press, 1993), p. 75.

3. John Frow, *Cultural Studies and Cultural Value* (Oxford: Oxford University Press, 1995).

4. Pierre Bourdieu, *The Rules of Art: Genesis and Structure in the Literary Field* (Stanford, CA: Stanford University Press, 1996), p. 148.

5. Howard Barker, *A Style and Its Origins* (London: Oberon Books, 2007).

6. Charles Lamb, *The Theatre of Howard Barker* (London: Routledge, 2005), p. 200.

7. Ibid.

8. Mark Brown (ed.), *Howard Barker Interviews 1980–2010* (Bristol: Intellect, 2011), p. 93.

9. Brown, *Howard Barker Interviews*, p. 94.

10. Brown, *Howard Barker Interviews*, p. 171.

11. The League of Gentlemen are four comic writers who created the eponymous, darkly comic television series (BBC, 1999–2002) and *Psychoville* (BBC, 2011).

12. Gareth MacLean, 'Odd Men Out', interview, *Guardian* (10 February 2001) http://shaninenovember.20m.com/html/guardian_article.html.

13. Dave Russell, *Looking North: Northern England and the National Imagination* (Manchester: Manchester University Press, 2004).

14. Pete Postlethwaite, *A Spectacle of Dust: The Autobiography* (London: Weidenfeld & Nicolson, 2011), p. 141.

15. David Nathan, 'Playwright Jim Cartwright has Finally Made It to the West End', *Independent*, 19 October 1992.

16. Jim Mulligan interviews Sarah Daniels on *Taking Breath*. First published in 1999. www.jimmulligan.co.uk/interview/sarah-daniels-taking-breath (accessed 6 May 2011).

17. Sarah Daniels, *Dust*, in Craig Slaight (ed.), *New Plays from A.C.T.'s Young Conservatory* (Hanover: Smith & Kraus, 2003), p. 181.

18. Jim Mulligan, 'Journey to the Centre of Yourself', interview with Sarah Daniels (2003) www.jimmulligan.co.uk/interview/sarah-daniels-dust (accessed 10 May 2011).

19. Review by Lennie Varvarides, British Theatre Guide, 2006. www.britishtheatreguide. info/reviews/virginiasister-rev.htm (accessed 4 October 2011).

20. Elaine Aston and Geraldine Harris, *Performance Practice and Process: Contemporary [Women] Practitioners* (Basingstoke: Palgrave, 2008), pp. 89, 98.

21. This is a misrecognition of the 'purity' of theatre in Bourdieu's terms. For a succinct discussion of Bourdieu's notion of cultural capital as the acquisition, inheritance or circulation of knowledges, competences and resources that become socially beneficial, see Pierre Bourdieu, 'Forms of Capital', in J. E. Richardson (ed.), *Handbook of Theory and Research for the Sociology of Education* (New York: Greenwood, 1986), pp. 241–58.

22. Elaine Aston, 'Geographies of Oppression – the Cross-Border Politics of (M)othering: *The Break of Day* and *A Yearning*', *Theatre Research International*, Vol. 24, No. 3 (1999), pp. 247–53; and Susan Carlson, 'Language and Identity in Wertenbaker's Plays', in Elaine Aston and Janelle Reinelt (eds), *The Cambridge Companion to Modern British Women Playwrights* (Cambridge: Cambridge University Press, 2000), pp. 134–49.

23. Timberlake Wertenbaker, *The Break of Day* (London: Faber and Faber, 1995), p. 46.

24. This was Francis Fukuyama's assertion in *The End of History and the Last Man* (New York: Free Press, 1992).

25. Cited in Maya E. Roth, 'Engaging Cultural Translations of History', in Maya E. Roth and Sara Freeman (eds), *International Dramaturgy: Translation and Transformation in the Theatre of Timberlake Wertenbaker* (Brussels: Peter Lang, 2008), pp. 155–76; at p. 173.

26. Alexis Greene (ed.), *Women Writing Plays: Three Decades of the Susan Smith Blackburn Prize* (Austin: University of Texas Press, 2006), p. 68.

27. Wertenbaker, 'First Thoughts on Transforming a Text', in Roth and Freeman (eds), *International Dramaturgy*, pp. 35, 37.

28. Wertenbaker, 'First Thoughts', p. 36.

29. Wertenbaker, 'First Thoughts', p. 39.

30. Elaine Aston, *Feminist Views on the English Stage: Women Playwrights 1990–2000* (Cambridge: Cambridge University Press, 2003).

31. Christopher B. Balme, 'Selling the Bird: Richard Walton Tully's *The Bird of Paradise* and the Dynamics of Theatrical Commodification', *Theatre Journal*, Vol. 57, No. 1 (2005), pp. 1–20; at p. 20.

32. For example, Ayckbourn is discussed in Michael Billington's volumes of collected theatre reviews, Peter Hall's memoirs and Richard Eyre's history of the British stage.

33. John Bull, 'The Establishment of Mainstream Theatre, 1946–1979', in Baz Kershaw (ed.), *The Cambridge History of British Theatre: Volume 3, Since 1895* (Cambridge: Cambridge University Press, 2004), pp. 326–48.

34. Heidi Stephenson and Natasha Langridge, *Rage and Reason: Women Playwrights on Playwriting* (London: Methuen, 1997), p. 46.

35. Stephenson and Langridge, *Rage and Reason*, p. 48.

36. Lynette Goddard has talked about Pinnock's desire to resist the essentialising forces at

work in commentary on black writing in *Staging Black Feminisms* (Basingstoke: Palgrave, 2007).

37. Winsome Pinnock, 'The Alfred Fagon Awards: the Best of Black British Playwriting?', *Guardian*, 14 December 2010 www.guardian.co.uk/stage/theatreblog/2010/dec/14/ alfred-fagon-award-black-playwrights (accessed 11 October 2011).

38. John Guillory, *Cultural Capital: The Problem of Literary Canon Formation* (Chicago: University of Chicago Press, 2003), p. 240.

39. For the two sides of the debate, see Allen Bloom, *The Closing of the American Mind* (New York: Simon & Schuster, 1988) and Lawrence Levine's *The Opening of the American Mind* (Boston, MA: Beacon Press, 1996), which champions women's writing and multicultural literature on to a universal canon.

40. Bourdieu, *Field of Cultural Production*, p. 110.

41. Claire MacDonald, 'Writing Outside the Mainstream', in Elaine Aston and Janelle Reinelt (eds), *The Cambridge Companion to Modern British Women Playwrights* (Cambridge: Cambridge University Press, 2000), pp. 235–52; at p. 245.

42. See Philip Auslander, *Presence and Resistance: Postmodernism and Cultural Politics in Contemporary American Performance* (Ann Arbor: University of Michigan Press, 1992) and Sally Banes, *Subversive Expectations: Performance Art and Paratheater in New York* (Ann Arbor: University of Michigan, 1998).

43. Cited in John Corner and Sylvia Harvey, *Enterprise and Heritage: Crosscurrents of National Culture* (London: Routledge, 1991), p. 67.

44. Fredric Jameson, *Postmodernism: or, the Cultural Logic of Late Capitalism* (London: Verso, 1991), p. 54.

45. See Ernesto Laclau and Chantal Mouffe, *Hegemony and Socialist Strategy* (London: Verso, 1985).

SELECT BIBLIOGRAPHY

Books on the 1980s

Brandt, George (ed.), *British Television Drama in the Eighties* (Cambridge: Cambridge University Press, 1993). Studies of important TV drama series, soaps and one-off dramas that reflected contemporary issues, such as *Boys from the Blackstuff* or *The Falklands Play*.

Friedman, Lester (ed.), *Fires were Started: British Cinema and Thatcherism* (London: Wallflower, 2006). Polemical analyses of the diversity of British films, and their response to Thatcherism, and a look at the changes in filmmaking in the decade.

McSmith, Andy, *No Such Thing as Society: A History of Britain in the 1980s* (London: Constable & Robinson, 2010). A very accessible and thorough view of social history in the 1980s.

Riddell, Peter, *The Thatcher Decade: How Britain Has Changed During the 1980s* (Oxford: Basil Blackwell, 1989). The political editor of the *Financial Times* offers a statistical and economic analysis of the decade.

Turner, Alwyn, *Rejoice! Rejoice! Britain in the Eighties* (London: Aurum Press, 2010). A lively and accessible account of the political upheavals of the decade with a sense of how culture responded.

Wu, Chin-Tao, *Privatising Culture: Corporate Art Intervention Since the 1980s* (London: Verso, 2002). A careful comparative UK/US analysis, in earlier chapters, of the way corporate finance changed fine art culture during the decade.

Key texts on theatre in the 1980s

Key texts on the period that offer both overview and case studies.

Bull, John, *Stage Right: Crisis and Recovery in British Contemporary Mainstream Theatre* (Basingstoke: Macmillan, 1994). A lively study of the fall and rise of the West End, and major mainstream playwrights.

Dorney, Kate and Ros Merkin (eds), *Glory of the Garden: Regional Theatre and the Arts Council 1984–2009* (Newcastle: Cambridge Scholars Press, 2010). Diverse voices from regional theatres reflect on the 1980s, policy initiatives and funding crises.

Edgar, David (ed.), *State of Play: Playwrights on Playwriting* (London: Faber and Faber, 1999). Edgar's polemical introduction sets the scene for a series of short think-pieces from leading playwrights of the 1980s.

Goodman, Lizbeth, *Contemporary Feminist Theatres: To Each Her Own* (London: Routledge, 1993). A study of the processes, practices and analyses of the plays and performances of feminist theatre makers in the 1970s and 1980s.

Jellicoe, Ann, *Community Plays: And How to Put Them On* (London: Methuen, 1987). Both a step-by-step guide to managing a community play, and useful insight into the place of theatre in community life.

Kershaw, Baz, 'Discouraging Democracy: British Theatre and Economics', *Theatre Journal* Vol. 51, No. 3 (1999), pp. 267–84. A thoughtful discussion of the complex implications for theatre and culture of Thatcherite economic policies, and beyond.

Osment, Philip (ed.), *Gay Sweatshop: Four Plays and Company* (London: Methuen Drama, 1989). Plays and working principles from the leading gay and lesbian activist group of the 1980s.

Owusu, Kwesi, *Black British Culture and Society: A Text Reader* (London: Routledge, 2000). Some useful contextual introductions to the range of black British arts practices, and interviews with playwrights in section two.

Peacock, D. Keith, *Thatcher's Theatre: British Theatre and Drama in the Eighties* (New York: Greenwood Press, 1999). Essential reading, a polemic and highly informed reading of impact of Thatcherite ideology on theatrical institutions, playwrights and plays.

Reinelt, Janelle, *After Brecht: British Epic Theater* (Ann Arbor: University of Michigan Press, 1994). A theoretically stimulating analysis of the Brechtian components left in left-wing British playwriting.

Shank, Theodore (ed.), *Contemporary British Theatre*, updated edn (London: Macmillan, 1994). A readable collection of essays on leading elements of the British theatre industry, from an American perspective.

Recommended texts on post-war British theatre

Aston, Elaine and Janelle Reinelt (eds), *The Cambridge Companion to Modern British Women Playwrights* (Cambridge: Cambridge University Press, 2000).

Billington, Michael, *State of the Nation: British Theatre Since 1945* (London: Faber and Faber, 2007).

Chambers, Colin, *Black and Asian Theatre in Britain: A History* (London: Routledge, 2011).

——, and Mike Prior, *Playwrights' Progress: Patterns of Postwar British Drama* (Oxford: Amber Lane Press, 1987).

Davis, Geoffrey and Anna Fuchs (eds), *Staging New Britain: Aspects of Black and South Asian British Theatre Practice* (Brussels: Peter Lang, 2006).

Devine, Harriet (ed.), *Looking Back: Playwrights at the Royal Court 1956–2006* (London: Faber and Faber, 2006).

Goodman, Lizbeth and Jane de Gay (eds), *Feminist Stages: Interviews with Women in Contemporary British Theatre* (Amsterdam: Harwood, 1996).

Griffiths, Trevor R., and Margaret Llewellyn-Jones (eds), *British and Irish Women Dramatists Since 1958: A Critical Handbook* (Buckingham: Open University Press, 1993).

Holdsworth, Nadine and Mary Luckhurst (eds), *A Concise Companion to Contemporary British and Irish Drama* (Oxford: Blackwell, 2008).

Heddon, Deirdre and Jane Milling, *Devising Performance: A Critical History* (Basingstoke: Palgrave, 2005).

Hewison, Robert, *Culture and Consensus: England, Art, and Politics Since 1940* (London: Methuen, 1995).

Innes, Christopher, *Modern British Drama 1890–1990* (Cambridge: Cambridge University Press, 1992).

Kershaw, Baz (ed.), *The Cambridge History of British Theatre: Since 1895*, volume 3 (Cambridge: Cambridge University Press, 2004).

Roberts, Philip, *The Royal Court Theatre and the Modern Stage* (Cambridge: Cambridge University Press, 1999).

Shellard, Dominic, *British Theatre Since the War* (New Haven, CT and London: Yale University Press, 1999).

Wandor, Michelene, *Post-War British Drama: Looking Back in Gender* (London: Routledge, 2001).

The playwrights

For each of the selected playwrights in this volume, a key critical text is listed, along with other useful recommended reading. Play editions are those cited in the chapters on each playwright.

Howard Barker

Plays

Barker, Howard, *Victory: Choices in Reaction* (London: John Calder, 1983).

——, *Howard Barker: Plays Two* (London: Oberon, 2006).

——, *The Last Supper* (London: John Calder, 1988).

Key text

Gritzner, Karoline and David Ian Rabey (eds), *Theatre of Catastrophe: New Essays on Howard Barker* (London: Oberon, 2006).

Recommended texts

Barker, Howard, *Arguments for a Theatre* (Manchester: Manchester University Press, 1989).

——, *Death, the One and the Art of Theatre* (Abingdon: Routledge, 2005).

——, *A Style and Its Origins* (London: Oberon, 2007).

Brown, Mark (ed.), *Howard Barker Interviews 1980–2010: Conversations in Catastrophe* (Bristol: Intellect, 2011).

Lamb, Charles, *The Theatre of Howard Barker* (London: Routledge, 2005).

Rabey, David Ian, *Howard Barker, Politics and Desire: An Expository Study of His Drama and Poetry, 1969–1987* (Basingstoke: Macmillan, 1989).

——, *Howard Barker, Ecstasy and Death: An Expository Study of His Drama, Theory and Production Work, 1988–2008* (London: Palgrave, 2009).

Shaughnessy, Robert, 'Howard Barker, the Wrestling School, the Cult of the Author', *New Theatre Quarterly*, Vol. 5, No. 19 (1989), pp. 264–71.

Jim Cartwright

Plays

Cartwright, Jim, *Plays: 1* (London: Methuen Drama, 1996).

——, *I Licked a Slag's Deodorant* (London: Methuen Drama, 1997).

——, *Hard Fruit* (London: Methuen Drama, 2000).

Key text

Pankratz, Anetee, 'Jim Cartwright', in Aleks Sierz, Martin Middeke and Peter Paul Schnierer (eds), *The Methuen Drama Guide to Contemporary British Playwrights* (London: Methuen Drama, 2011), pp. 62–81.

Recommended texts

Chaudhuri, Una, *Staging Place: The Geography of Modern Drama* (Ann Arbor: University of Michigan Press, 1995).

Kershaw, Baz (ed.), *The Cambridge History of British Theatre: Since 1895*, volume 3 (Cambridge: Cambridge University Press, 2004).

Little, Ruth and Emily McLaughlin (eds), *The Royal Court Theatre: Inside Out* (London: Oberon, 2007).

Peacock, D. Keith, *Thatcher's Theatre: British Theatre and Drama in the Eighties* (New York: Greenwood Press, 1999).

Piper, Francis, 'Contemporary Writers: Jim Cartwright, Critical Perspective', British Council, http://literature.britishcouncil.org/jimcartwright.

Sarah Daniels

Plays

Daniels, Sarah, *Plays 1* (London: Methuen Drama, 1991).

——, *Plays 2* (London: Methuen Drama, 1994).

Key text

Dymkowski, Christine, 'Breaking the Rules: The Plays of Sarah Daniels', *Contemporary Theatre Review*, Vol. 5, No. 1 (1996), pp. 63–75.

Recommended texts

Aston, Elaine, 'Daniels in the Lion's Den: Sarah Daniels and the British Backlash', *Theatre Journal*, Vol. 47, No. 3 (1995), pp. 393–403.

——, *Feminist Theatre Practice: A Handbook* (London: Routledge, 1999).

——, *An Introduction to Feminism and Theatre* (London: Routledge, 1995).

Bartleet, Carina, 'Sarah Daniels' Hysteria Plays: Re-presentations of Madness in *Ripen Our Darkness* and *Head-Rot Holiday*', *Modern Drama*, Vol. 46, No. 2 (2003), pp. 241–60.

Carlson, Susan, *Women and Comedy: Rewriting the British Theatrical Tradition* (Ann Arbor: University of Michigan Press, 1991).

Cousin, Geraldine, *Women in Dramatic Place and Time: Contemporary Female Characters on Stage* (London: Routledge, 1996).

Davis, Tracy C., '*Extremities* and *Masterpieces*: A Feminist Paradigm of Art and Politics', in Helene Keyssar (ed.), *Feminist Theatre and Theory* (Houndmills: Macmillan, 1996), pp. 137–54.

Goodman, Lizbeth, *Contemporary Feminist Theatres: To Each Her Own* (London: Routledge, 1993).

Goodman, Lizbeth and Jane de Gay (eds), *Feminist Stages: Interviews with Women in Contemporary British Theatre* (Amsterdam: Harwood Academic Publishers, 1996).

Griffin, Gabriele, 'Violence, Abuse and Gender Relations in the Plays of Sarah Daniels', in Elaine Aston and Janelle Reinelt (eds), *The Cambridge Companion to Modern British Women Playwrights* (Cambridge: Cambridge University Press, 2000), pp. 194–211.

Haedicke, Susan, 'Doing the Dirty Work: Gendered Versions of Working Class Women in Sarah Daniels' *The Gut Girls* and Israel Horovitz's *North Shore Fish*', *Journal of Dramatic Theory and Criticism*, Vol. 8, No. 2 (1994), pp. 77–88.

Remnant, Mary, 'Introduction', in Mary Remnant (ed.), *Plays by Women: Volume Six* (London: Methuen, 1987), pp. 7–12.

Timberlake Wertenbaker

Plays

Wertenbaker, Timberlake, *Plays One* (London: Faber and Faber, 1996).

Key text

Carlson, Susan, 'Language and Identity in Wertenbaker's Plays', in Elaine Aston and Janelle Reinelt (eds), *Cambridge Companion to Modern British Women Playwrights* (Cambridge: Cambridge University Press, 2000), pp. 134–49.

Recommended texts

Carlson, Susan, 'Issues of Identity, Nationality, and Performance: The Reception of Two Plays by Timberlake Wertenbaker', *New Theatre Quarterly*, Vol. 9, No. 3 (1993), pp. 267–89.

Dahl, Mary Karen, 'Constructing the Subject: Timberlake Wertenbaker's *The Grace of Mary Traverse*', *Journal of Dramatic Theory and Criticism*, Vol. 7, No. 2 (1993), pp. 149–59.

Dymkowski, Christine, '"The Play's The Thing": The Metatheatre of Timberlake Wertenbaker', in Nicole Boireau (ed.), *Drama on Drama: Dimensions of Theatricality on the Contemporary British Stage* (Basingstoke: Macmillan, 1997), pp. 121–35.

Freeman, Sara, 'Tragedy *After Darwin*: Timberlake Wertenbaker Remakes "Modern" Tragedy', *Comparative Drama*, Vol. 44, No. 2 (2010), pp. 201–27.

——, 'Adaptation *After Darwin*: Wertenbaker's Evolving Texts', *Modern Drama*, Vol. 45, No. 4 (2002), pp. 646–62.

Roberts, Philip and Max Stafford-Clark, *Taking Stock: The Theatre of Max Stafford-Clark* (London: Nick Hern Books, 2007).

Roth, Maya E. and Sara Freeman (eds), *International Dramaturgy: Translation and Transformations in the Theatre of Timberlake Wertenbaker* (Brussels: Peter Lang, 2008).

Stafford-Clark, Max, *Letters to George: The Account of a Rehearsal* (London: Nick Hern Books, 1989).

Sullivan, Esther-Beth, 'Hailing Ideology, Acting in the Horizon, and Reading Between Plays by Timberlake Wertenbaker', *Theatre Journal*, Vol. 5, No. 2 (1993), pp. 139–54.

Wertenbaker, Timberlake, 'The Importance of Being Uncomfortable', pamphlet version of the Royden B. Davis, S.J. Chair Lecture, given 27 April 2006 at the Gonda Theatre, Davis Performing Arts Center, Georgetown University, Washington, DC. Published by Georgetown University.

——, Introductory Remarks on *The Thebans*. Radio broadcast, BBC Radio 3, 10 December 2006.

——, 'The Voices We Hear', in Edith Hall, Fiona Macintosh and Amanda Wrigley (eds), *Dionysus Since 69: Greek Tragedy at the Dawn of the New Millennium* (Oxford: Oxford University Press, 2004), pp. 361–8.

——, 'Dancing with History', in Marc Maufort and Franca Bellarsi (eds), *Crucible of Cultures: Anglophone Drama at the Dawn of the New Millennium* (Brussels: Peter Lang, 2002), pp. 17–23.

——, 'About Then: History Plays', in David Edgar (ed.), *State of Play: Playwrights on Playwriting* (London: Faber and Faber, 1999), pp. 73–6.

Wilson, Ann, '*Our Country's Good*: Theatre, Colony, and Nation in Wertenbaker's Adaptation of *The Playmaker*', *Modern Drama*, Vol. 34, No. 1 (1991), pp. 23–34.

Winston, Joe, 'Recasting the Phaedra Syndrome: Myth and Morality in Timberlake Wertenbaker's *Love of the Nightingale*', *Modern Drama*, Vol. 38, No. 4 (1995), pp. 510–19.

INDEX

Note: Play titles are entered in the index under authors' names, if known. Page references in **bold type** denote main references to topics.

NOTES ON CONTRIBUTORS

Sara Freeman is Assistant Professor of Theatre Arts at the University of Puget Sound. In 2007 she received the Gerald Kahan Award for the best essay in Theatre Studies by a younger scholar from the American Society of Theatre Research for an article on the history of Joint Stock Theatre Company. Dr Freeman is the co-editor of *International Dramaturgy: Translation and Transformations in the Theatre of Timberlake Wertenbaker* (Brussels: Peter Lang, 2008) and *Public Theatres and Theatre Publics* (Newcastle: Cambridge Scholars Press, 2012). She is a consulting editor for *Theatre History Studies*, the journal of the Mid America Theatre Conference.

Sarah Goldingay is Lecturer in Drama at the University of Exeter. Her main research interests lie in the practice of culture, religion and spirituality and its performance in contemporary British society. Her recent work as a theatre producer has been with Howard Barker as his executive producer. Forthcoming publications include a special edition of *Studies in Theatre and Performance* on Barker that she is co-editing. Dr Goldingay continues to work as a researcher in the areas of pain, pilgrimage and the construction of belief as a performed process, as well as a performance practitioner.

David Lane is a dramaturg, playwright and academic based in Bristol. He is the author of *Contemporary British Drama* (Edinburgh: Edinburgh University Press, 2010) and articles on dramaturgy and new writing. He is currently Acting Course Convenor on the MA Writing for Performance at Goldsmiths College. He works in new writing and artist development with various theatres and companies in the south west, and has written several plays for young people which have toured both nationally and regionally.